Citizen Attitudes Toward Local Government, Services, and Taxes

Citizen Attitudes Toward Local Government, Services, and Taxes

Floyd J. Fowler, Jr.

Ballinger Publishing Company • Cambridge, Mass.
A Subsidiary of J. B. Lippincott Company

Copyright © 1974 by Ballinger Publishing Company. All rights reserved. No part of this publication may be reproduced, stored in a retrieval system, or transmitted in any form or by any means, electronic mechanical photocopy, recording or otherwise, without the prior written consent of the publisher.

Library of Congress Catalog Card Number: 74-9976

International Standard Book Number: 0-88410-408-7

Printed in the United States of America

Library of Congress Cataloging in Publication Data

Fowler, Floyd J
        Citizen attitudes toward local government, services, and taxes.

        1. Municipal government—United States—Public opinion. 2. Municipal services—United States—Finance—Public opinion. 3. Public opinion—United States. I. Title.
JS341.F69   301.15'43'352073   74-9976
ISBN 0-88410-408-7

Contents

List of Figures	ix
List of Tables	xiii
Foreword	xxi
Author's Preface	xxiii
Introduction	xxv

Chapter One
About This Report — 3

The Potential Value of an Attitude Survey — 3
Utilization Problems — 4

Chapter Two
Methods and Procedures — 9

Methodology — 9
Reliability of the Survey Data — 15
Conclusion — 23

Chapter Three
The Ten Cities — 25

Population and Housing Data — 25
Socio-Economic Characteristics — 28
Evaluating Inter-City Differences — 28

Chapter Four
Priorities — 37

What Are The Most Important Problems For Local Governments
  to Work On? — 37
Are These All Equally Important to People? — 45
How Do Groups Within Cities Differ From One Another
  in Their Priorities? — 47
Can Peoples' Responses With Respect to Priorities
  Be Summarized? — 54

Chapter Five
Balancing the Local Budget — 57

Did People In Cities Think Local Taxes Are Too High? — 57
How Did The Answers to This Question Compare With Interest
  in Increased Service Expressed in Other Parts of the Interview? — 59
In What Ways Did People Think Their Local Tax Money Was
  Poorly Spent? — 71
Were There Sources From Which Increased Revenues Could
  Be Raised? — 76
How Would The Data Be Summarized? — 83

Chapter Six
Housing — 87

How Does Housing Differ Between The Ten Cities? — 87
What Were The Relative Costs of Owning and Renting
  A Place to Live? — 88
Other Than Costs, What Problems Were There With
  Housing? — 96
Did People Think That Local Government Should Play A
  Role in Providing Low-Cost Housing? — 105
How Has Urban Renewal Affected People In Cities? — 107
What Other Roles Did Citizens Feel The Local Government
  Should Play in Relation to Housing? — 113
How Can The Housing Data Be Summarized? — 119

Chapter Seven
Transportation — 125

How Did Most People Get Around In Cities? — 125
Who Used The Public Transportation System? — 133

Would More People Ride The Public Transportation System If It Were Improved?	138
What Did People Say About Financing Public Transportation?	140
What About Those People Who Wanted to Make It Easier to Drive?	145
How Would The Data Be Summarized?	145

Chapter Eight
Law and Order 147

Were People In Cities Afraid?	147
What Types of Crimes Are People Concerned About?	149
How Did People Rate Their Police Force?	159
What Were The Implications of The Data?	165

Chapter Nine
Teaching the Children 171

To What Extent Did City Residents Rely On The Public Schools?	171
How Did People In Central Cities Feel About Their School Systems?	176
What Changes Did People Want In Their School Systems?	185
What About The Problem of Racial Integration of Schools?	189
How Would One Summarize The Data On The Schools in Central Cities?	194

Chapter Ten
Images of City Government 199

What Was The Perception of City Government Efficiency?	199
What Was The Perception of Honesty in City Government?	200
To What Extent Were City Governments Seen As Responsive to People's Needs?	200
What Accounted For The Way People Rated Their City Government Overall?	211
How Would The Data Be Summarized?	217

Chapter Eleven
Conclusion 219

Policy Implications	219
Findings	220

Appendix A
Tables A–1 Thru A–13 223

Appendix B
The Questionnaire 231

About the Author 243

List of Figures

4-1	Number of Items on Which a Majority Voted for Increased Expenditure, by City	48
5-1	Percent Who Say Local Taxes Are Too High, by Race	60
5-2	Percent Who Prefer to Raise Local Taxes Rather Than Cut Services, by Race	65
5-3	Percent Who Prefer to Raise Taxes Rather Than Cut Services, by Home Tenure	66
5-4	Percent Who Say They Do Not Get Adequate Services for Their Local Tax Dollars, by Race	70
5-5	Percent Who Are Willing to Tax Church Property, by Race	81
6-1	Percent Who Own Homes, by Race	90
6-2	Percent Who Pay a Quarter or More of Annual Income for Housing, by Condition of Housing	94
6-3	Percent of Total Population Who Think Cost of Their Housing is "About Right," by City	95
6-4	Percent Who Think They Pay Too Much for Housing, by Race	97
6-5	Percent Who Pay a Quarter or More of Annual Income for Housing, by Race	98
6-6	Percent Who Said There Was a Serious Problem with Their Housing, by City	99
6-7	Percent of Renters Who Say Their Housing Is Seriously in Need of Maintenance, by City	103
6-8	Percent Who Would Accept or Favor Low-Income Housing in Their Own Neighborhood, by Race	109
6-9	Percent Who Would Accept or Favor Low-Income Housing in Their Own Neighborhood, by Home Tenure	110

x List of Figures

6–10	Percent Who Say Urban Renewal Has Made Their City a Better Place to Live, by Race	112
6–11	Percent Who Say Local Agencies Enforce Housing Inspection Code "Not Too Well" or "Not Well at All," by Race	116
6–12	Percent Who Say Local Agencies Enforce Housing Inspection Code "Not Too Well" or "Not Well at All," by Home Tenure	117
6–13	Percent Who Want to Spend More Money on Housing Inspection, by Home Tenure	121
6–14	Percent Who Want to Spend More Money on Housing Inspection, by Race	122
7–1	Percent Who Own a Car, by City	126
8–1	Percent Who Say They Feel "Very Safe" or "Pretty Safe" in Their Neighborhoods Alone at Night, by Race	151
8–2	Percent Who Say They Feel "Very Safe" or "Pretty Safe" in Their Neighborhoods Alone at Night, by Sex	152
8–3	Percent Who Feel There Is More Crime in Their Neighborhood Than Rest of City, by Race	154
8–4	Percent Who Rate Police Protection in Their Neighborhoods "Very Good" or "Good Enough," by Race	163
8–5	Percent Who Say Police Come Right Away, by Race	166
8–6	Percent Who Say Police Treat People "Very Good" or "Good Enough," by Race	168
9–1	Percent of Households Using the Public Schools, by City	173
9–2	Percent of Those Who Chose Schools as One of the Three Most Important Areas for Increased Effort and Who Said the Quality of Education in Their Schools Was "Good Enough" or "Very Good," by City	178
9–3	Percent Rating Quality of Neighborhood School as "Very Good" or "Good Enough," by Population with School Age Children vs. Population without Children	179
9–4	Percent Who Rate Quality of Neighborhood Schools as "Very Good" or "Good Enough," by Families Using Public Schools vs. Families Using Other Schools	181
9–5	Percent Who Say Neighborhood Schools Are "Better" or "Same" as Rest of City, by Race	182
9–6	Percent Who Say Quality of Education in Neighborhood Schools Is "Very Good" or "Good Enough," by Race	183
9–7	Percent Who Say Parents Have Enough Say in School Policy, by Race	191
9–8	Percent Who Say Integration Has Been a "Serious" or "Some" Problem, by City	192

9–9	Percent Who Say Integration Has Been a "Serious" or "Some" Problem, by Race	193
9–10	Percent Who Say Assigning Children to Schools in Other Neighborhoods Is a "Good Idea," by Race	195
9–11	Percent of Blacks Who Say They Are Willing to Have Their Children Bused, by City	196
9–12	Percent of Whites Who Say They Are Willing to Have Their Children Bused, by City	197
10–1	Percent Who Say There Is "Some" or "A Great Deal" of Illegal Activity among Local Officials, by Race	202
10–2	Percent Who Say Local Officials Concerned about Same Problems "A Little" or "Hardly at All," by Race	207
10–3	Percent Who Rate the Way in Which the City Is Run "Excellent" or "Very Good," by Race	215

List of Tables

2-1	Interview Length, by City	10
2-2	Interview Results, by City	13
2-3	Sex of Wrong Respondents, Compared with Sex of Right Respondents, by City	14
2-4	Approximate Sampling Errors for the Citizen Attitude Study	16
2-5	Sampling Errors of Differences	17
2-6	Whether Children under 18 Years in the Household of Non-Respondents, by City	21
2-7	Ethnicity of Non-Respondents, by City	21
2-8	Comparison Between Census Figures and Citizen Attitude Survey Figures for Owner Occupancy	22
2-9	Comparison Between Census Figures and Citizen Attitude Survey Figures for Percent of Blacks in the Population	22
3-1	Population in the Ten Cities	26
3-2	Type of Housing Unit, by City	27
3-3	Home Tenure, by City	29
3-4	Ethnicity of Adults, by City	30
3-5	Religion of Adults, by City	31
3-6	Total Family Income, by City	32
3-7	Education of Adults, by City	33
3-8	Household Composition	34
4-1	Attitudes of People Toward Spending for Selected Services	40
4-2	In Which Three Areas are Increased Efforts by Local Government Most Needed?	43
4-3	How Much of a Problem is Drug Use Among Young People?	44
4-4	Ways in Which City Government can Help with Drug Problem, by City	44

xiv List of Tables

4–5	Services In Which the Local Agencies Should Spend More Money	46
4–6	On Which Three Areas are Increased Efforts Most Needed?	47
4–7	Which Three Areas Should Local Government Cut Back On?	49
4–8	Items Willing to Cut Back On	50
4–9	Rank Order of Items on Which Citizens Want to "Spend More"	51
4–10	Number of Items on Which a Majority voted for Increased Expenditure by Education, Income, Race, and Home Tenure	52
5–1	How People Rate the Level of Local Taxes, by City	58
5–2	Percent Who Say Local Taxes Are Too High, by Education	58
5–3	Percent Who Say Local Taxes Are Too High, by Income	61
5–4	Median Effective Rate of Annual Property Tax for Single-Family Homes as Percent of Sales Price, by City	61
5–5	Attitude Toward Raising Local Taxes Rather Than Cutting Services, by City	62
5–6	Percent Who Want to Spend More on Many Services, by Preference for Raising Taxes or Cutting Services and by City	62
5–7	Percent Who Want to Spend More on Few Services, by Preference for Raising Taxes or Cutting Services and by City	64
5–8	Percent Who Prefer to Raise Local Taxes Rather Than Cut Services, by Education	64
5–9	Percent Who Prefer to Raise Local Taxes Rather Than Cut Services, by Income	67
5–10	Do People Think They Get Adequate Services for Their Local Tax Dollar?, by City	69
5–11	Percent Who Think They Are Not Getting Adequate Services for Their Tax Dollar, by Education	69
5–12	Percent Who Say They Do Not Get Adequate Services for Their Tax Dollar, by Income	72
5–13	Why Don't People Get Their Money's Worth?, by City	72
5–14	Attitudes Toward City Pay Scale, by City	74
5–15	Should Local Tax Money Help Pay for Trash and Garbage?	74
5–16	Should Local Tax Money Help Pay for Libraries and Museums?	75
5–17	Should Local Tax Money Help Pay for Public Transportation?	75
5–18	Percent Who Say Local Taxes Should Help Pay for Public Transportation, by Education	77
5–19	Should Private Schools Retain Their Tax Exempt Status?	77
5–20	Should the Church Retain Its Tax Exempt Status?	78
5–21	Percent Who Are Willing to Tax Private School Property, by Education	78
5–22	Percent Who Are Willing to Tax Church Property, by Education	80
5–23	Percent Who Are Willing to Tax Church Property, by Religion	80

5-24	Best Way of Raising Additional Tax Money, by City	82
5-25	Two Best Ways of Raising Additional Tax Money, by City	82
5-26	Best Way of Raising Additional Tax Money, by Income	84
5-27	Percent Who Chose Income Tax as Best Method of Raising Additional Tax Money, by Education	85
5-28	Percent Who Chose Property Tax as Best Way to Raise Additional Tax Money, by Age and by Home Tenure	85
6-1	Percent Who Own Homes, by Income	89
6-2	Total Monthly Payments for Housing, by Home Tenure and by City	89
6-3	Cost of Housing as Percent of Total Annual Income by Home Tenure	91
6-4	Percent Who Pay a Quarter or More of Their Family Income for Housing, by Income	93
6-5	Percent of Citizens Who Spend Less Than 15 Percent for Housing of Total Family Income, by Income	93
6-6	Percent Who Think They Pay Too Much for Housing, by Income	100
6-7	Reason Why House or Neighborhood is Not a Good Place to Live, by City	100
6-8	Percent Who Say There is a Serious Problem With Their Housing, by Income	102
6-9	Percent Who Say There is a Serious Problem With Their Housing, by Race	102
6-10	Percent of Renters Who Say Their Housing is Seriously in Need of Maintenance, by Race	104
6-11	Percent of Renters Who Say Their Housing is Seriously in Need of Maintenance, by Income	104
6-12	Percent of Housing Rated Dilapidated or Deteriorating, by Race	105
6-13	Percent of Housing Rated Dilapidated or Deteriorating, by Income	106
6-14	Should Local Government Play a Role in Providing More Low- and Moderate-Cost Housing?	106
6-15	Attitude Toward Low-Cost Housing in Citizens' Neighborhood, by City	108
6-16	Percent Who Would Accept or Favor Low-Income Housing in Their Own Neighborhood, by Income	108
6-17	Percent Who Say They Have Been Personally Affected by Urban Renewal, by City	111
6-18	Percent Forced to Move by Urban Renewal, by Race and by Income	111
6-19	Effect of Urban Renewal on the City as a Place to Live, by City	114

6-20	Percent Who Say Urban Renewal Has Made Their City a Better Place to Live, by Income	114
6-21	How Well do Local Agencies do in Inspecting Houses and Effecting Needed Repairs?	115
6-22	Percent Who Say Local Agencies Enforce Housing Inspection Code "Not Too Well" or "Not Well at All," by Income	115
6-23	Percent Who Say Local Agencies Enforce Housing Inspection Code "Not Too Well" or "Not Well at All," by Education	118
6-24	Percent Who Want More Money Spent on Housing Inspection, by Education	118
6-25	Percent Who Want More Money Spent on Housing Inspection, by Income	120
7-1	Type of Transportation Used Most Often, by City	128
7-2	Percent Who Own a Car, by Income and by Age	128
7-3	How Often Public Transportation Is Used, by City	129
7-4	Pattern of Car and Transit Use, by Income	131
7-5	Percent Who Use Public Transportation at Least Once a Week, by Number of Cars Owned	132
7-6	Percent Who Ride Public Transportation Almost Every Day, by Number of Cars Owned	132
7-7	Percent Who Mention Public Transportation as Type Transportation Most Often Used, by Income, Race, and Age	134
7-8	Should City Improve Public Transportation or Make Driving Easier?	135
7-9	Percent Who Say City Should Improve Public Transportation Rather Than Making Driving Easier by Income, Race, and Car Ownership	136
7-10	Response of Those Who Never Use Public Transportation to "Should City Improve Public Transportation or Make Driving Easier."	136
7-11	Would Changes in Public Transportation Increase Usage?	139
7-12	Percent Who Say Changes in Public Transportation Would Increase Usage, by Income and by Race	139
7-13	Type of Improvement Mentioned to Increase Usage of Public Transportation, by City	141
7-14	Percent Who Say Tax Money Should Help Support Public Transportation	143
7-15	Percent Who Say Tax Money Should Help Support Public Transportation, by Income	143
7-16	Percent Who Say Tax Money Should Help Support Public Transportation, by Education	144
7-17	Percent Who Want Type of Change to Make Driving Easier, by City	144

8-1	How Safe People Feel in Their Neighborhoods Alone at Night, by City	148
8-2	Percent Who Say They Feel "Very Safe" or "Pretty Safe" in Their Neighborhoods Alone at Night, by Education	148
8-3	Percent Who Say They Feel "Very Safe" or "Pretty Safe" in Their Neighborhoods Alone at Night, by Income	150
8-4	Percent Who Say They Feel "Very Safe" or "Pretty Safe" in Their Neighborhoods Alone at Night, by Age	150
8-5	How Citizens Feel About the Relative Amount of Crime in Own Neighborhoods, by City	153
8-6	Percent Who Feel There is More Crime in Their Neighborhood Than Rest of City, by Income	153
8-7	Percent of People Who Chose Problem as Important for City Government to Work On, by City	155
8-8	Number of Crimes Against Household Members in Past Year per 100 Households, by City	157
8-9	Burglary and Car Theft Rates per 100 Households from Citizen Attitude Survey and Police Records, by City	159
8-10	Rating of Police Protection in Neighborhood, by City	160
8-11	Percent Who Rate Police Protection in Their Neighborhoods "Very Good" or "Good Enough," by Income	162
8-12	Percent Who Rate Police Protection in Their Neighborhoods "Very Good" or "Good Enough," by Education	162
8-13	Percent Who Rate Police Protection in Their Neighborhoods "Very Good" or "Good Enough," by Age	164
8-14	People's Perception of Amount of Time for Police to Answer Calls, by City	164
8-15	Percent Who Say Police Respond to Calls Quickly, by Income	167
8-16	Rating of Way Police Treat People in Neighborhood, by City	167
8-17	Percent Who Say Police Treat People "Very Good" or "Good Enough," by Age	169
9-1	Type of School Families Send Children To, by City	172
9-2	Type of School Catholic Families Send Children To, by City	174
9-3	Percent Who Support Public Funding for Parochial Schools, by Religion and by Race	175
9-4	Should Tax Money go to Support Parochial Schools?	175
9-5	Quality of Education in Neighborhood Schools, by City	177
9-6	Percent Who Say Education in Neighborhood Schools is "Very Good" or "Good Enough," by Income	184
9-7	Percent Who Say Education in Neighborhood Schools is "Very Good" or "Good Enough," by Education	184

9–8	Ways Cited to Improve Neighborhood Schools, by City	186
9–9	Percent Who Want Selected Additional Courses Taught in Schools, by City	187
9–10	Percent of Blacks Who Mention Black Studies as Course Which Should be Taught in Public Schools, by City	187
9–11	Do Parents Have Enough Say in School Policy?	188
9–12	Ways in Which Parents Should Have More Say for Those Who Want More Say, by City	190
10–1	Citizens' Perception of Honesty of Local Officials Compared to Most Other People, by City	201
10–2	Citizens' Perception of Amount of Illegal Activity among Local Officials, by City	201
10–3	Percent Who Say There is "Some" or "A Great Deal" of Illegal Activity among Local Officials, by Education	203
10–4	Percent of Citizens Who Mention Types of Illegal Activity of Local Officials, by City	204
10–5	Perception of Degree to Which Officials Are Concerned About the Same Problems as Citizens, by City	205
10–6	Percent Who Say Local Officials Concerned About Same Problems "A Little" or "Hardly at All," by Education	208
10–7	Percent Who Say Local Officials Concerned About Same Problems "A Little" or "Hardly at All," by Income	208
10–8	Ways in Which People Can Make Themselves Heard by Local Government, by City	209
10–9	Ways in Which People Can Make Themselves Heard by Local Government, by Race	210
10–10	Ways in Which People Can Make Themselves Heard by Local Government, by Education	212
10–11	Rating of the Way in Which the City Is Run, by City	213
10–12	Percent Who Rate the Way in Which the City Is Run "Excellent" or "Very Good," by Education	214
10–13	Percent Who Rate the Way in Which the City Is Run "Excellent" or "Very Good," by Income	214
10–14	Correlations of Selected Measures with Rating of How City Government is Run	216

APPENDIX TABLES

A–1	Sex of Respondents by City	224
A–2	Age of Respondents by City	224
A–3	Education of Respondents by City	225
A–4	Family Income by City	225

A-5	Ethnicity by City	226
A-6	White Protestant and White Catholic Respondents by City	226
A-7	Presence of Minor Children in the Household by City	227
A-8	Whether Households Will Send or Are Sending Their Children to Public Schools by City	227
A-9	Condition of Housing by City	228
A-10	Tenure by City	228
A-11	Renters by Race by City	229
A-12	Renters by Income by City	229
A-13	Number of Cars Owned by Respondents' Families by City	230

Foreword

What do city residents think about city services, taxes, and the condition of local government? What are the implications of these opinions for the way our cities are governed? Insightful answers to these and related questions appear in this book, which is the result of a unique ten city survey of citizens' attitudes toward local government. The survey was conducted by the Urban Observatory Program, for which the National League of Cities serves as the coordinating Secretariat under a contract with the Department of Housing and Urban Development.

The views and preferences of citizens are, of course, a major criteria for evaluating and developing public policies and programs. Attitude surveys have received increasing attention as a means of making these criteria operational. Such surveys provide information that reflects reliably the opinions of the entire citizenry, rather than just the vocal few. Dr. Floyd J. Fowler's analyses of the Urban Observatory survey data are an extremely useful contribution to our understanding of inter-city patterns of citizens' preferences. Knowledge of these patterns provides decision-makers and policy analysts with a comparative context and a sense of perspective with respect to their local problems.

In an era of increasing responsibilities for local governments, there is an acute need for more and better tools for policy analysis and program evaluation. This report is a useful contribution in that regard.

This volume is the first in a series of Urban Observatory Program comparative studies. The series will be based on the multi-city research projects conducted by the Urban Observatories.

The National League of Cities is therefore pleased to present Dr. Fowler's study to the public, to urban researchers, but, even more importantly, to city officials.

Tom Bradley
Mayor of the City of Los Angeles
President, National League of Cities

Author's Preface

This book should not be viewed as *the final report* or *the analysis* for two reasons. First, in each city there were separate analyses that were much more specifically geared to policy issues and local implications. In some ways, the local reports are more important to the main goal of the project—local policy impact—than this overall view. Second, the data are very extensive. No one report can adequately deal with the potential of the project. Herein, an attempt has been made to present the basic findings and to look at the most obvious tabulations, which turns out to be a substantial undertaking. However, there is much more analysis to be done throughout.

In keeping with the goal of addressing the main questions that were raised as study objectives, there is not a unifying theme or message presented. There were a lot of different questions in the minds of the study planners. Their questions were not unified. Although an attempt has been made to present each topic in an organized way, an integration across topics could have been imposed and probably would have selected out some important data. However, if there is a theme, it is that assumptions about how citizens feel often are not justified. There are exceptions to many of the seemingly most obvious generalizations. Policy-making would be more efficient and effective if it took into account data such as these.

References to other research are not included in the document. There is basically a dearth of multi-city studies. The heterogeneity of the relationships found in the ten cities simply highlighted the fruitlessness of reference to individual community study findings. Doing a respectable job on the literature in each of the subject areas covered in the study seemed impossible; the scholarship was doomed to be uneven at best. A comparison with the other recent multi-city survey project, done for the Kerner Commission, was considered. Since the comparability was only partial, though significant, it was decided not to include it.

The format of the data presentation was chosen to highlight the questions that gave rise to the measures in each section and to increase the readability of the report. Throughout the book, an attempt has been made to minimize the technical presentations that would make the task of understanding the findings more formidable for non-researchers. Most of the numbers discussed are presented as tables in the text, however, for the book is also meant to serve as a reference and resource.

When I undertook this project, it seemed a near impossible job to coordinate nine separate field operations and synthesize the research interests of ten different cities. I had visions of irate scholars insisting on the inclusion of their favorite measures, vetoes from city officials concerned about having negative sentiment measured and, worst of all, field operations that would get halfway through and then bog down. These things did not happen; and it is a tribute to all those involved that they did not.

Altogether, the fact of the project is excellent proof that academic scholars and people in political positions, despite differences in the day-to-day pressures and issues they must fact, can work together smoothly for the common good.

So many people were essential to the success of this project that it is impossible to list them all. Each city hall had one or more staff people involved. There were field supervisors, numbering at least nine, and over 300 interviewers, who did the really important work. However, the following were the people who worked with me most closely and who generally were responsible for the analyses of the data at the local level.

Albuquerque

Susan Johnson
Frieda Prickett

Atlanta

Timothy Ryles
Frank Steggert

Baltimore

Warren Houze

Boston

Bradbury Seasholes

Denver

Warren Weston

Kansas City

C. J. Hein
David Klassen

Milwaukee

Miriam Palay

Nashville

Nicholas Sieviking

San Diego

Oscar Kaplan
Robert Ontell

Introduction

This was one of the first two "national agenda projects" undertaken as part of the Urban Observatory Program. The Urban Observatory Program is a unique and innovative effort to assist city officials in resolving the myriad of problems now facing the nation's cities. The Program is jointly sponsored by the Department of Housing and Urban Development and the Office of Education of the Department of Health, Education, and Welfare, with the National League of Cities serving as the Urban Observatory Secretariat. It is thus an interdepartmental program, utilizing HUD funds for research projects and federal Office of Education funds from Title I of the Higher Education Act for service and training activities.

The Program is designed to carry out coordinated, comparative research in ten urban areas, which is a distinguishing feature in itself. The research undertaken is based upon an agenda of priorities established by the participating cities in cooperation with academic consultants in order to utilize the skills and disciplines of various universities in solving urban problems.

Thus, the Urban Observatory approach attempts to achieve three objectives:

1. It seeks to develop a reservoir of comparable, reliable data of general application to the nation's cities in their efforts to resolve the ills that now beset urban America.
2. It endeavors to address the research needs of city executives and administrators.
3. It attempts to build a set of institutional relationships between local public officials and local universities and colleges to help develop and improve public policy and governmental action on urban problems.

Each local observatory is organized in such a way as to promote optimum cooperation between participating institutions of higher learning and the local governments within the local governments of a metropolitan area. Responsibility for establishing this organization and designating a fiscal agent is vested in the local government officials.

The research agenda is developed solely by the participating institutions and local governments, although it is subject to final approval by the Department of Housing and Urban Development and reviewed by the Office of Education. The research undertaken falls into two categories: (1) national research projects carried out simultaneously by four or more Observatories using comparable research methodology and (2) local research projects of major interest to only one Observatory city. The national research projects are jointly agreed upon by the participating institutions and local governments, but they must be projects that the local chief executives believe will assist in the solution of pressing urban problems.

The ten cities participating in this project are: Albuquerque; Atlanta; Baltimore; Boston; Denver; Kansas City, Kansas; Kansas City, Missouri; Milwaukee; Nashville; and San Diego. In terms of Urban Observatory membership, Cleveland, which did not participate in this particular project, is actually the tenth member, with the two Kansas Cities being considered as a single unit. Since there are two city governments involved, however, we include Kansas City, Kansas, and Kansas City, Missouri, as two separate cities, which maintains a total of ten member cities in the project. The basic design called for comparable surveys in each of these ten cities to collect data on citizen views relevant to local services and policies.

Consistent with the Urban Observatory concept, the project was organized as a consortium. The author served as the project director, and was ultimately responsible for technical research decisions. In each city, there was an academic social scientist and one or more representatives of the local government administration who represented their city's interests in the project. Together with staff members of the National League of Cities, these local representatives, working with the project director at each step, were primarily responsible for the choice of research objectives addressed in the survey. They were also responsible for analysis, interpretation, and dissemination of the data for their respective cities. The data collection took place in the summer of 1970. Details of the research process are presented in Chapter 2.

Citizen Attitudes Toward Local Government, Services, and Taxes

Chapter One

About This Report

This book, reporting one of the more ambitious projects in the field of urban studies yet to be undertaken, is a product of a unique experiment both in inter-city and in university–city government cooperation. At the simplest level, this is a report of some 4,300 interviews—taken with cross-section samples—of adults in ten major United States cities who were asked about their views on city government, city services, and city problems. Although the size and scope of the project is impressive, the distinctive part of the program is the emphasis on making the research relevant and meaningful to city officials and citizens, as well as academic researchers.

THE POTENTIAL VALUE OF AN ATTITUDE SURVEY

From the inception of this project, the question of how the survey data would most benefit city government has been a major concern. Our orientation to this problem and the answers we came up with form an essential foundation for this book. The fact that a survey of citizens was one of the first projects selected by Urban Observatory members suggests that local officials have an interest in obtaining more information about the citizens they serve. Although some descriptive information about residents, such as their use of services or their experience with crime, was obtained, the focus of the project was measurement of the subjective side of citizens, attitudes, including:

1. Their perceptions of the way city government is run;
2. Their evaluation of local government and services;
3. Their values or priorities regarding increased services or changes in local policy.

3

Such information is not easy to obtain. While local officials frequently hear the views of people they personally know, of community leaders, or of people who speak out, it is difficult or impossible for them to know the extent to which such spokesmen are representative of the population as a whole or to know how much weight to attach to one view as compared to another. Elections and referenda do have the potential for broad-based expression of preference, but the extent to which it is realized depends on the voter turn-out. The information about citizen views transmitted through voting may be limited or difficult to interpret. For instance, referenda are taken on only a relatively small number of topics and usually only after a complex problem has been reduced to a small number of policy alternatives. Further, choices between candidates seldom can be interpreted unambiguously as expressions of policy preference. Since there are usually only one or two key issues on which candidates differ, the range of issues to which election results apply is consequently limited.

A properly executed sample survey, however, can measure citizen views in a representative way. Through surveys, opinions can be gathered in proportion to the number of people in a city who hold them; and surveys provide a way not only to measure representative opinions on a wide range of issues but to explore the reasons they are held. Having such information should be helpful to city officials in making decisions that best reflect the needs and interests of their constituency. Knowing the priorities of citizens and the sources of their satisfaction or dissatisfaction with local services provides one potentially important basis for decisions and policy. The potential value of an attitude survey is fairly easy to present. However, there are, in reality, some important reasons why surveys often do not make as useful or important a contribution to local government officials as theory would suggest they could.

UTILIZATION PROBLEMS

One commonly raised issue is the extent to which data based on a sample are accurate. There can be, of course, error in survey data as is possible in almost every other kind of information. (The factors affecting the accuracy of survey data are discussed in some detail in Chapter 2.) However, the limits of the accuracy of survey data, if they are carefully collected, probably constitute the least important problem to be discussed here. In most cases, the fact that the figures presented in this book could, by chance, vary five or even ten percentage points will not significantly alter their policy implications.

A more significant problem is the kind of answers people can give about their attitudes and opinions. The survey process requires people to use words to describe their feelings, which is not an easy task. The standard survey strategy is to give respondents words that describe feelings—"very good, good, fair or poor"—and ask them to choose the category closest to their own view. Because all respondents are relating to the same words, their answers can be compared. On the average, people who say "very good" are more positive than those who say "good." Such data can be used comparatively: one group is more or less positive than another; one individual is more positive about one service than another. Such statements can be very useful in setting priorities, but they do not provide an absolute standard. They do not lend themselves to identifying the number of people who find a service "intolerable," or when "too many" people are dissatisfied. Relative answers, in fact, are usually a sufficient base on which to make choices; but there is often some frustration to users of data who would prefer absolute answers: Are most people satisfied with this service, or not?

People also are much better at identifying problems than designing or assessing solutions for them. A person can report which services he needs and uses, which aspects of city government he perceives to be in need of change, and which problems he sees as most important. However, problem solutions require information about costs, manpower, political and organizational constraints that few citizens are likely to have. Thus, survey data can be very useful in telling officials where to direct their attention; but the development of policy cannot usually be derived directly from the survey data.

Indeed, in addition to the difficulty people have in suggesting problem solutions, the policy implications of attitudinal data are also made unclear by our lack of knowledge about how closely attitudes are tied to reality. If people are dissatisfied with the quality of education in their schools, the obvious response might be to make the schools better, if possible. However, how people rate schools involves a complex combination of what they know about the schools—or think they know; what they expect of the schools; and how they apply their criteria. Some of these factors can be measured in a carefully constructed survey instrument. Nonetheless, we still need to know a great deal more about how attitudinal data relate to specific service characteristics to realize the policy-making potential of survey research.

Perhaps the most important problem, however, lies not in any limitations of the data, but rather in the difficulty of having the data used to the extent that the information is beneficial in making decisions. This problem, of course, applies to information in general, not just survey research data; and it is a problem that the Urban Observatory concept attempts to address directly.

There are at least five conditions that must be met in order for information about citizen attitudes to be used and useful:

> 1. *Those considering policy or making decisions must want such information.* If the reasons for making a given decision on other grounds are sufficiently compelling, information about citizen attitudes may be irrelevant, or even distracting. The fact that this project was proposed by and executed with city officials is at least an endorsement in principle by those cities of the value of this kind of information.

2. *The information available must be relevant to the policies or decisions being considered.* The involvement of city officials in defining research objectives and reviewing the questionnaire was designed to maximize the likelihood of relevance. However, it is an inherent difficulty in such research to have data that are specific enough to be helpful in individual decisions.

3. *The data must be available when issues are being considered.* The cliché about the uselessness of the large report on the bookshelf is not a joke. The difficulty of disseminating throughout a city hall the knowledge of what kind of information is available so that someone would even know to look for it is enormous. Data will not be used if the relevant people do not know what is available.

4. *The research findings must be in a usable form.* This means the analyst must anticipate the kinds of questions that will be asked of the data, so that the needed answers are in the right form. It also means that he must present his findings so that the meaning is clear to non-researchers. Clarity of presentation is not a universal strength of research reports.

5. *The policy implications of the findings must be feasible to accomplish.* There clearly are constraints within which city officials must operate. It is usually impossible to know in advance, of course, what the research findings will be. However, a reality that possibly can limit the value of research is that political, fiscal or organizational factors may be present that make it impossible for officials to respond appropriately to research findings.

The organization of the research was designed to increase the likelihood that these conditions would be met—that the data would be used by city officials. The effort made in that respect was probably unique in the annals of survey research. However, the problems to be overcome were indeed substantial, and the effort was no doubt more successful in some cities than in others.

Because the cities do not constitute a probability sample of cities, it was concluded that it was not appropriate to combine the data from all cities. In addition, the power to state how often a given relationship occurred constitutes a strength of this study, and by keeping the cities separate, we can take advantage of that ability.

The percentages given all add up to 100. Tenths of percent are not presented, because that would imply a precision the data do not have. When the rounding resulted in a total other than 100, the smallest change possible was made to produce a 100 percent total.

Because only one adult was interviewed in a household, the data on individual attitudes properly should be weighted by the number of adults in the household. A number of distributions were tabulated with and without this weighting, and the effect of weighting on figures was consistently found to be trivial. The figures in the text generally are not weighted by the number of adults in the household. It is indicated by footnote if they are.

Responses of population sub-groups were sometimes percentagized on the basis of all those responding, excluding those for whom answers were not ascertained. When this was the case and when the average rate of "not ascertained" responses exceeded 3 percent, there is a footnote to that effect in the table, for there is the possibility of bias due to systematic non-response among some groups.

The number of cases on which percentages are based are an index of the reliability of the figures, as we discuss in Chapter 2. Often, the number of cases is presented in the table. However, for multi-dimensional tables, it was very difficult to format; and so numbers not found in tables can be found in Appendix A.

Chapter Two

Methods and Procedures

The study was designed so that virtually identical surveys could be conducted in each of the ten cities. This chapter describes the procedures that were used, as well as the way those procedures were carried out in each city.

METHODOLOGY

The Questionnaire

Development of the questionnaire entailed meshing the interests of city halls and academic researchers, as well as attempting to achieve an optimum balance of all the most important issues in the ten cities. The questionnaire development began with a meeting in Albuquerque at which the local project directors, together with representatives from their local city halls, discussed and then ordered various issues for research in terms of local interest and concern. At that meeting, some consensus was achieved on the general issues to be addressed in the questionnaire. After the meeting, this consensus was translated by the project director into a more specific set of written objectives that was sent to each city for comments and criticisms. The main topics were:

Perceptions of city government, including such issues as efficiency, honesty, and the problem of the city as an employer;
The school system, including perceptions and views relevant to school administration;
Concern about law and order, including perceptions of police efficiency, police-community relations and concern about crime;
Transportation, including use of and attitudes toward both mass transportation systems and the automobile and problems;
Housing, including problems and ideas on solutions to those problems;
Taxation, including attitudes toward present forms of taxation, alternative

forms of taxation and the related issues of alternative sources of revenue and reductions in expenditures;

Priorities, including both areas in which increased effort and less effort are needed.

At this point, a pretest questionnaire was developed. At the same time that it was sent to each city for review, it was pretested in Nashville and Boston with about 25 interviews in each city. The comments from city representatives on the questionnaires plus the results of the pretest were then incorporated into a final questionnaire, which is reproduced in full in Appendix B.

The core questionnaire was administered in each city to the selected sample. In addition, the research staff in each city had the option of adding a set of supplemental questions to this core questionnaire for the interviews in their city. The questionnaire was designed to be administered in slightly under an hour without a supplement, slightly over an hour with a supplement. Table 2-1 presents the median length of the total interview by city. The median for the core questionnaire was about an hour, with the supplements adding another 10 to 20 minutes when they were used.

Sampling

The probability samples were drawn by Dr. Bernard Lazerwitz, Public Opinion Survey Unit, University of Missouri.[1] In each city, each household within the geographic boundaries of the city itself—but not the suburbs, if they were part of a different political division—was given an equal chance of falling into the sample. Samples were designed to yield between 450 and 500 interviews in eight cities, assuming a 75 percent response rate. In Kansas City, Kansas, and Kansas City, Missouri, the desired yield was 250 and 400 respectively, so that separate estimates could be made for each city.

In each city, the basis for the sample was the most recent R. L. Polk

Table 2-1. Interview Length, by City

City	Median Length (Minutes)
Albuquerque	61
Atlanta*	60
Baltimore*	70
Boston*	83
Denver	76
Kansas City, Kansas*	82
Kansas City, Missouri*	81
Milwaukee	56
Nashville*	73
San Diego	53

*Local Supplements were added to the core questionnaire.

Methods and Procedures 11

City Directory. However, the procedures were so designed that the quality of the sample was in no way dependent upon the accuracy or completeness of the City Directory inasmuch as:

1. If the City Directory indicated a single unit address, the interviewer checked the address and included all units associated with that address. Omitted units that were associated with what the City Directory indicated were single-family addresses were thus included.
2. At addresses that the City Directory indicated were multiple unit addresses, the City Directory listing of units were not relied on, but rather the interviewers went out and listed all housing units at the address; and a selection was based on the interviewer's listing, not on the City Directory.
3. A sample of blocks was selected and interviewers checked these blocks for addresses that did not appear at all in the City Directory. This block supplement procedure corrected for those cases in which an address was missing entirely from the City Directory.

The procedure entailed selecting specific housing units for which no substitutions could be made. Clusters of about five addresses per selected block were chosen to reduce travel costs.

Field Sampling Procedures

The interviewers were given assignments of cover sheets, each of which had the address of a specific housing unit on it. These were made out for single-family units at Public Opinion Survey Unit, University of Missouri, and after the listing procedure, for multi-unit and block supplement samples, either at P.O.S.U. or locally. Once addressed cover sheets had been assigned, the interviewer proceeded as follows:

1. An advance letter describing the sponsorship and purposes of the research was mailed to the address.
2. The interviewer called at the household. The first step was to ascertain that there was only one housing unit associated with the address on the cover sheet. If there was more than one, he or she made out separate cover sheets for each additional unit and they were included in the assignment.
3. When the interviewer made contact with a household, he or she listed each household member based on information given by any responsible adult in the household. The adults were then numbered in a specified way. A table, stamped on each cover sheet, indicated the number of the person who was to be interviewed. The tables were so structured that each adult in a household had an equal chance of being selected as the respondent. Since only one adult per household was to be interviewed, this procedure insured that the samples would have appropriate proportions of men, women, aged, and young

adults. This procedure is described in more detail in L. Kish, *Survey Sampling* (New York: John Wiley, 1965). All persons 18 years of age or older were defined as adults and were eligible to be the chosen respondent. Households that did not include anyone 18 or older were dropped from the sample.
4. Once the respondent had been identified, the interviewer either interviewed the person, if he or she was home, or arranged a more convenient time. No substitutions were permitted once a respondent had been selected.
5. Interviewers were required to make at least six calls, at least two of them in the evening or on a weekend, before they could turn in a cover sheet as a "non-interview" by reason of the respondent being "not at home." In many cases more than six calls were made. Before a refusal was accepted, it was usual for a second interviewer to try to explain the value of the study to the reluctant respondent.

Field Staffs

It was decided at an early stage that to maximize local involvement and to enhance local capability to conduct survey research, field work would be contracted to a local university-related organization in each city, rather than to a single national organization. In four cities, Milwaukee, Boston and the two Kansas Cities[2] there were existing university field organizations that maintained continuing staffs of interviewers and supervisors. In a fifth city, San Diego, no organization existed but there was a faculty member who had done a great deal of survey research and had a core staff of interviewers available that he had trained and who were experienced. In Atlanta, several surveys had also recently been done under the aegis of Georgia State University, and there was, as a result, a core of trained interviewers around which to build a staff. In the other four cities, Nashville, Denver, Albuquerque and Baltimore, new staffs had to be recruited and trained to do the interviewing.

Field Coordination

An interviewer instruction manual was prepared by the project director and used in all cities. Prior to the onset of field work, the project director met with each of the field supervisors to go over questions, problems, and procedures. Supervision and training, however, was all done at a local level. The only additional central involvement, in addition to answering specific questions that came up, was to review some of the early interviews from each city to catch major problems and misunderstandings.

On the average, about 20 interviewers were used in each city. It was not possible to begin field work simultaneously in all locations. The earliest interviews were taken in late June, 1970; the last was completed in October. In most cities, the data collection was accomplished in a period of six weeks to two months.

Quality of Field Work

One would expect some variability in the quality of field work, considering the differences among cities in experience with this kind of project. It is very difficult to obtain precise measures of the quality of field work, but the following are some dimensions normally considered.

Response rates are a function both of the effectiveness of the interviewing staff and the characteristics of the population to be interviewed. Response rates are almost always higher in rural areas than in urban areas and higher in single-family houses than in high-density apartment houses. Some of the cities have a considerable amount of suburban-type housing, others relatively little. The response rates varied from 64 percent to 82 percent. The median was 73 percent (Table 2-2). Undoubtedly, some of the variation in response rates was due to the different levels of experience between staffs. In Denver, where the response rate was lowest, the staff was composed of students who had not interviewed before.[3] Generally, however, there was no particular correlation between response rates and whether or not a wholly new staff was used. Overall, the response rates probably were not very different from the experience of established staffs in central cities for projects of this type. However, one of the problems of central city survey work is that response rates tend to be lower than is desirable and below those obtained for other populations.

Interviewers were instructed to record verbatim answers to the open questions. On the closed questions, if the respondent did not choose one of response alternatives, the interviewer was not to summarize his answer by checking a box. Interviewers were trained to ask the questions exactly as worded. If probing was required to get a fuller, more relevant answer, they were trained to probe non-directively—that is, by using such phrases as "anything else," "how

Table 2-2. Interview Results, by City

City	Number of Occupied Units Selected	Number of Interviews Completed	Response Rate*
Albuquerque	592	471	80%
Atlanta	639	469	73%
Baltimore	651	500	77%
Boston	713	507	71%
Denver	557	357	64%
Kansas City, Kansas	281	193	69%
Kansas City, Missouri	570	383	67%
Milwaukee	587	443	75%
Nashville	584	426	73%
San Diego	634	517	82%

*Percentage of occupied units selected at which an interview was completed.

do you mean that," "tell me more," which are standard probes that do not suggest answers to respondents.

It was very difficult to assess how well the interviewers followed these procedures. The quality of the verbatim recording was the only aspect that could be fairly well observed. On this dimension, coders rated Milwaukee, the Kansas Cities, Boston, and Albuquerque to be above average. With a couple of exceptions, the quality of interviewing appeared to be "satisfactory" to "good" on those dimensions that could be evaluated.

Respondent Selection

Selecting the respondent in each household involved numbering adults in a pre-determined way and then applying a selection table stamped on the cover sheet to identify the one adult to be interviewed. As Table 2–3 shows, interviewers in some cities had difficulty in performing this task properly, probably because it was new to some of the supervisors.

Perusal of the interviews shows, however, that the errors were almost all in numbering the adults. This is a non-biasing error. Once adults were numbered, the selection table was applied properly. When there was evidence of selection of the most convenient respondent or other such biasing procedures, the interview was not accepted. As the Table 2–3 shows, wrong respondents were about equally divided between men and women. Hence, these deviations from the design should not affect the quality of the data in any way.

Table 2–3. Sex of Wrong Respondents, Compared with Sex of Right Respondents, by City

City	Number of Males: Wrong Respondents	Number of Males Who Would Have Been Interviewed If Procedure Had Been Applied Correctly in These Households	Total Number of Wrong Respondents
Albuquerque	0	1	2
Atlanta	5	2	10
Baltimore	1	0	1
Boston			
Denver	3	3	8
Kansas City, Kansas	1	3	4
Kansas City, Missouri	2	2	
Milwaukee	0	1	1
Nashville	28	16	47
San Diego	4	2	9

Note: In each household there was one person who was to be interviewed. In some cases, the interviewer incorrectly selected the adult to be interviewed, which resulted in a "wrong respondent."

Coding

All interviews were mailed to the Joint Center for Urban Studies, Cambridge, Massachusetts, where a carefully trained group of coders translated the answers into numbers that were then punched onto cards and read onto tape for computer analysis. One interview in ten was independently coded and compared with the original coding to identify coders who needed further training or codes that were problematic as well as to obtain estimates of coding reliability. Coding reliability was better than 98 percent for most variables. In addition, over 250 checks for internal consistency of coding were made before analysis began.

RELIABILITY OF THE SURVEY DATA

Properly executed surveys of carefully selected samples of a population produce figures on the whole population that are quite reliable. However, it is very important for users of survey data to be aware of the limitations of the reliability of survey data and to exercise appropriate caution in reaching conclusions from such information.

Types of Error

There are three potential sources of error in survey data: sampling error, response error, and non-response bias.

Sampling Error. Sampling error, or sampling variability, is not biasing—that is, it does not consistently produce estimates that are different from true population values. However, because any sample of a population may be slightly different from other samples that might be drawn from that population, sample figures must be treated as estimates that in fact may be a little higher or lower than the actual figures. Thus, if a sample indicated that 50 percent of the households in a city were homeowners, the actual figure might be 48 percent or 52 percent. Fifty percent would be the best estimate; there is no reason to think that a properly drawn sample systematically would underestimate or overestimate homeowners. However, in using the figure, one should be aware that the true figure could vary from 50 percent by a few percentage points either way.

One can calculate how far the true population value could by chance differ from the sample estimate. For reasons that are mysterious but widely accepted, it is most usual to report a range around the sample figure within which one can be 95 percent certain that the true population value will fall. Thus, it is usual to say that 50 percent of the households in the city are homeowners, with a confidence interval of 5 percentage points. This statement would mean that there are 95 chances in 100 that the true population figure is between 45 percent and 55 percent. It also means that 50 percent is the most likely figure and that as estimates get further from 50 percent they are increasingly less likely to be the true population figure.

There are two things that affect the variability of a sample estimate: the size of the sample and the percentage of the sample purported to have a characteristic.[4] *Ceteris paribus*, the larger the sample the smaller will be the range of sampling variability around a figure based on the sample. Moreover, there is a wider range of uncertainty around an estimate that 50 percent of the population are homeowners than there is around an estimate that 10 or 90 percent are homeowners. Note that for this purpose, 10 and 90 percent are equivalent; for saying that 10 percent of the population are homeowners is equivalent to saying that 90 percent are not homeowners. The reliability of the two statements based on the same sample is the same. Table 2-4 presents average sampling variabilities for different percentage figures and sample sizes. The table should be used as a gauge to the reliability of sample figures. The chances are 95 in 100 that the true population figure lies in the range of the sample percentage plus or minus the number of percentage points shown in the table.[5]

Example:
There are 100 black households in the sample; 50 percent are homeowners.

The table presents a figure of 11 percentage points for samples of 100 and percentages around 50 percent.

Thus the chances are 95 in 100 that between 39 and 61 percent of all black households in the city are homeowners.

Table 2-4. Approximate Sampling Errors for the Citizen Attitude Study *(Chances are 95 in 100 that the central value lies within the reported value, plus or minus the number of percentage points shown in this table.)*

Sample Size	Sampling Errors for Reported Percentage Around				
	5 or 95%	10 or 90%	20 or 80%	30 or 70%	50%
50	–	–	12	14	15
100	–	7	9	10	11
200	3	5	6	7	8
300	3	4	5	6	6
400	2	3	4	5	6
500	2	3	4	5	5

Note: The actual sampling errors were not computed for this study. The figures in Tables 2-4 and 2-5 are about 10 percent higher than a simple random sample would yield. Actual calculations of sampling errors for many variables from comparable samples indicate these estimates to be reasonable or conservative. However, they are only average estimates; and the actual sampling errors for any given variable may be higher or lower than the estimates given here.

In addition to knowing the reliability of population estimates, people are also interested in the reliability of obtained differences between groups. For example, if in a sample, older people were more often homeowners than younger people, one would want to know if there really was a difference in the population, or if this difference could be due to chance variability of the sample. In other words, if another sample were drawn, what are the chances that older people would be homeowners more often than young adults?

Again, how big a difference is needed depends on the size of the samples and the percentage figures involved. Table 2–5 presents estimates of the differences required to be 95 percent confident that two groups in fact differ in the way the sample indicates.

Table 2–5. Sampling Errors of Differences *(When a percentage difference between two different sub-groups exceeds the figures in the table, the chances are 95 in 100 that the two sub-groups are in fact different.)*

Size of Sample or Group	75	100	200	350	500
For Proportions from About 30% to 70%					
75	15	14	13	12	12
100		13	12	11	10
200			10	9	8
350				7	7
500					6
For Proportions Around 20% or 80%					
75	13	13	11	10	10
100		11	10	9	9
200			8	7	7
350				6	6
500					5
For Proportions Around 10% or 90%					
75	10	10	8	8	8
100		9	8	7	7
200			6	6	6
350				5	5
500					4
For Proportions Around 5% or 95%					
200			5	4	4
350				4	3
500					3

Example:
There are 190 persons over 65 in the sample; 36 percent own homes. There are 93 persons under 30 in the sample; 23 percent own houses. There is thus a 13 percentage point difference between the two groups.

The table shows that when comparing groups sized about 200 and about 100 for percentages near 30 percent, a 12 percentage point difference is needed to be 95 percent confident that there is a real difference between the two groups in the population.

The difference found in the sample is that large, and one can conclude that the two groups are in fact probably different.

Statistical Tests. "Statistical significance," which is the way scientists refer to a relationship or difference that probably is real and not chance, is not the same as social or political significance. Differences as small as 4 or 5 percentage points may be statistically significant; i.e., they indicate real differences between groups. However, that does not necessarily mean that they are important social differences.

On the other hand, tests of significance are useful as a guard against taking too seriously differences or relationships that may not be real. The preceding tables show that groups differing by 10 or even 15 percentage points may not be "significantly" different if the samples of these groups are small. Such differences, while possibly politically significant, should be taken as suggestive—differences that need to be further documented.

When one is dealing with samples of 100 or more, it is relatively unusual for a really important difference not also to be statistically significant. However, when samples drop below 100, sampling variability rises sharply and much more caution is required.

One final note: when samples drop much below 50, the sampling variability is usually sufficiently great that even presenting the figures may be more misleading than illuminating.

Response Error. Response error refers to errors in the data resulting from either the interviewer or the respondent failing to do the job he is supposed to do. The most readily identifiable result is information that is "not ascertained"—that is, the respondent did not give a codable answer to a question. Such events occur when the respondent does not know or is unwilling to give the answers, or when the interviewer fails to probe an inadequate initial answer by the respondent.

The number of such answers is usually small, but in a few cases, it may be larger. It often is reasonable to assume that "not ascertained" answers are random events. However, there are at least two types of situations when this may not be reasonable. First, people who do not know very much about a topic are most likely to give inadequate answers to attitude questions. In this respect, the people who give "not ascertained" responses may be systematically different from those who answer the question. Second, certain types of presumably sensitive questions—such as those regarding income—show patterns of the people not likely to answer. In the case of income, those with incomes at the extremes— either high or low—are more likely not to answer. Excluding the "not ascertained" answers from a distribution is, in effect, assuming that they are random, not systematic, occurrences.

Other kinds of response error are harder to identify. When an interviewer does not record an answer completely, when a respondent slants his answer in the direction he thinks will please the interviewer, when an interviewer probes directively, errors occur that are difficult to identify later. In general, we rely on careful, thorough training of interviewers to keep such errors to a minimum. We think for most purposes they are not prevalent enough to affect conclusions based on the data. However, it is not possible to estimate where, or how often, such errors might have occurred.

Non-Response Bias. Non-response bias occurs because all people selected in the sample are not interviewed. Even when every effort is made, there is always a certain percentage of a sample that either cannot be reached or will not agree to participate. Insofar as the non-respondents (those selected but not interviewed) differ from those interviewed, the sample of interviews is a biased sample of the population—that is, it is systematically different from the population. Note how this differs from sampling error, which is not systematic, or biased, but simply a random, chance deviation from the true population.

When response rates (the percentage of the selected sample actually interviewed) is 85 percent or above, the effect of non-response usually is relatively slight on most percentage distributions. As response rates get lower, the researcher has to be increasingly concerned with the characteristics of those in the population not represented in his data. It is obviously not feasible to measure all of the ways non-respondents differ from respondents. However, interviewers were asked to write down as much information as they could learn about those whom they could not interview. Comparison of respondents and non-respondents on a city-by-city basis shows the following trends.

In most cities there was a slight tendency for there to be too few households with only one adult among those at which an interview was taken. The order of magnitude of this trend is that between one-fifth and one-fourth of the households in most cities had only one adult but one-fourth to one-third of the non-interview households contained only one adult. The effect of this bias is fairly insignificant.

Of somewhat more significance is the fact that households in which there were no minor children were over represented among the non-respondents (Table 2-6). There were no children in around one-half of the households in most cities, but closer to two-thirds of those in the sample who were not interviewed had no children. Although interviewers did not always get this information on households not interviewed, there can be little question that households with children were slightly over represented in the study samples.

Another fairly clear pattern, at least in those seven cities where blacks constitute a substantial portion of the population, is that blacks were probably somewhat over represented in the interviewed sample (Table 2–7). The response rates in most cities were better in the black community than in the white community.

It is reasonable to ask how much non-responses affected the data. A couple of extreme examples may be helpful. Although the large number of cases—one-third to one-half—for which interviewers did not get the needed information mean the figures are only estimates, they will illustrate the magnitude of the effect that non-response can have on data.

The lowest response rate obtained was 64 percent in Denver. Denver was also extreme in that 51 percent of the households interviewed did not have any children, whereas 65 percent of the non-interviews for which interviewers obtained household composition information did not have any children. Yet even in this extreme case, one would estimate that 55 percent of all selected households had no children, only 4 percent different from the estimate based only on those actually interviewed. In general, most of the estimates for the effect of non-response that we can make are smaller than the 4 percent effect noted above. However, there was one extreme case with respect to racial composition that illustrates how important and serious non-response bias can be.

In Baltimore, the response rate was a respectable 78 percent. However, the response rate was much better in the black community than in the white community. A little over half of all those interviewed were black; but only 12 percent of all the non-respondents were black. From the sample of interviews, one would estimate that 52 percent of the population was black. However, adding the non-response data changed the estimate to 43 percent. Such a differential response is most unusual to find in survey research. In most of the cities, the inclusion of estimates of the racial composition of the non-respondents would change the population estimates by less than two or three percentage points. Nonetheless, the Baltimore experience illustrates well the potential of non-response to bias sample survey data. While other attitudinal and demographic differences related to these biases cannot be measured, the above are issues that should be carefully considered in interpreting the data.

Comparisons with Census

One way to estimate the effects of sampling variability and non-response is to compare the characteristics of the samples with census data. Tables 2–8 and 2–9 present these comparisons for owner occupancy and race of household. It is apparent that the estimates of owner occupancy and black

Methods and Procedures 21

Table 2–6. Whether Children Under 18 Years in the Household of Non-Respondents, by City

Response	Albuquerque	Atlanta	Baltimore	Boston	Denver	Kansas City, Kansas	Kansas City, Missouri	Milwaukee	Nashville	San Diego
No Children	25%	32%	31%	62%	31%	46%	53%	56%	39%	38%
Children	31	18	16	18	17	20	21	26	23	30
Not Ascertained	44	50	53	20	52	34	26	18	38	32
Total	100%	100%	100%	100%	100%	100%	100%	100%	100%	100%
(N)	(137)	(170)	(141)	(206)	(197)	(68)	(187)	(146)	(154)	(95)

Table 2–7. Ethnicity of Non-Respondents, by City

Ethnicity	Atlanta	Baltimore	Boston	Kansas City, Kansas	Kansas City, Missouri	Milwaukee	Nashville
White	57%	87%	67%	84%	80%	80%	75%
Black	27	12	15	13	11	15	6
Not Ascertained	16	1	18	3	9	5	19
Total	100%	100%	100%	100%	100%	100%	100%
(N)	(170)	(141)	(206)	(68)	(187)	(146)	(154)

Note: Albuquerque, Denver, and San Diego are not represented in this table because their black populations are too small.

Table 2–8. Comparison Between Census Figures and Citizen Attitude Survey Figures for Owner Occupancy

	Albuquerque	Atlanta	Baltimore	Boston	Denver	Kansas City, Kansas	Kansas City, Missouri	Milwaukee	Nashville	San Diego
U.S. Census	65%	41%	45%	27%	50%	63%	65%	47%	60%	51%
Citizen Attitude Survey	66%	45%	46%	26%	53%	66%	68%	47%	64%	46%

Table 2–9. Comparison Between Census Figures and Citizen Attitude Survey Figures for Percent of Blacks in the Population

	Albuquerque	Atlanta	Baltimore	Boston	Denver	Kansas City, Kansas	Kansas City, Missouri	Milwaukee	Nashville	San Diego
U.S. Census	2%	51%	46%	16%	9%	20%	22%	15%	20%	8%
Citizen Attitude Survey	3%	45%	52%	20%	7%	25%	20%	14%	18%	5%

Note: Census figures include those in group quarters, while Citizen Attitude data relate only to the population housing units.

occupancy from the U. S. Census figures and the survey samples generally are very similar, and the differences that did occur are almost all within the range of normal sampling variability.

CONCLUSION

Anyone who is using data should know how far the data can be generalized and be aware of the ways in which the data can lead, or simply enable, a mind to reach an unjustified conclusion. At the same time, though there is error, these survey data, taken as a body and used well, provide reliable information not otherwise available. There are many bases other than surveys on which conclusions are reached about how people feel and what they think. None is error-free, however; and for most it is difficult or impossible to estimate the type and magnitude of error. It is hard to make a case that any method is more adequate at portraying a total population's views in a non-biased fashion than a properly conceived and executed survey.

NOTES TO CHAPTER TWO

1. A more detailed description of the sampling procedure is available on request from the National League of Cities Secretariat.
2. The Survey Research Laboratory, University of Wisconsin; the Joint Center for Urban Studies of M.I.T. and Harvard; and the Public Opinion Survey Unit, University of Missouri, respectively.
3. The use of students as interviewers was discouraged; and only in Denver—where there was reliance on a graduate student program in which students were older than average—was there any significant amount of interviewing done by students.
4. The number of cases on which a percentage is based is usually presented in each table. In some cases, the presentation of data for sub-groups made this procedure difficult. The N's for major analytic sub-groups for each city are in Appendix A.
5. The estimated sampling errors may be higher for sub-groups that are highly clustered. Thus, for example, if one were looking at figures for neighborhood areas or for groups that may be concentrated geographically, a more conservative interval might be appropriate.

Chapter Three

The Ten Cities

It is important to understand some of the differences between the participating cities in order to better understand the responses citizens gave regarding city problems and city services.[1]

POPULATION AND HOUSING DATA

The cities differ in size, as well as location. Populations range from about 170,000 in Kansas City, Kansas, to close to 910,000 in Baltimore (Table 3-1). It is probably very significant that they also differ in the extent to which they include all of the metropolitan area. Less than one-fourth of Greater Boston residents live in the city of Boston, for example, while the cities of Nashville and Albuquerque encompass most of their metropolitan area populations. In a majority of the cities, central cities include about half the metropolitan population. A related issue is population density. Those cities with high density (such as Boston and Baltimore) may be better able to support certain services than other cities (for example, mass transportation); but at the same time, higher population density may contribute to the incidence of other problems.

The cities differ considerably in their housing stock (Table 3-2). Cities that had early growth and substantial suburbs outside the city have relatively fewer detached single-family houses. In Albuquerque and the two Kansas Cities, about three-fourths or more of the housing is in single-family structures, and over half of the housing units are single-family houses in seven of the cities. However, in Baltimore and Boston, where two- to four-family houses and row houses are dominant, only about 10 percent of all housing units are single-family structures. In Milwaukee, only 40 percent of the housing units are single-family structures. Atlanta is distinctive in that over 30 percent of the housing in the city is in buildings with five or more units.

The kind of housing in a city will influence the kinds of housing

Table 3-1. Population in the Ten Cities

City	1970 Population[a]	Percent of SMSA Population in Central City	Persons Per Square Mile	Black Population	Percent of Population That Is Black
Albuquerque	243,751	77	4,200	5,400	2
Atlanta	496,973	35	3,700	255,000	51
Baltimore	905,759	44	11,600	420,200	46
Boston	641,071	23	13,900	104,700	16
Denver	514,678	42	7,600	47,000	9
Kansas City, Kansas	168,213	13[b]	3,900[c]	34,300	20
Kansas City, Missouri	507,087	41[b]	3,900[c]	112,000	22
Milwaukee	717,099	51	8,000	105,100	15
Nashville	448,003	83	850	87,900	20
San Diego	696,769	51	3,600	53,000	8

[a]1970 population figures include persons living in group quarters.
[b]Kansas City SMSA population includes both Kansas City, Kansas, and Kansas City, Missouri.
[c]Average persons per square mile for Kansas City, Kansas, and Kansas City, Missouri.

Table 3-2. Type of Housing Unit, by City

Type of Housing Unit	Albuquerque	Atlanta	Baltimore	Boston	Denver	Kansas City, Kansas	Kansas City, Missouri	Milwaukee	Nashville	San Diego
Single-Family House	85%	52%	10%	9%	60%	78%	74%	41%	70%	68%
2 to 4 Family or Row	8	12	77	60	16	9	11	38	14	13
5 or More Apartments	4	32	10	27	20	8	10	17	13	15
Other	2	2	2	3	1	4	4	3	1	2
Not Ascertained	1	2	1	1	3	1	1	1	2	2
Total	100%	100%	100%	100%	100%	100%	100%	100%	100%	100%
(N)[a]	(471)	(469)	(500)	(507)	(357)	(193)	(383)	(443)	(426)	(517)

Note: The source of these figures and all other figures presented is the Citizen Attitude Survey sample data, unless otherwise noted.
[a] In this and all subsequent tables, N refers to the number of cases (interviews) on which a percentage distribution is based.

problems people have. Along with other things, the kind of housing also will affect the rate of home ownership in a city (Table 3-3). As an average, about half the housing units in these cities are occupied by the owners; the other half by renters. In Boston, however, less than one-third of all housing units are owner-occupied, while in Albuquerque, Nashville and the two Kansas Cities, about two-thirds are. Along with size and physical differences, there are also differences in the population that lives in a city. Close to one-half the people in Atlanta and Baltimore are black, but blacks account for less than 10 percent of those living in San Diego, Denver, and Albuquerque (Table 3-4). In the rest of the cities, around a fifth of the population is black. As a consequence, adequate samples of the black population were obtained in only seven cities: Boston, Baltimore, Atlanta, Milwaukee, Nashville and the two Kansas Cities. In Kansas City, Kansas, the number of blacks in the sample was marginal and should be treated with caution. People of Spanish descent constitute a quarter of the Albuquerque population and over 10 percent of the Denver population. There are substantial Catholic populations in Boston and Milwaukee (more than half) as well as in Albuquerque (about 40 percent), as can be seen on Table 3-5. The attitudes of Catholics and people of Spanish descent are only infrequently singled out for analysis in this report.[2]

SOCIO-ECONOMIC CHARACTERISTICS

Another important consideration is the socio-economic characteristics of a city's population. The figures on income are hard to interpret because of regional differences in salary scales and costs of living (Table 3-6). Education, however, may be more meaningful (Table 3-7). It is noteworthy, for example, that over 40 percent of the adults in Albuquerque and San Diego have attended college, compared with less than one-fourth of the adults in Baltimore, Milwaukee, and Kansas City, Kansas. There also are differences among cities in the prevalence of various household types (Table 3-8). In Boston and Atlanta, for example, almost one-third of all households consist of single individuals or unrelated roommates; by contrast in Baltimore, Nashville, and Albuquerque, such households constitute only one-sixth of all households. The former cities have a correspondingly lower rate of families—that is, married couples and families with children.

EVALUATING INTER-CITY DIFFERENCES

The list of differences between the cities could be extended almost without end. The importance of the complexity of inter-city differences is very important in interpreting the data that follow. When the residents of two cities differ markedly in the way they answer a question, there are likely to be many plausible explanations because every pair of cities differs in so many ways.

There are at least three classes of differences to be examined in most

Table 3-3. Home Tenure, by City

Home Tenure	Albuquerque	Atlanta	Baltimore	Boston	Denver	Kansas City, Kansas	Kansas City, Missouri	Milwaukee	Nashville	San Diego
Owns	66%	45%	46%	26%	53%	66%	68%	47%	64%	56%
Rents	31	55	53	73	46	34	30	52	34	41
Other	2	*	*	1	*	*	1	1	1	3
Not Ascertained	1	*	*	*	1	*	1	*	1	*
Total	100%	100%	100%	100%	100%	100%	100%	100%	100%	100%
(N)	(471)	(469)	(500)	(507)	(357)	(193)	(383)	(443)	(426)	(517)

*Less than 0.5 percent.

Table 3-4. Ethnicity of Adults, by City

Ethnicity	Albuquerque	Atlanta	Baltimore	Boston	Denver	Kansas City, Kansas	Kansas City, Missouri	Milwaukee	Nashville	San Diego
White, not of Spanish Descent	67%	55%	56%	76%	77%	70%	75%	84%	79%	83%
White of Spanish Descent	27	1	1	2	13	2	3	1	1	6
Black	3	44	43[a]	20	7	25	20	14	18	5
Other	2	*	*	2	1	2	2	1	1	5
Not Ascertained	1	*	*	*	2	1	*	*	1	1
Total	100%	100%	100%	100%	100%	100%	100%	100%	100%	100%
(N)	(471)	(469)	(500)	(507)	(357)	(193)	(383)	(443)	(426)	(517)

[a]Adjusted for differential non-response, 52 percent of interviews were with blacks.
*Less than 0.5 percent.

Table 3-5. Religion of Adults, by City

Religion	Albuquerque	Atlanta	Baltimore	Boston	Denver	Kansas City, Kansas	Kansas City, Missouri	Milwaukee	Nashville	San Diego
Protestant	56%	91%	71%	31%	64%	78%	75%	48%	89%	64%
Catholic	41	6	23	59	28	20	22	50	8	30
Other	2	2	5	9	6	1	2	2	2	5
Not Ascertained	1	1	1	1	2	1	1	*	1	1
Total	100%	100%	100%	100%	100%	100%	100%	100%	100%	100%
(N)	(471)	(469)	(500)	(507)	(357)	(193)	(383)	(443)	(426)	(517)

*Less than 0.5 percent.

Table 3-6. Total Family Income, by City

Income	Albuquerque	Atlanta	Baltimore	Boston	Denver	Kansas City, Kansas	Kansas City, Missouri	Milwaukee	Nashville	San Diego
Less than $5,000	22%	30%	20%	33%	24%	29%	23%	26%	20%	20%
$5,000 to $9,999	33	32	40	35	41	41	33	33	33	30
$10,000 to $14,999	19	16	22	16	16	18	25	24	20	25
$15,000 or More	17	17	13	10	12	9	15	10	15	20
Not Ascertained	9	5	5	6	7	3	4	7	12	5
Total	100%	100%	100%	100%	100%	100%	100%	100%	100%	100%
(N)	(471)	(469)	(500)	(507)	(357)	(193)	(383)	(443)	(426)	(517)
Median Income (in dollars)	8,700	7,400	8,400	6,900	7,800	7,400	8,900	8,500	8,300	9,500

Table 3-7. Education of Adults, by City

Education	Albuquerque	Atlanta	Baltimore	Boston	Denver	Kansas City, Kansas	Kansas City, Missouri	Milwaukee	Nashville	San Diego
8 Years or Less	12%	18%	21%	19%	14%	16%	16%	21%	20%	7%
Some High School	12	19	23	18	13	27	12	20	17	11
High School Graduate	34	26	34	35	37	39	40	36	29	38
Some College	21	18	14	13	20	14	21	15	20	28
College Graduate or Higher Degree	20	19	8	14	16	4	11	8	13	16
Not Ascertained	1	*	*	1	*	*	*	*	1	*
Total	100%	100%	100%	100%	100%	100%	100%	100%	100%	100%
(N)	(471)	(469)	(500)	(507)	(357)	(193)	(383)	(443)	(426)	(517)

*Less than 0.5 percent.

Table 3-8. Household Composition

Household Composition	Albuquerque	Atlanta	Baltimore	Boston	Denver	Kansas City, Kansas	Kansas City, Missouri	Milwaukee	Nashville	San Diego
One Person	15%	22%	15%	23%	19%	16%	18%	18%	12%	19%
Unrelated Persons	3	6	1	6	5	1	3	4	2	4
Married Couple	21	17	18	20	18	25	22	21	25	24
Married Couple, with Children	46	34	38	30	40	41	44	40	44	42
Other with Children	11	14	22	15	14	13	11	12	12	8
Other	4	7	6	6	3	4	2	5	4	3
Not Ascertained	*	*	*	*	1	*	*	*	1	*
Total	100%	100%	100%	100%	100%	100%	100%	100%	100%	100%
(N)	(471)	(469)	(500)	(507)	(357)	(193)	(383)	(443)	(426)	(517)

*Less than 0.5 percent.

cases: the historical and present nature of the problem, the way city officials have addressed the problem, and the perceptions and needs of the citizens. Let us take, as an example, citizen ratings of the "quality of education children get in the public schools." When the average rating differs between two cities, it could be because school officials in one city are, in fact, doing a better job of hiring and supervising teachers, planning curricula, providing educational goals. Before judging the school officials, however, one would also want to consider the difficulty of the school situation: the fiscal resources, the amount of community support, the prevalence of learning and social problems in the school population. Moreover, one would want to consider the characteristics of the residents who rated the schools. People may differ markedly in what they know about schools, what they expect a school system to do, and in their own individual needs and interests. Many tables that follow show greater differences in attitude between groups within cities than between cities. An evaluation of a service is always a joint product of what is being judged and who is doing the judging.

There are places in our discussion where differences in city populations such as those presented in this chapter clearly help to explain city differences in attitude responses. In general, however, it is difficult to be confident of explanations of why city averages differ because of the multitude of possible explanatory factors. In particular, the step from a citizen service rating to a direct assessment of the quality of administration in a city is a difficult one and one that we seldom have adequate data in this study alone to make.

NOTES TO CHAPTER THREE

1. Population figures in this chapter are from the 1970 census. Other figures are based on the survey data. It is important to notice that the survey data relate only to the population in housing units; those living in dormitories or institutional settings were not included. The census includes people in "group quarters" with total counts, and in some of the published population descriptions. Census and the survey data are comparable only when the reference is to the population in housing units.
2. Because there are only two cities for which there were samples of Spanish, large enough to be reliable, the ability to generalize about them was quite limited. It was felt that the strength of this analysis was to identify general trends in cities and that the distinctive views of Spanish respondents could be most appropriately addressed in the local reports in the two cities where the samples are adequate.

Chapter Four

Priorities

City officials are constantly faced with choices in determining the direction of city problems, programs, and services. Often the direction of such decisions is determined by practical limitations—money and manpower. Some choices are based on cost/benefit analyses; others are responses to voices loud enough to be heard above the crowd. Only rarely is the city official equipped with adequate data on the sentiment of the population as a whole which he can use to weight other factors in selecting programs and services to improve or to cut back.

The situation is paradoxical, however; not all of the people in a city are well informed about all the issues, even though they pay the taxes that support city-provided services. Individual citizens' attitudes are a combination of their knowledge of the issue and their personal values; yet a survey of these attitudes can be an important measure of public support.

Although the ten cities in this Citizen Attitude Survey cannot be assumed to be a representative sample of all cities, some of the data do suggest very consistent patterns across cities on some of the issues raised. The results of the survey are presented from two points of view: the identification of issues on which citizens believe the city should increase their expenditures, and the identification of issues which citizens perceive as important. Both viewpoints are useful considerations for the city official who is concerned with public support in decision making.

WHAT ARE THE MOST IMPORTANT PROBLEMS FOR LOCAL GOVERNMENTS TO WORK ON?

Sixteen items were chosen that were thought to characterize major service areas people might be concerned about. These items were selected after extensive discussion among the research and city participants. A key criterion for inclusion on the list was that the item be a local problem—either one that entailed local tax money or at least one that local policy could effect. Thus, foreign policy and Social Security were excluded. Freeways, welfare, low-cost housing, transportation and medical care are problem areas in which the role of city government varies from city-to-city, but they were local concerns frequently enough to justify inclusion. In those cases for which more than one resource was available to address a problem, the wording focussed on the problem area.

People were given the list and asked whether they thought the local government ought to be spending "more" than at present, the "same," or "less" on each one. The items were:

Public schools.
Police patrolling the streets at night.
Giving tickets and towing cars parked in illegal places.
Street lighting.
Cleaning and repairing streets.
Providing medical care to people who cannot afford to pay for it themselves.
Cleaning up parks and playgrounds for small children.
Places for teen-age boys to go when they want to play a game, have some recreation, or a good time.
Trash and garbage collection.
Inspecting and making owners clean up houses that are run down or have rats or other safety hazards.
Helping kids and others who are on drugs.
Building low-cost housing.
Controlling air pollution.
Improving public transportation.
Building freeways.
Welfare and aid for dependent children (AFDC).

People were then asked to select the three most important areas for increased effort.

How Do People Rank These Issues?

There are two ways to deal with these data: (1) the percentage of people in each city who said that more money should be spent on a given service, and (2) the frequency with which a service was selected as one of the most important areas for increased effort. These two approaches gave similar, but far from identical, orderings. In some cases, many people thought an area needed more expenditure, but not too many people thought it was among the three most important areas for increased effort. Using the data from either one of these questions, however, one reaches the conclusion that the item on the list about which there was most sentiment for increased effort was "helping kids and others who are on drugs."[1]

In every city, about 70 percent or more of the people said the city should be spending more on this problem, as shown in Table 4–1. In all cities, this was also one of the most cited items when people were asked to choose the three most important items for increased effort (Table 4–2). These data parallel the answers to the direct question of whether or not people considered drugs to be a serious problem in their city (Table 4–3). Between 65 and 95 percent of the people in the ten cities said that drug use among young people was a "serious" problem.

Do People Want to Help Drug Users, Or Do They Want to Catch Them and Punish Them?

Undoubtedly what they want to do is stop drug use. When we asked people what cities should be going about the drug problem, the answers covered both law enforcement and therapeutic approaches (Table 4–4). Around one-third of the people focused on law enforcement and getting the drug sellers in one way or another. Another 25 percent of the people in cities wanted more direct control of drug users—that is, stiffer laws, more law enforcement, and so on. Altogether, those who were primarily using the police and law enforcement techniques on users or sellers to stop drug use constituted over one-half of the people who wanted to do something more about the drug problem. On the other hand, around 12 percent of the people answering the question thought drug education was the strategy to use; another 10 percent focused on treatment centers and counseling. Altogether roughly 25 percent of the people in the cities focused on education and treatment, rather than law enforcement. Thus, probably more peoples' first response to the problem is the law enforcement rather than the therapeutic approach to the problem. Nonetheless, when the question was phrased as "helping kids on drugs," a large number of people responded positively.

What's The Second Priority Item?

The next highest degree of consensus was that the cities should spend more money on inspecting houses and making owners clean up substandard or hazardous conditions (Table 4–1). Most of the population in every single city thought the city should be spending more money on this sort of activity. The rate was quite constant among all cities—between 55 and 72 percent of the adults in the population. It is notable, however, that when people were asked for their choice of the three most important issues, inspecting houses was seldom selected, as can be seen in Table 4–2.

What Are the Next Most Important Issues?

The two mentioned above, drugs and house inspection, stand out because they were supported by majorities in all cities. Next in line, there were six or seven services that were bunched closely together.

Majorities in six or seven cities said more money should be spent on

Table 4-1. Attitudes of People Toward Spending for Selected Services

Item	Albuquerque	Atlanta	Baltimore	Boston	Denver	Kansas City, Kansas	Kansas City, Missouri	Milwaukee	Nashville	San Diego
Public Schools										
Spend more	53	61	72	66	47	59	59	38	60	45
Spend same	41	32	23	26	46	33	37	55	35	45
Spend less	4	3	3	2	3	6	3	5	1	7
Police Patrolling										
Spend more	50	59	70	70	46	56	66	41	62	33
Spend same	45	33	20	24	48	36	32	52	33	61
Spend less	2	4	8	3	2	6	2	2	2	3
Ticketing & Towing										
Spend more	6	19	8	14	4	12	8	8	11	5
Spend same	53	45	27	35	36	46	44	48	44	51
Spend less	37	31	63	47	53	40	47	40	40	40
Street Lighting										
Spend more	36	41	36	31	45	42	42	26	39	34
Spend same	57	50	55	60	44	53	53	67	54	62
Spend less	5	6	6	5	9	4	4	6	4	3
Cleaning & Repairing Streets										
Spend more	52	57	49	56	41	54	64	26	61	25
Spend same	43	38	41	39	54	42	34	69	35	71
Spend less	3	2	9	3	1	3	1	4	2	2
Medical Care for Poor										
Spend more	45	62	73	65	44	64	58	55	64	42
Spend same	41	28	23	26	43	29	35	35	29	44
Spend less	9	6	2	6	7	5	6	7	3	8

Cleaning Parks & Playgrounds										
Spend more	24	47	49	55	29	43	27	23	42	21
Spend same	66	44	42	38	61	51	65	68	50	71
Spend less	7	5	7	4	7	5	8	6	4	4
Recreation for Teenage Boys										
Spend more	49	61	69	62	46	55	49	46	56	49
Spend same	41	31	23	28	44	37	44	47	36	44
Spend less	6	4	6	7	7	6	7	5	4	4
Trash & Garbage Collection										
Spend more	40	48	33	24	15	33	44	21	33	11
Spend same	52	47	60	71	78	59	47	73	61	85
Spend less	5	2	6	3	3	6	7	4	2	2
Inspecting Houses										
Spend more	55	69	72	72	61	66	66	61	59	56
Spend same	34	25	24	23	30	30	30	32	32	35
Spend less	6	3	2	1	4	3	3	5	4	3
Helping Kids on Drugs										
Spend more	75	83	86	81	68	79	75	69	79	77
Spend same	21	12	11	12	21	18	24	23	16	18
Spend less	2	2	2	3	4	2	—	5	2	3
Low-Cost Housing										
Spend more	49	58	66	68	50	52	45	52	52	41
Spend same	34	27	24	20	31	34	39	30	34	38
Spend less	14	11	9	9	13	11	15	16	9	16

Table 4-1. (cont.)

Item	Albuquerque	Atlanta	Baltimore	Boston	Denver	Kansas City, Kansas	Kansas City, Missouri	Milwaukee	Nashville	San Diego
Control Air Pollution										
Spend same	47	63	50	62	62	43	55	55	52	61
Spend more	43	24	29	25	25	34	33	33	37	33
Spend less	7	8	19	8	7	20	11	9	6	4
Improved Public Transportation										
Spend same	29	52	49	50	63	33	43	36	30	36
Spend more	55	35	40	38	25	47	49	48	51	51
Spend less	11	8	9	8	7	17	7	14	13	10
Building Freeways										
Spend more	20	36	17	18	25	22	22	12	31	11
Spend same	57	43	36	32	45	51	52	38	49	65
Spend less	22	17	45	46	24	26	26	48	16	22
Welfare & AFDC										
Spend more	38	51	59	41	25	43	40	31	41	24
Spend same	44	34	28	35	40	44	41	42	44	51
Spend less	15	10	11	20	27	12	17	24	9	20

Note: Percentages do not total 100 percent because "not ascertained" responses are omitted.

Table 4-2. In Which Three Areas Are Increased Efforts by Local Government Most Needed?

Item	Albuquerque	Atlanta	Baltimore	Boston	Denver	Kansas City, Kansas	Kansas City, Missouri	Milwaukee	Nashville	San Diego
Public Schools	41	41	43	39	30	41	40	21	46	32
Police Patrolling	25	23	35	43	19	37	43	28	30	17
Ticketing & Towing	1	2	1	2	1	6	2	2	2	1
Street Lighting	10	7	6	7	5	17	10	8	6	9
Cleaning & Repairing Streets	18	11	9	10	9	16	23	7	20	8
Medical Care for Poor	23	27	32	32	24	28	34	35	33	25
Cleaning Parks & Playgrounds	5	7	5	6	3	3	3	5	6	6
Recreation for Teen-age Boys	21	19	17	15	15	23	11	20	19	25
Trash & Garbage Collection	14	16	6	4	6	9	19	6	8	4
Inspecting Houses	17	16	22	21	22	21	17	29	15	18
Helping Kids on Drugs	50	46	55	44	47	40	46	48	46	63
Low-Cost Housing	15	16	22	26	16	12	7	23	13	13
Control Air Pollution	23	22	12	15	39	16	19	25	16	39
Public Transportation	6	12	6	11	29	8	7	11	7	17
Building Freeways	3	5	1	1	4	1	5	4	5	2
Welfare & AFDC	16	19	23	13	12	18	14	17	12	12

Note: Percentages represent population which chose area as one of three most important for increased effort. Percentages will add to about 300 percent (minus those not responding), reflecting the fact that each person had an opportunity to choose three areas.

44 Citizen Attitudes Toward Local Government, Services, and Taxes

Table 4-3. How Much of a Problem is Drug Use Among Young People?

Response	Albuquerque	Atlanta	Baltimore	Boston	Denver	Kansas City, Kansas	Kansas City, Missouri	Milwaukee	Nashville	San Diego
Serious Problem	82%	80%	94%	89%	77%	65%	79%	75%	71%	86%
Some Problem	13	15	6	7	15	25	16	19	23	9
A Little Problem	2	2	*	1	2	3	3	3	4	4
No Problem at All	1	1	*	*	3	2	1	*	*	*
Not Ascertained	2	2	*	3	3	5	2	3	2	1
Total	100%	100%	100%	100%	100%	100%	100%	100%	100%	100%
(N)	(471)	(469)	(500)	(507)	(357)	(193)	(383)	(443)	(426)	(517)

*Less than 0.5 percent.

Table 4-4. Ways in Which City Government Can Help with Drug Problem, by City

Item	Albuquerque	Atlanta	Baltimore	Boston	Denver	Kansas City, Kansas	Kansas City, Missouri	Milwaukee	Nashville	San Diego
Law Enforcement against Sellers	16	24	27	20	20	15	17	23	17	17
Law Enforcement against Users	17	20	18	11	18	13	17	21	15	18
Drug Education	14	10	7	12	13	8	10	11	13	16
Treatment and Counseling	8	8	17	19	9	6	4	5	5	8
Other	5	3	5	4	6	1	2	5	4	4
Nothing Needed	33	26	30	26	27	26	20	28	33	32

Note: Figures are the percentage of the population in each city giving each type of response. Because some people gave no codable response and others more than one, percentages do not add to 100 percent.

the following services: schools, police patrolling the streets, cleaning and repairing streets, medical care for those who cannot afford it, low-cost housing, and controlling air pollution. These, along with recreation for teen-age boys, were services in which the support for increased expenditure in the median city was over 50 percent. Thus, these seven services constitute a second group about which there is considerable support, in many cities (at least half) for increased expenditure (Table 4–1 and 4–5).

ARE THESE ALL EQUALLY IMPORTANT TO PEOPLE?

When people were asked to choose the most important three services for increased effort, some of these items were cited considerably more often than others (Table 4–2 and Table 4–6). Schools, and to a lesser extent, police and medical care for the poor, were singled out, along with drugs, as the areas in which increased efforts were most important.

It is important to note that there was no consensus on any item as one of the important issues. Even "drugs" was selected as one of the three most important problems by less than half the people in most cities. The percentage of citizens in cities that supported increased effort on a service is a good index of the breadth of citizen interest in a service; the percent that said it was one of the "most important" may be a better index of intensity of feeling. Both figures are meaningful; there is no right answer about which is a better index of priority.

Which Services Would People be Willing to Cut Down On?

There was a very consistent tendency for people to be much more willing to increase expenditures for the services in the list than to decrease them (Table 4–1). There were only four services for which less than a majority in any city wanted increased expenditures: ticketing and towing illegally parked cars, street lighting, trash and garbage collection, and building freeways. There was only one city in which there was majority sentiment for increased expenditure for cleaning up parks.

Of all the services listed, the only item which a majority was willing to spend less on was towing illegally parked cars, and that occurred in only two cities.

When people were asked where they would be willing to cut back, if cuts had to be made, ticketing and towing illegally parked cars and building freeways were consistently among the most often cited, as shown in Tables 4–7 and 4–8. The other selections for cut-backs were spread around a number of items, with none being among the top three in more than a few cities.

Table 4-5. Services on Which The Local Agencies Should Spend More Money

Service	No. of Cities in Which a Majority Voted to Spend More	Median Percent Voting to Spend More	Median Rank Among Items in Percent Voting to Spend More
Public Schools	7	59%	4
Police Patrolling	7	57%	5
Ticketing & Towing	0	8%	16
Street Lighting	0	36%	12
Cleaning & Repairing Streets	6	53%	7
Medical Care for Poor	7	60%	3
Cleaning Parks & Playgrounds	1	35%	13
Recreation for Teen-age Boys	5	52%	8
Trash & Garbage Collection	0	33%	14
Inspecting Houses	10	64%	2
Helping Kids on Drugs	10	78%	1
Low-Cost Housing	7	52%	9
Control Air Pollution	7	55%	6
Public Transportation	3	39%	11
Building Freeways	0	21%	15
Aid For Dependent Children	2	40%	10

Table 4-6. On Which Three Areas Are Increased Efforts Most Needed?

Service	Median Percent Mentioning as One of Three Most Important Items	Number of Cities in which It Was One of the Three Most Cited Items
Public Schools	41%	9
Police Patrolling	21%	5
Ticketing & Towing	2%	0
Street Lighting	8%	0
Cleaning & Repairing Streets	10%	0
Medical Care for Poor	32%	3
Cleaning Parks & Playgrounds	5%	0
Recreation for Teen-age Boys	19%	0
Trash & Garbage Collection	7%	0
Inspecting Houses	19%	1
Helping Kids on Drugs	46%	10
Low-Cost Housing	15%	0
Control Air Pollution	21%	2
Public Transportation	9%	0
Build Freeways	3%	0
Welfare & AFDC	15%	0

Did People in Some Cities Consistently Oppose Increased Services?

Very definitely—citizens of San Diego, Milwaukee, and Denver were least likely to give majority support for increased expenditures for services. Citizens of Baltimore, Boston, and to a lesser extent, Atlanta, were consistently more positive than those in other cities about spending more for services (Figure 4-1).

How Did The Order of Priorities Vary From City-to-City?

There were a few services, such as control of air pollution and police patrolling the streets at night, which varied in importance from city-to-city. However, when the items within each city were ranked on the basis of the percentage of people in a city who said they wanted more money spent on a service, the consistency from city-to-city is most notable (Table 4-9). In general, one would say that the major differences between cities tended to be in the willingness or interest of citizens in spending more money on services. With a few exceptions, the order in which they would work on services was quite similar.

HOW DO GROUPS WITHIN CITIES DIFFER FROM ONE ANOTHER IN THEIR PRIORITIES?

The most obvious way groups differed was in their concern for increased services. Less educated, those with lower incomes, renters, and blacks generally were

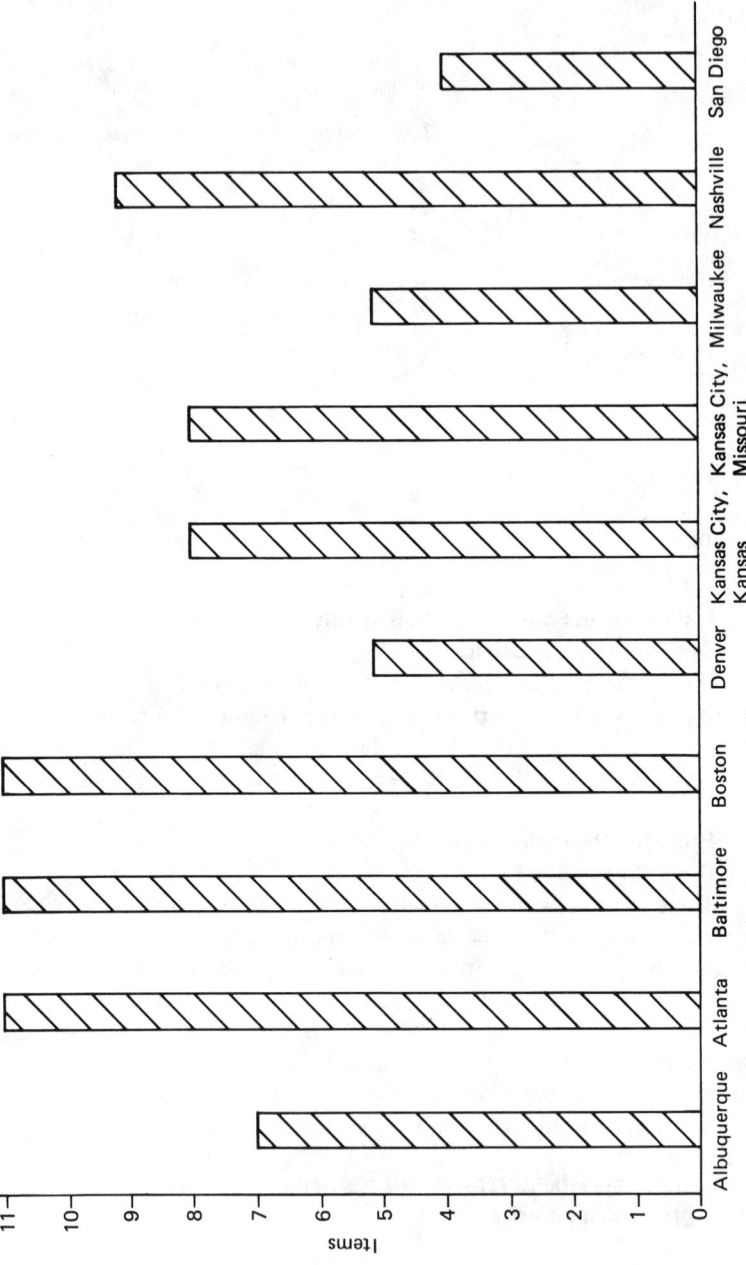

Figure 4–1. Number of Items on Which a Majority Voted for Increased Expenditure, by City

Table 4–7. Which Three Areas Should Local Government Cut Back On?

Item	Albuquerque	Atlanta	Baltimore	Boston	Denver	Kansas City, Kansas	Kansas City, Missouri	Milwaukee	Nashville	San Diego
Public Schools	3	3	3	4	6	4	3	6	2	7
Police Patrolling	4	6	8	4	3	7	4	5	3	5
Ticketing & Towing	59	55	73	60	57	62	62	54	58	59
Street Lighting	14	17	21	18	15	18	9	14	21	10
Cleaning & Repairing Streets	10	10	13	10	9	7	9	11	9	12
Medical Care for Poor	8	5	2	6	6	8	4	4	2	8
Cleaning Parks & Playgrounds	17	12	11	10	14	15	24	13	17	17
Recreation for Teenage Boys	12	13	8	10	10	14	14	11	10	12
Trash & Garbage Collection	8	8	10	13	10	10	14	10	10	9
Inspecting Houses	11	8	3	4	6	4	7	5	10	10
Help Kids on Drugs	2	3	1	2	2	1	1	4	2	3
Low-Cost Housing	18	15	11	11	10	14	19	14	15	26
Control Air Pollution	16	20	28	17	11	38	26	13	20	11
Public Transportation	31	19	18	18	12	33	22	24	34	26
Building Freeways	41	42	66	68	45	47	51	67	41	44
Welfare & AFDC	15	15	12	19	28	13	19	21	11	24

Note: Figures are weighted for number of adults. Percentages represent population which chose area as one of three to be cut back on. "No response" data (5% average) not shown. Percentage total about 300 percent, reflecting three choices per respondent.

50 Citizen Attitudes Toward Local Government, Services, and Taxes

Table 4–8. Items Willing to Cut Back On

Service	Median Percent Mentioning as One of Three Willing to Cut Back On	Number of Cities in which It Was One of the Three Most Cited to Cut Back On
Public Schools	3%	0
Police Patrolling	5%	0
Ticketing & Towing	59%	10
Street Lighting	16%	0
Cleaning & Repairing Streets	10%	0
Medical Care for Poor	5%	0
Cleaning Parks & Playgrounds	14%	0
Recreation for Teen-age Boys	11%	0
Trash & Garbage Collection	10%	0
Inspecting Houses	6%	0
Helping Kids on Drugs	2%	0
Low-Cost Housing	14%	1
Control Air Pollution	18%	4
Public Transportation	22%	3
Building Freeways	46%	10
Welfare & AFDC	17%	2

more likely to say that more money should be spent on services, and they generally had a majority asking for these increases for a larger number of services (Table 4–10). However, there was not much disagreement about what was most important. The pattern tended to be that the above mentioned groups wanted increased effort on the same problems as the people in the city as a whole, but in addition wanted more services in some areas of less interest to all citizens.

In order to establish a basis for comparison between groups in cities, it was decided, somewhat arbitrarily, that "support" for a service would be defined as any service on which a majority in at least seven cities wanted to increase expenditures. The following is a breakdown of "supported" services by total family income:

Less than $5,000–	*$5,000 to $9,999–*	*$10,000 or more–*
Schools	Schools	Schools
	Police	Police
Streets		
Teen recreation	Teen recreation	
Medical care	Medical care	
Inspect houses	Inspect houses	Inspect houses
Drugs	Drugs	Drugs
Low-cost housing	Low-cost housing	
Air pollution	Air pollution	Air pollution
Welfare		

Table 4-9. Rank Order of Items on Which Citizens Want to "Spend More"

Item	Albu-querque	Atlanta	Baltimore	Boston	Denver	Kansas City, Kansas	Kansas City, Missouri	Milwaukee	Nashville	San Diego
Public Schools	3	5	3	5	6	4	5	8	5	5
Police Patrolling	5	7	5	3	7	5	3	7	3	10
Ticketing & Towing	16	16	16	14	16	16	16	16	16	16
Street Lighting	12	14	13	13	11	9	12	11	12	9
Cleaning & Repairing Streets	4	9	11	9	10	7	4	12	4	11
Medical Care for Poor	9	4	2	6	9	3	6	4	2	6
Cleaning Parks & Playgrounds	14	13	10	10	12	11	15	13	10	13
Recreation for Teen-age Boys	6	6	6	7	8	6	8	6	7	4
Trash & Garbage Collection	10	12	14	15	15	14	10	14	13	15
Inspecting Houses	2	2	4	2	4	2	2	2	6	3
Helping Kids on Drugs	1	1	1	1	1	1	1	1	1	1
Low-Cost Housing	7	8	7	4	5	8	9	5	8	7
Control Air Pollution	8	3	9	8	3	10	7	3	9	2
Public Transportation	13	10	12	11	2	13	11	9	15	8
Building Freeways	15	15	15	16	14	15	14	15	14	14
Welfare & AFDC	11	11	8	12	13	12	13	10	11	12

Note: Ordering based on percentage who said they wanted to spend more.

Table 4–10. Number of Items on Which a Majority Voted for Increased Expenditure by Education, Income, Race, and Home Tenure

	Albuquerque	Atlanta	Baltimore	Boston	Denver	Kansas City, Kansas	Kansas City, Missouri	Milwaukee	Nashville	San Diego
Education										
Less than High School	7	13	11	12	7	9	9	6	8	6
High School Graduate	6	13	9	10	5	6	7	5	7	3
Any College	5	10	9	11	5	8	8	3	9	5
Income										
Less than $5,000	9	13	13	11	7	10	11	7	10	4
$5,000 to $9,999	7	13	11	9	5	9	8	6	8	6
$10,000 or More	6	8	9	9	4	5	7	4	7	4
Race										
White		9	8	10		6	6	4	9	
Black		13	11	13		10	12	9	14	
Home Tenure										
Owner	7	10	13	10	5	7	7	4	8	3
Renter	7	13	11	11	8	9	8	6	10	7

The only item not "supported" by the lowest income group but supported by those with higher incomes was increased police patrols; and it happens that this item was asked for by a majority in the lowest income group in six of the ten cities. Street cleaning and repair and increased payments for people on welfare and AFDC was an issue supported among the low-income people but much less so among those with higher incomes. Teen-age recreation facilities, low-income medical care programs, and low-cost housing were less supported by those in the highest income category than by those with medium or low incomes.

The same procedure for owners and renters yields the following list:

Owners—	*Renters—*
Schools	Schools
Police	
	Streets
Medical care	Medical care
	Teen recreation
Inspect houses	Inspect houses
Drugs	Drugs
	Low-cost housing
Air pollution	Air pollution

It can be seen that only increased police patrols was more favored by owners than by renters. Street maintenance, teen-age recreation, and low-cost housing were supported by renters but not owners.

The same procedure was used to compare blacks and whites. Since their answers could be compared in only seven cities, the criterion used was that a majority asked for more to be spent on a service in at least five of the seven cities.

Blacks—	*Whites—*
Schools	Schools
Police	Police
Street lights	
Streets	
Medical care	Medical care
Parks and playgrounds	
Teen-age recreation	
Inspect houses	Inspect houses
Drugs	Drugs
	Air pollution
Welfare	

There are more differences between blacks and whites than for any of the other comparisons: blacks were much more concerned about improved services than whites. Again, however, blacks supported all the same service priorities that whites did, with the exception of air pollution control. In addition, however, they supported street lighting, street maintenance, park and playground maintenance, teen-age recreation facilities, and increased payments to those on AFDC and welfare.

In almost all of the comparisons made, the differences between groups reflected the differing level of concern about increased services as much as they reflected a different way of ordering priorities. Nonetheless, to the extent that there are services that are viewed as in need of improvement by a majority of blacks and those with low incomes, but not so much by whites and those with higher incomes, there is a problem for policy makers.

CAN PEOPLE'S RESPONSES WITH RESPECT TO PRIORITIES BE SUMMARIZED?

There was the most consensus in cities that working on the drug problem and inspecting houses were areas in which increased expenditure was needed. There was then a group of six or seven services that majorities in more cities than not said deserved increased funding. These probably constitute the priority issues.

There was not so much consensus when people were asked to select the three most important problems for increased effort. No one issue was selected by a majority of people in a majority of the ten cities as one of the three most important problems. There are no simple answers to the question of priorities. However, the number of people in a city who would "vote" for increased expenditures for a service is probably as good an index as we have for priorities. The following is a summary of the consensus among cities.

Seven out of ten cities had a majority in favor of spending more on school systems. The only three in which this was not the case were Denver, Milwaukee, and San Diego. Those were the same three cities in which there was not a majority for increased police patrolling the streets at night. It was notable that there was a lot of variation between cities in their rankings of expenditure for police patrols.

Increased medical care for the poor, low-cost housing and air pollution control also received majority support in seven or eight cities. The three cities in which a majority did not want to increase expenditure for medical care were Denver, Albuquerque, and San Diego. Similarly, San Diego, Albuquerque, and Kansas City, Missouri, did not have majority support for low-cost housing. Exceptions to majority support for air pollution control occurred in Albuquerque and Kansas City, Kansas. Support for air pollution control varied a lot between cities; it was the second or third most supported item in Atlanta, Denver, Milwaukee, and San Diego while being very close to the middle in other cities.

In six of the ten cities, a majority supported increased expenditure to clean and maintain streets. In Denver, Milwaukee, San Diego, and Baltimore a majority did not support increases in this area. Although this ranked around the middle in most cities, it was the fourth most cited item in Albuquerque; Kansas City, Missouri; and Nashville. In five cities a majority would increase expenditures for teen recreation. Public transportation was supported by majorities in only three cities—Boston, Atlanta, and Denver.

Increased payments to people on welfare and AFDC were favored by majorities in Atlanta and Baltimore. None of the cities had a majority who wanted to cut back money for this service. Finally, a majority in only one city, Boston, favored spending more money on cleaning up parks and recreation facilities.

Four items on the list did not receive majority support for increased expenditure in any city: trash and garbage collection, building freeways, street lighting, and ticketing and towing illegally parked cars. At the same time, no city had a majority in favor of spending less on the first three items. Ticketing and towing was the only item on the list which received a majority in favor of spending less in any city. Most citizens in Baltimore and Denver were willing to spend less on towing and ticketing illegally parked cars.

When people were asked which three items they would cut back on if a choice had to be made, only two received a majority in any city. Cutting back expenditures on ticketing and towing illegally parked cars was supported by a majority in every city. Cutting expenditures for building freeways received majority support in four cities. No other item received a majority in favor of cutting back expenditures in any city.

NOTES TO CHAPTER FOUR

1. The data by city of whether people want to spend more, less or the present amount on items are all presented in Table 4–1. The responses to which items are most important for increased expenditures are in Table 4–2. These two tables will be referred to throughout the chapter.

Chapter Five

Balancing the Local Budget

It is a common perception among city officials that there is a continuing cry for reduced taxes and, at the same time, an increasing demand both for the expansion of existing services and for the performance of new services. It is also generally believed that poor people, blacks, and renters want more services than do others; that homeowners and people with high incomes want reduced taxes.

In this chapter, these common perceptions are examined in light of the answers provided to questions of citizens' attitudes toward tax levels and the adequacy of city services.

The concern about local taxes among people in cities is considered along with citizens' feelings about some alternative approaches to local problems of budgetary priorities. The results are also correlated with education and income levels among those surveyed.

DID PEOPLE IN CITIES THINK LOCAL TAXES ARE TOO HIGH?

Attitudes varied from city-to-city (Table 5-1). There were four cities in the study in which more than half the citizens said that local taxes were too high: Baltimore; Boston; Milwaukee; and Kansas City, Kansas. In contrast, there were six other cities in which only one-third of the population said their local taxes were too high. Indeed, in Nashville almost one-fifth of all adults thought taxes were too low to pay for needed services. There were quite a few people in every city that thought taxes were too high; a third of the population is significant. However, if one were to say that a majority of people did not think that local taxes were too high, he would be correct more often than not.

Table 5-1. How People Rate the Level of Local Taxes, by City

Response	Albuquerque	Atlanta	Baltimore	Boston	Denver	Kansas City, Kansas	Kansas City, Missouri	Milwaukee	Nashville	San Diego
Too High	27%	35%	68%	67%	38%	53%	35%	67%	27%	28%
About Right	57	50	28	22	50	39	48	27	47	60
Too Low	11	9	4	7	4	5	13	3	19	6
Not Ascertained	5	6	*	4	8	3	4	3	7	6
Total	100%	100%	100%	100%	100%	100%	100%	100%	100%	100%
(N)	(471)	(469)	(500)	(507)	(357)	(193)	(383)	(443)	(426)	(517)

*Less than 0.5 percent.

Table 5-2. Percent Who Says Local Taxes Are Too High, by Education

	Albuquerque	Atlanta	Baltimore	Boston	Denver	Kansas City, Kansas	Kansas City, Missouri	Milwaukee	Nashville	San Diego
Less than High School Graduate	52%	50%	74%	76%	54%	62%	58%	73%	43%	43%
High School Graduate	28%	32%	68%	78%	41%	43%	38%	71%	27%	31%
Any College	18%	28%	56%	56%	29%	46%	18%	57%	16%	25%

Note: The number of cases on which the percentages in this and subsequent tables are based are in Appendix A when not included in the table itself.

Are Certain Segments of The Population
Particularly Concerned About High Taxes?

The most common pattern was for the less educated and those with lower incomes to be more likely to say that taxes were too high (Tables 5-2 and 5-3). As shown in Figure 5-1, blacks tended to say taxes were too high more often than whites. However, these generalizations are less accurate in those four cities where there was most concern about taxes: Boston; Milwaukee; Baltimore; and Kansas City, Kansas. In particular, the higher-income people reported nearly as much concern about high taxes as those with low incomes in these cities.

How Did People's Perceptions Correspond
With the Real Level of Their Taxes?

The three cities in which the most people said taxes are too high were also those with the highest effective rate of property tax for single-family houses.[1] The order of the ten cities using this index was nearly identical to the order of cities with respect to the rate at which citizens said taxes were "too high." Considering the fact it is likely that virtually no one in a city knows the effective tax rate, Table 5-4 is a very good testimony to the degree to which reality is reflected in people's attitudes.

Would People Rather Raise Local Taxes
or Cut Services, if a Choice Had to be Made?

As one would expect from the above, cities varied considerably in this respect as well (Table 5-5). In six of the ten cities, more people wanted taxes raised than wanted services cut. The two cities most willing to raise taxes were Nashville and Atlanta. There was only city—Milwaukee—in which there was a clear majority of the population that preferred to cut services rather than raise taxes. In the other three cities, the balance seemed to be about 50–50 between those who would prefer to cut services and those who would prefer to raise taxes if a choice had to be made.

HOW DID THE ANSWERS TO THIS QUESTION COMPARE WITH INTEREST IN INCREASED SERVICE EXPRESSED IN OTHER PARTS OF THE INTERVIEW?

Although there is not a simple answer, there was a tendency for those cities in which people thought taxes were too high to also be those cities in which citizens were most interested in increased expenditure on services. First of all, of the three cities in which there was most concern about taxes—Boston, Baltimore, and Milwaukee—the citizens of two of those were most likely to ask for increased services. In Boston, for example, a majority wanted increased expenditures on 11 of the 16 service areas; yet 67 percent of the citizens of Boston thought the

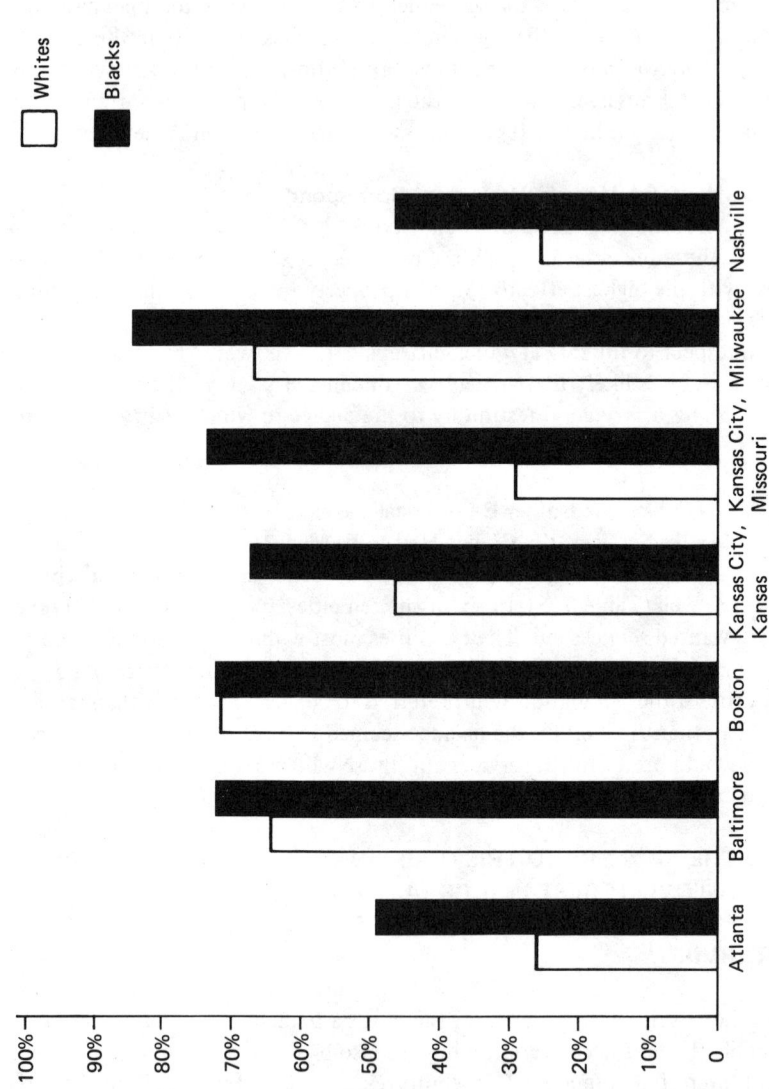

Figure 5-1. Percent Who Say Local Taxes Are Too High, by Race

Table 5-3. Percent Who Say Local Taxes Are Too High, by Income

	Albuquerque	Atlanta	Baltimore	Boston	Denver	Kansas City, Kansas	Kansas City, Missouri	Milwaukee	Nashville	San Diego
Less than $5,000	41%	47%	74%	69%	47%	67%	62%	64%	39%	37%
$5,000 to $9,999	31%	41%	75%	73%	43%	42%	42%	66%	30%	28%
$10,000 or More	17%	22%	58%	69%	30%	51%	22%	71%	22%	25%

Table 5-4. Median Effective Rate of Annual Property Tax for Single-Family Homes as Percent of Sales Price, by City

	Albuquerque	Atlanta	Baltimore	Boston	Denver	Kansas City, Kansas	Kansas City, Missouri	Milwaukee	Nashville	San Diego
Percent[a]	1.30	2.41	3.47	3.01	2.03	2.17	1.60	3.31	1.33	2.02
Order of Citizen Concern About High Taxes[b]	10	6	1	3	5	4	7	2	9	8

[a]U. S. Bureau of the Census, *Census of Governments*, 1967.
[b]Citizen Attitude Survey, 1970. Rank ordering of cities based on percent who says taxes "too high."

Table 5-5. Attitude Toward Raising Local Taxes Rather Than Cutting Services, by City

Response	Albuquerque	Atlanta	Baltimore	Boston	Denver	Kansas City, Kansas	Kansas City, Missouri	Milwaukee	Nashville	San Diego
Taxes Raised	53%	61%	54%	42%	44%	44%	50%	32%	59%	48%
Services Cut	41	31	41	44	44	50	42	59	26	44
Not Ascertained	6	8	5	14	12	6	8	9	15	8
Total	100%	100%	100%	100%	100%	100%	100%	100%	100%	100%
(N)	(471)	(469)	(500)	(507)	(357)	(193)	(383)	(443)	(426)	(517)

Table 5-6. Percent Who Want to Spend More on Many Services, by Preference for Raising Taxes or Cutting Services and by City

	Albuquerque	Atlanta	Baltimore	Boston	Denver	Kansas City, Kansas	Kansas City, Missouri	Milwaukee	Nashville	San Diego
Taxes Raised	54%	67%	56%	57%	58%	*	58%	*	81%	*
Services Cut	46	33	44	43	42	*	42	*	19	*
Total	100%	100%	100%	100%	100%	*	100%	*	100%	*
(N)	(63)	(160)	(153)	(139)	(55)	(37)	(83)	(37)	(102)	(24)

Note: "Many" was defined as eleven or more.
*Too few cases to be reliable.

taxes were too high. A similar pattern existed in Baltimore. On the other hand, the people in Milwaukee were fairly consistent. A majority said the taxes were too high; a majority would rather cut services than raise taxes; and in general Milwaukee citizens were among the lowest in asking for increased expenditures for various services.

Did The Same People Ask for More Services and No Further Tax Increases?

Tables 5–6 and 5–7 present the relationship between the number of services on which people wanted to spend more money and their preference for raising taxes or cutting services, if a choice had to be made. People had some tendency to be consistent. Those who wanted more spent on many services generally were more willing to raise taxes, but there were three cities in which that was not the case. Moreover, an average of about 40 percent of those who wanted more spent on many services would prefer to cut services than raise taxes. Thus, wanting more spent on services is related to a willingness to raise taxes, but the two ideas are far from closely linked in people's minds.

How Did Segments of The Population Differ?

There was a clear tendency in most cities for better-educated people to be more willing to raise taxes than less-educated people, despite the fact that the less-educated people were more likely to ask for increased expenditures on services (Table 5–8). By income, there was no difference in willingness to raise taxes in five of the ten cities (Table 5–9). In those cities where there was a relationship, those people with high incomes were more willing to raise taxes than those people with low incomes. Generally, of course, people with low incomes were more likely to ask for increased expenditures on services than those with high incomes. Although blacks were more likely than whites to want increased expenditures for services in almost all areas, in general, they were very similar to whites in their degree of willingness to raise taxes rather than cut services (Figure 5–2).

The one group that was most consistent was renters (Figure 5–3). Renters consistently asked for more services than home owners, and they were more willing to increase taxes. This may have something to do with the indirect way the property tax is passed along to renters. However, this tendency should not be emphasized too greatly. While the difference is always in the same direction, in some cities the difference between renters and owners is not statistically significant, and in others, it is significant but not particularly large.

How Were People Able to Want More Services and Yet Not be Willing to Raise Taxes?

First of all, people are not necessarily rational or consistent. Whether it has to do with their own budgets or the city budget, many people are probably

Table 5-7. Percent Who Want to Spend More on Few Services, by Preference for Raising Taxes or Cutting Services and by city

	Albuquerque	Atlanta	Baltimore	Boston	Denver	Kansas City, Kansas	Kansas City, Missouri	Milwaukee	Nashville	San Diego
Taxes Raised	52%	56%	53%	44%	44%	37%	44%	27%	61%	50%
Services Cut	48	44	47	56	56	63	56	73	39	50
Total	100%	100%	100%	100%	100%	100%	100%	100%	100%	100%
(N)	(234)	(139)	(139)	(140)	(178)	(71)	(143)	(254)	(157)	(317)

Note: "Few" was defined as zero to six.

Table 5-8. Percent Who Prefer to Raise Local Taxes Rather Than Cut Services, by Education

	Albuquerque	Atlanta	Baltimore	Boston	Denver	Kansas City, Kansas	Kansas City, Missouri	Milwaukee	Nashville	San Diego
Less than High School Graduate	34%	58%	49%	45%	36%	39%	46%	31%	54%	39%
High School Graduate	60%	59%	61%	41%	53%	57%	51%	37%	71%	51%
Any College	70%	77%	68%	64%	63%	56%	65%	41%	81%	59%

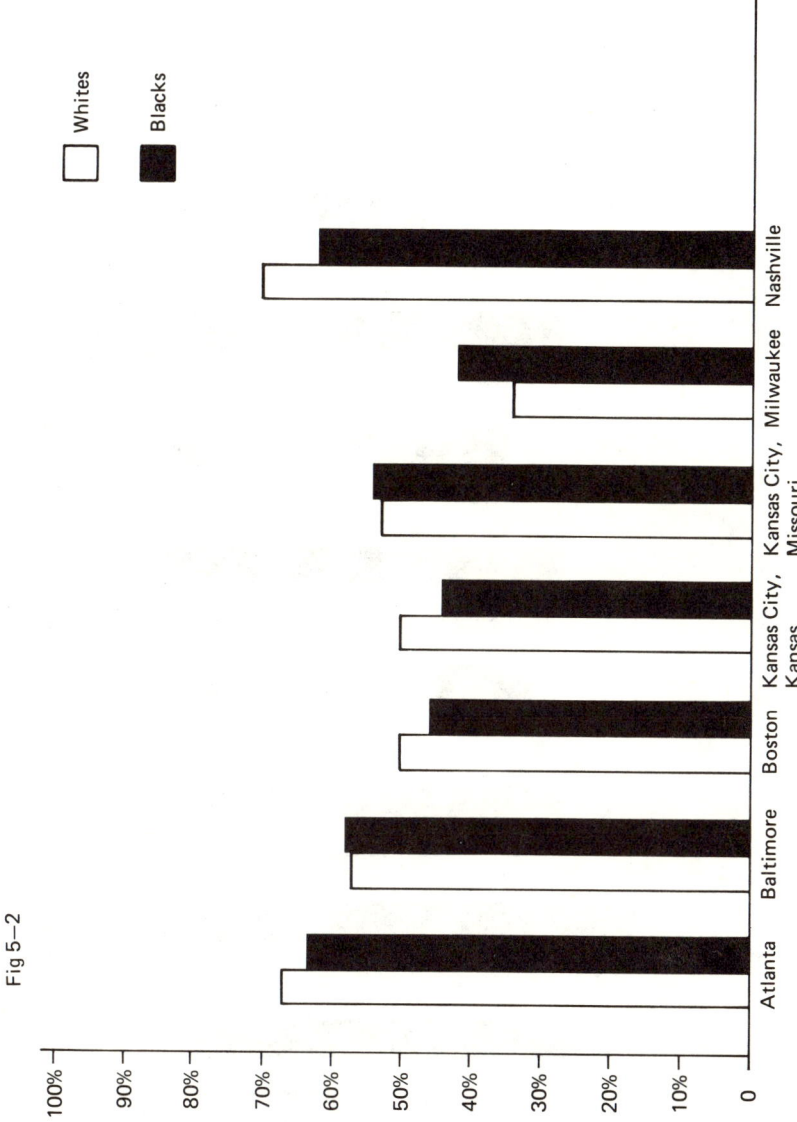

Figure 5-2. Percent Who Prefer to Raise Local Taxes Rather Than Cut Services, by Race

66 Citizen Attitudes Toward Local Government, Services, and Taxes

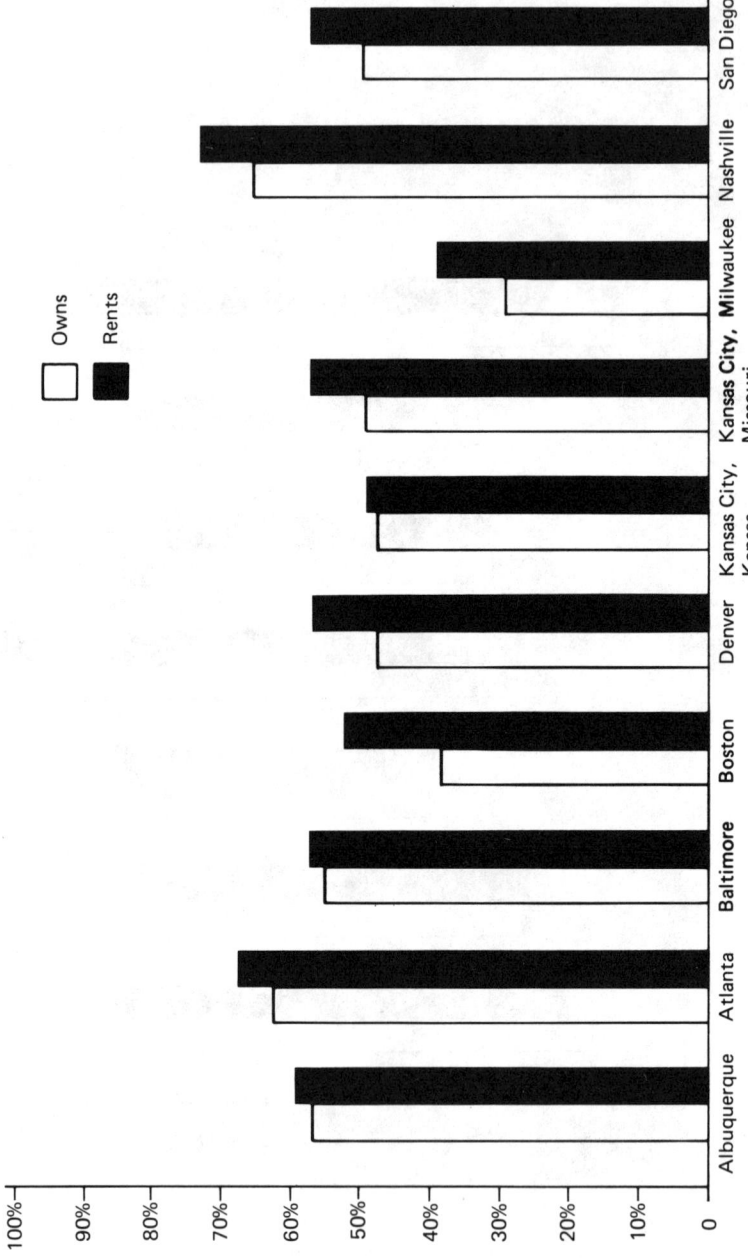

Figure 5-3. Percent Who Prefer to Raise Taxes Rather Than Cut Services, by Home Tenure

Table 5–9. Percent Who Prefer to Raise Local Taxes Rather Than Cut Services, by Income

	Albuquerque	Atlanta	Baltimore	Boston	Denver	Kansas City, Kansas	Kansas City, Missouri	Milwaukee	Nashville	San Diego
Less than $5,000	43%	57%	46%	51%	51%	47%	36%	30%	53%	40%
$5,000 to $10,000	59%	68%	55%	49%	53%	49%	53%	35%	70%	52%
$10,000 or More	68%	70%	69%	52%	56%	52%	62%	40%	75%	58%

guilty of wanting to get more for their dollar than, in fact, they can buy. On the other hand, there are some explanations that people can have that would make this view less inconsistent. One of them is that they are not getting their money's worth for their tax dollars. People who feel that way may be justified in thinking that services should be increased without increasing taxes.

We asked people directly whether they thought they got their money's worth in services from their tax dollars in their cities. There were extreme differences between cities in the answers to this question, although the answers did follow a pattern (Table 5-10). At one extreme was San Diego, the only city in which a majority of citizens said they thought they received their money's worth for their tax dollars. San Diego was a city in which relatively few people asked for increased services. It was also a city in which few people thought the taxes were too high. Albuquerque and Denver were two other cities where more than the average number of people thought they received their money's worth. In both of these cities, the demand for increased services tended to be moderately low, while the concern about the cost of taxes also tended to be moderately low. Thus, those cities in which people were relatively satisfied with their services and not too concerned with their taxes were also cities in which people thought they were getting their money's worth.

At the other extreme were Baltimore and Boston, where there was consensus that the taxes were too high; and there was considerable demand for increased services. In each of these cities, more than 70 percent of the adult population thought they were not getting their money's worth for the taxes they paid.

How About Groups Within Cities?

There was not a difference by education in all cities (Table 5-11). When there was, however, less-educated people were less likely to think that they were getting their money's worth than better-educated people. The same was true by income—that is, low-income people, when there was a difference by income, were less likely to think they were getting their money's worth for local taxes (Table 5-12). The most striking difference, however, was by race. In all seven cities in which blacks and whites could be compared, blacks were less likely to think they were getting their money's worth for the tax dollar; in most cities the difference was statistically significant (Figure 5-4). There was a very constant pattern, then, for those populations in which support for more services and concern about taxes were high to be also more likely than others to think that tax money was not well used.

It is not the purpose of this study to try to evaluate the legitimacy of a citizen perception—that money is or is not being spent efficiently. However, what people perceive is a reality itself. When there is a widespread feeling among citizens that they are not getting their money's worth, that constitutes a city problem. If nothing else, this perception provides a justification for demanding increased services without increased taxation.

Table 5-10. Do People Think They Get Adequate Services for Their Local Tax Dollar?, by City

Response	Albuquerque	Atlanta	Baltimore	Boston	Denver	Kansas City, Kansas	Kansas City, Missouri	Milwaukee	Nashville	San Diego
Yes	47%	39%	27%	21%	46%	25%	26%	35%	36%	64%
No	46	53	72	70	44	65	62	56	58	29
Not Ascertained	7	8	1	9	10	10	12	9	6	7
Total	100%	100%	100%	100%	100%	100%	100%	100%	100%	100%
(N)	(471)	(469)	(500)	(507)	(357)	(193)	(383)	(443)	(426)	(517)

Table 5-11. Percent Who Think They Are Not Getting Adequate Services for Their Tax Dollar, by Education

	Albuquerque	Atlanta	Baltimore	Boston	Denver	Kansas City, Kansas	Kansas City, Missouri	Milwaukee	Nashville	San Diego
Less than High School Graduate	52%	68%	73%	77%	57%	78%	73%	70%	64%	37%
High School Graduation	56%	63%	75%	81%	54%	62%	76%	60%	64%	32%
Any College	44%	43%	65%	79%	44%	73%	61%	47%	57%	29%

70 Citizen Attitudes Toward Local Government, Services, and Taxes

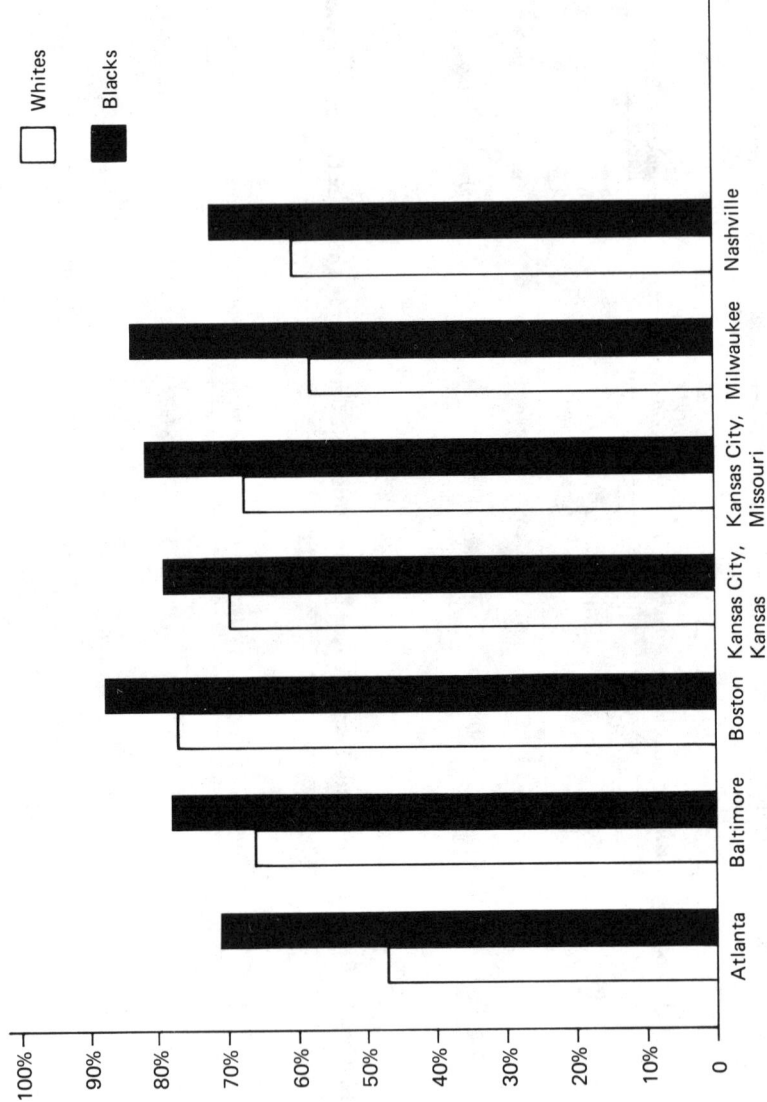

Figure 5-4. Percent Who Say They Do Not Get Adequate Services for Their Local Tax Dollar, by Race

IN WHAT WAYS DID PEOPLE THINK THEIR LOCAL TAX MONEY WAS POORLY SPENT?

There were two kinds of answers that stood out when we asked people why they thought they did not get their money's worth (Table 5-13). One answer was that money was spent on the wrong things/wrong priorities. The other was that there was inefficient administration: somehow money was lost in the process of collecting the taxes and delivering the services. These two responses accounted for more than half of the answers given in most cities. Two other answers that were common, though less prevalent, were that political graft or unequal distribution of services was responsible for people not getting their money's worth.

Besides Reducing Inefficiency, Whatever The Cause, Was There Any Way in Which People Would Favor Reducing City Expenditures?

To begin with, on the long list of services that we presented to people on which they could want to "spend more," "spend the same," or "spend less," there was no service on which the majority of the people in more than two cities wanted to spend less (See Table 4-1). In two cities, a majority was willing to spend less on ticketing and towing illegally parked cars, and, of course, that represents a relatively small portion of the city budget. Even building freeways, which was one of the least popular items on the list, did not receive a majority for "cutting down" in any city, although 48 percent of those in Milwaukee would spend less on that item, along with 45 percent in Boston and Baltimore.

When we asked people which of the items on the list they would cut, if they had to cut somewhere, freeways and towing and ticketing cars were the only two that came anywhere close to getting a majority in any city. The rest of the responses were spread among many items—none of which amounted to anywhere near a consensus. Thus, there was very little basis for saying that people were willing to cut basic services.

How About Economizing on City Salaries?

People were asked directly if they thought city salaries should be higher, were about right, or should be lower (Table 5-14). In all but one city, less than 8 percent of the population thought city salaries should be lower. The exception was Milwaukee, where about 18 percent of the adults thought city salaries should be lower, but an equal percentage of adults in Milwaukee thought city salaries should be higher. In six of the ten cities, more than 40 percent of the population thought that city salaries should be higher. In three cities—Albuquerque, Atlanta, and Baltimore—over one-half the people thought that city salaries should be higher. Thus, cutting city salaries was not a very popular way to cut city expenditures.

Table 5-12. Percent Who Say They Do Not Get Adequate Services for Their Tax Dollar, by Income

	Albuquerque	Atlanta	Baltimore	Boston	Denver	Kansas City, Kansas	Kansas City, Missouri	Milwaukee	Nashville	San Diego
Less than $5,000	51%	66%	74%	75%	57%	66%	66%	54%	57%	36%
$5,000 to $9,999	54%	61%	75%	83%	58%	68%	75%	64%	68%	37%
$10,000 or More	43%	44%	68%	79%	38%	77%	67%	62%	57%	24%

Table 5-13. Why Don't People Get Their Money's Worth?, by City

Response	Albuquerque	Atlanta	Baltimore	Boston	Denver	Kansas City, Kansas	Kansas City, Missouri	Milwaukee	Nashville	San Diego
Wrong Priorities	32%	18%	30%	24%	22%	42%	25%	37%	33%	37%
Unequal Distribution of Services	5	17	14	7	14	10	14	10	18	11
Inefficient Administration	39	26	20	29	37	20	31	26	27	28
Political Graft	8	13	13	25	12	18	15	6	14	7
Unequal Taxes	7	14	8	8	8	3	7	13	4	10
Other	9	12	15	7	7	7	8	8	5	7
Total	100%	100%	100%	100%	100%	100%	100%	100%	100%	100%
(N)	(169)	(163)	(292)	(303)	(127)	(90)	(163)	(167)	(174)	(113)

Note: Includes only responses from those who said they did not get their money's worth.

What About User Charges as a Means of Reducing City Expenditures?

Four specific kinds of services, which in some communities are not supported by tax money, were considered. This list included trash and garbage collection, museums, libraries, and public transportation. The question was whether these services should be wholly supported by people who use them, rather than being supported (in part or wholly) by local taxes.

When we asked whether trash and garbage collection should be paid for out of taxes or whether people should pay for them on their own, pluralities ran from 67 percent to 96 percent in favor of tax-supported collection in 9 out of 10 cities (Table 5-15). In Kansas City, Missouri, the response was more evenly divided; 50 percent to 48 percent, with 2 percent undecided.

A similar question was asked about museums and libraries: should city taxes help to pay for these services or should they be paid for entirely by the people who use them? (See Table 5-16.) Here again in every case, large majorities of citizens in every city supported tax help for both of these institutions. Perhaps that response is noteworthy in light of the fact that it is likely a minority of the citizens regularly use these facilities in any given city.

The question with respect to public transportation was whether tax money should help to pay the cost of public transportation or whether fares should pay the entire cost (Table 5-17). In five of the ten cities, a majority of the people said fares should pay the entire cost of public transportation. Among these cities were Milwaukee and Baltimore, where use of public transportation runs higher than in some other cities. (See Chapter 7.) It may be significant, however, that there was a very strong education relationship (Table 5-18). People who had attended college were more likely to favor a tax supplement to public transportation, even though their rate of use tended to be lower than average. It is possible that the public as a whole did not understand the economics of public transportation very well. Nonetheless, in two cities—Nashville and Baltimore again—a majority of those people who had been to college favored having fares pay the entire cost of public transportation, although these majorities were not very great.

How Would Citizen Views of Reduced Expenditures be Summarized?

The data relate to four basic ways in which cities could reduce expenditures from tax money. First, some people in all cities thought that somehow administrative overhead could be reduced or efficiency could be increased. Obviously, anyone would be in favor of that, but it was beyond the scope of this study to know how much potential for savings of this type actually existed.

Second, city salaries could be reduced, as a way of reducing the cost of services and administration. However, in most cities there was virtually no support for cutting city salaries; there was much more support to raise them.

Table 5-14. Attitudes Toward City Pay Scale, by City

Response	Albuquerque	Atlanta	Baltimore	Boston	Denver	Kansas City, Kansas	Kansas City, Missouri	Milwaukee	Nashville	San Diego
Should Be Higher	52%	58%	56%	32%	27%	48%	44%	17%	44%	23%
About Right	30	24	36	43	50	32	33	51	37	55
Should Be Lower	3	1	4	6	7	4	4	18	2	4
Not Ascertained	15	17	4	19	16	16	19	14	17	18
Total	100%	100%	100%	100%	100%	100%	100%	100%	100%	100%
(N)	(471)	(469)	(500)	(507)	(357)	(193)	(383)	(443)	(426)	(517)

Table 5-15. Should Local Tax Money Help Pay for Trash and Garbage?

Response	Albuquerque	Atlanta	Baltimore	Boston	Denver	Kansas City, Kansas	Kansas City, Missouri	Milwaukee	Nashville	San Diego
Paid by Taxes	67%	90%	96%	89%	77%	75%	50%	85%	73%	79%
People Pay for Their Own	28	8	4	8	16	23	48	12	24	19
Not Ascertained	5	2	*	3	7	2	2	3	3	2
Total	100%	100%	100%	100%	100%	100%	100%	100%	100%	100%
(N)	(471)	(469)	(500)	(507)	(357)	(193)	(383)	(443)	(426)	(517)

*Less than 0.5 percent.

Table 5-16. Should Local Tax Money Help Pay for Libraries and Museums?

Response	Albuquerque	Atlanta	Baltimore	Boston	Denver	Kansas City, Kansas	Kansas City, Missouri	Milwaukee	Nashville	San Diego
Paid by Taxes	62%	67%	67%	60%	64%	62%	53%	58%	65%	71%
Paid by People Who Use Them	32	28	31	32	25	36	44	37	30	25
Libraries Only	1	1	*	1	1	*	*	1	1	1
Not Ascertained	5	4	2	7	10	2	3	4	4	3
Total	100%	100%	100%	100%	100%	100%	100%	100%	100%	100%
(N)	(471)	(469)	(500)	(507)	(357)	(193)	(383)	(443)	(426)	(517)

*Less than 0.5 percent.

Table 5-17. Should Local Tax Money Help Pay for Public Transportation?

	Albuquerque	Atlanta	Baltimore	Boston	Denver	Kansas City, Kansas	Kansas City, Missouri	Milwaukee	Nashville	San Diego
Yes	53%	54%	48%	53%	60%	37%	46%	39%	37%	54%
No	40	40	51	36	27	58	47	51	58	40
Not Ascertained	7	6	1	11	12	5	7	10	5	6
Total	100%	100%	100%	100%	100%	100%	100%	100%	100%	100%
(N)	(471)	(469)	(500)	(507)	(357)	(193)	(383)	(443)	(426)	(517)

Third, basic services could be cut back. There were plenty of people in all cities who would generally rather cut back services than further increase taxes, though this was the clear majority view only in Milwaukee. It was much harder to find any specific services that a substantial portion of any city's population would be willing to cut back. Illegal parking control and building freeways, neither of which are very significant portions of most city budgets, were the only two areas for which there was any substantial amount of support for service reduction.

Finally, theoretically at least, some of the services and facilities that are usually tax-supported could be put on a break-even, fee-for-service basis. This approach might not reduce the cost of the service to the community, but it would distribute the cost on the basis of use and reduce the amount collected for taxes. However, public transportation was the only service considered for which there was majority citizen support in any city for not having tax subsidies; and this was true in only five cities.

Thus, the survey responses do not give a great deal of help in figuring out how to control city budgets by reducing expenditures in popular ways.

WERE THERE SOURCES FROM WHICH INCREASED REVENUES COULD BE RAISED?

There are two types of property in most cities that presently are not taxed—that owned by private schools and universities and that owned by churches. People were asked specifically whether they would be willing to change the laws affecting taxation of property owned by schools and churches.

A majority of those in nine of the ten cities were willing to change the laws with regard to taxation of private schools (Table 5–19). Furthermore, a majority in seven of the ten cities was willing to change the laws with respect to the taxation of church property (Table 5–20). Atlanta citizens were the only ones not willing to tax either of these institutions. Baltimore and Kansas City, Missouri, citizens were not willing to tax churches but were willing to tax school property.

Did These Patterns Hold Up for All Segments of the Population?

One might expect people who had been to college to be less willing to change the tax-exempt status of educational institutions. However, college-educated people were significantly more reticent about this in only Albuquerque and Nashville (Table 5–21). In three other cities, this segment of the population was more willing to tax school property, though not significantly so. In general, it can be said that it was very difficult to identify a group within most cities that was not predominantly willing to change the laws with respect to the tax exempt status of private schools and universities.

Table 5-18. Percent Who Say Local Taxes Should Help Pay for Public Transportation, by Education

	Albuquerque	Atlanta	Baltimore	Boston	Denver	Kansas City, Kansas	Kansas City, Missouri	Milwaukee	Nashville	San Diego
Less than High School Graduate	49%	48%	49%	54%	59%	30%	41%	41%	38%	45%
High School Graduate	50%	55%	46%	57%	73%	35%	43%	43%	32%	32%
Any College	68%	71%	48%	75%	74%	67%	65%	59%	47%	66%

Table 5-19. Should Private Schools Retain Their Tax Exempt Status?

Response	Albuquerque	Atlanta	Baltimore	Boston	Denver	Kansas City, Kansas	Kansas City, Missouri	Milwaukee	Nashville	San Diego
Law Should Change	54%	42%	58%	65%	53%	52%	51%	57%	58%	54%
Law Should Not Change	43	52	41	31	41	41	46	39	38	42
Not Ascertained	3	6	1	4	6	7	3	4	4	4
Total	100%	100%	100%	100%	100%	100%	100%	100%	100%	100%
(N)	(471)	(469)	(500)	(507)	(357)	(193)	(383)	(443)	(426)	(517)

78 Citizen Attitudes Toward Local Government, Services, and Taxes

Table 5-20. Should the Church Retain Its Tax Exempt Status?

Response	Albuquerque	Atlanta	Baltimore	Boston	Denver	Kansas City, Kansas	Kansas City, Missouri	Milwaukee	Nashville	San Diego
Law Should Change	60%	42%	47%	63%	53%	43%	51%	56%	66%	64%
Law Should Not Change	37	55	52	34	41	46	42	39	32	33
Not Ascertained	3	3	1	3	6	11	7	5	2	3
Total	100%	100%	100%	100%	100%	100%	100%	100%	100%	100%
(N)	(471)	(469)	(500)	(507)	(357)	(193)	(383)	(443)	(426)	(517)

Table 5-21. Percent Who Are Willing to Tax Private School Property, by Education

	Albuquerque	Atlanta	Baltimore	Boston	Denver	Kansas City, Kansas	Kansas City, Missouri	Milwaukee	Nashville	San Diego
Less than High School Graduate	63%	45%	59%	66%	56%	57%	54%	59%	66%	61%
High School Graduate	60%	42%	53%	70%	56%	54%	58%	64%	62%	59%
Any College	45%	46%	67%	72%	58%	65%	49%	57%	54%	52%

The data on taxing churches were a little more complicated. In general, it can be said that better-educated people were more in favor of taxing churches than less-educated people (Table 5-22). That statement holds true in eight of the ten cities to a statistically significant degree. There was not much difference by religion in willingness to tax churches (Table 5-23). In the cities in the sample that had significant Catholic populations, there was no difference between Catholics' willingness to change the law about taxing churches and that of the city population as a whole. Those of Spanish descent among the Catholics, however, were more against church taxation than others. Blacks seemed to constitute an identifiable group that was less willing to tax the churches than others, significantly so in most cities (Figure 5-5).

It is hard to know whether these expressions of opinion reflected changes in ideology over a period of time or simply a desperation for other sources of income for cities; we do not even know whether these figures represented a change from the past. It is significant to note that a few people specifically said that they would change the laws only with respect to property that was not being used for church purposes. However, there seems to be little doubt that some change in the laws regarding taxation of schools and churches was politically feasible in most of the cities at the time of this survey.

If Taxes Had to Be Raised, What Did People Think Was The Best Way to Be Taxed?

People were given the choice of five types of taxation: (1) tax on property, (2) tax on income (which was not specified whether it was graduated or not), (3) sales tax, (4) tax on utilities, and (5) tax on automobile owners. They were asked which form of taxation they would most prefer if taxes had to be raised, and then what their second choice would be.

There was one answer that stood out in every single city as being the most popular way to raise additional tax money (Table 5-24). In every city, more people selected the sales tax as the first choice than any of the alternatives. With five alternatives, it was not surprising that there was not a majority for the sales tax as a first choice; about 40 percent on the average chose the sales tax over the others. However, in every city more than half the adults—an average of over 60 percent—chose the sales tax as one of the two best ways to raise increased tax revenue (Table 5-25).

How About the Tax on Earnings?

In general, a tax on earnings had the second most support. In one city—Kansas City, Missouri—a majority of the citizens mentioned it as one of the two preferred forms of taxation, though there was even more support for the sales tax. In most cities, 20 to 30 percent less of the population selected the income tax than selected the sales tax (Table 5-25).

Table 5-22. Percent Who Are Willing to Tax Church Property, by Education

	Albuquerque	Atlanta	Baltimore	Boston	Denver	Kansas City, Kansas	Kansas City, Missouri	Milwaukee	Nashville	San Diego
Less than High School Graduate	46%	36%	41%	53%	48%	51%	48%	53%	55%	65%
High School Graduate	61%	37%	50%	63%	52%	48%	55%	59%	73%	63%
Any College	71%	57%	57%	82%	65%	58%	60%	63%	76%	70%

Table 5-23. Percent Who Are Willing to Tax Church Property, by Religion[a]

	Albuquerque	Atlanta	Baltimore	Boston	Denver	Kansas City, Kansas	Kansas City, Missouri	Milwaukee	Nashville	San Diego
Catholic	68%	*	60%	66%	50%	*	55%	57%	*	67%
Protestant	67%	56%	55%	74%	63%	58%	56%	61%	70%	70%

[a]Table includes whites only.
*Too few cases to be reliable.

Balancing the Local Budget 81

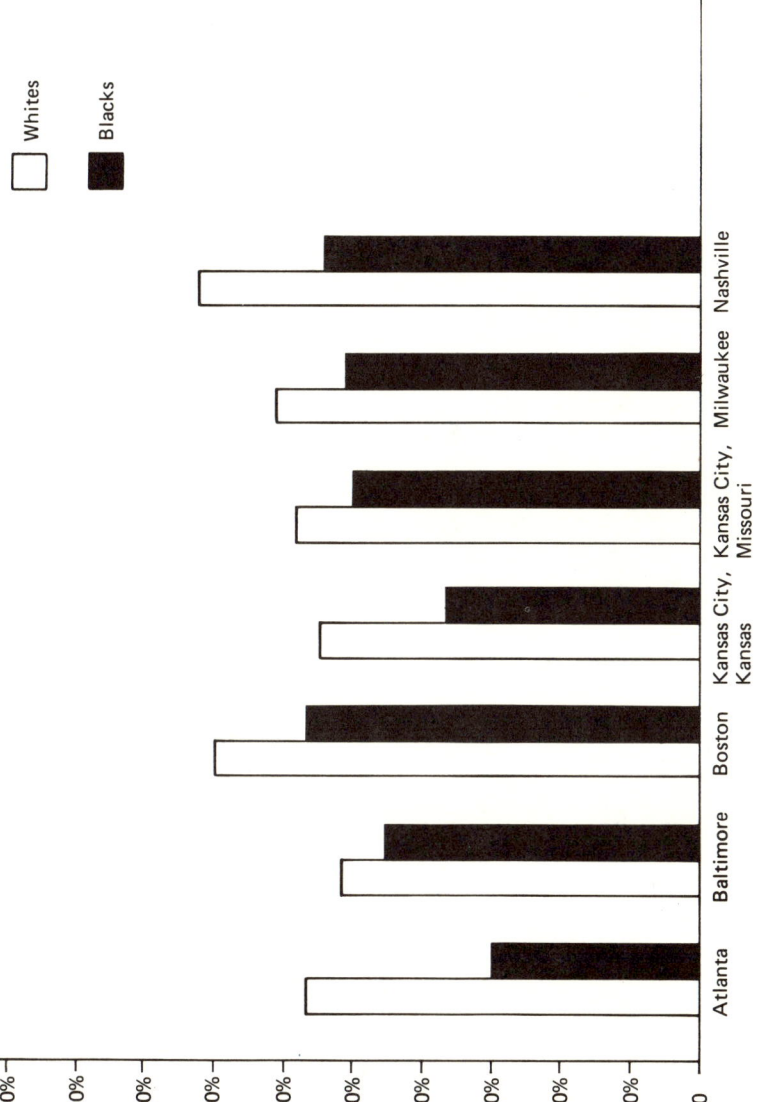

Figure 5-5. Percent Who Are Willing to Tax Church Property, by Race

Table 5-24. Best Way of Raising Additional Tax Money, by City

	Albuquerque	Atlanta	Baltimore	Boston	Denver	Kansas City, Kansas	Kansas City, Missouri	Milwaukee	Nashville	San Diego
Property Tax	9%	14%	15%	15%	9%	6%	6%	8%	16%	13%
Income	20%	17%	10%	16%	23%	23%	28%	22%	21%	15%
Utilities Tax	13%	10%	14%	12%	11%	8%	3%	10%	7%	11%
Sales Tax	41%	42%	37%	35%	33%	47%	44%	28%	31%	44%
Car Owners' Tax	9%	13%	17%	14%	12%	11%	12%	23%	18%	10%
Other	1%	*	2%	1%	1%	*	*	2%	*	1%
Not Ascertained	7%	4%	5%	7%	10%	5%	7%	7%	7%	6%
Total	100%	100%	100%	100%	100%	100%	100%	100%	100%	100%
(N)	(471)	(469)	(500)	(507)	(357)	(193)	(383)	(443)	(426)	(517)

*Less than 0.5 percent.

Table 5-25. Two Best Ways of Raising Additional Tax Money, by City

Tax Form	Albuquerque	Atlanta	Baltimore	Boston	Denver	Kansas City, Kansas	Kansas City, Missouri	Milwaukee	Nashville	San Diego
Tax on Property	23%	29%	27%	23%	23%	18%	15%	16%	29%	23%
Tax on Income	41	37	24	30	39	40	56	38	37	35
Tax on Utilities	32	29	33	30	27	24	16	32	24	33
Sales Tax	62	62	64	57	62	76	73	52	60	66
Tax Car Owners	26	30	36	31	27	29	26	41	37	27
Other	1	1	5	2	2	*	*	3	1	2
Not Ascertained	15	12	11	20	20	13	14	18	12	14
(N)	(471)	(469)	(500)	(507)	(357)	(193)	(383)	(443)	(426)	(517)

*Less than 0.5 percent.
Note: Figures total 200 percent, reflecting two choices per respondent.

What Was The Extent of Support for The Property Tax?

The property tax was clearly the least popular way to raise increased tax funds. In six of the ten cities, it was clearly at the bottom; in the other four, it was separated from the bottom by only a few percentage points (Table 5–25).

Did All Segments of the Population Favor The Sales Tax Equally?

Although all groups did not favor the sales tax equally, it was the favored tax among almost all groups in almost all cities. There was a clear tendency for those with high incomes to select the sales tax as the first choice more than those with incomes under $5,000 per year (Table 5–26). Differences ranged from 4 percentage points to 32 percentage points between the extreme income groups in this respect. Nevertheless, even among those with incomes under $5,000, the sales tax was the first choice of the most people in eight of the ten cities. The chief rival among this group was the tax on automobile owners; rates of automobile ownership were relatively low among the low-income group in many cities.

Other differences among groups included the general tendency for better-educated people to be more likely than others to choose an income tax, perhaps reflecting the fact that much sophisticated opinion considers a tax on earnings to be potentially the fairest (Table 5–27). Renters and people under 30 were somewhat more favorable toward the property tax than others (Table 5–28). None of these trends, however, affected the basic ordering of preference very much. For most cities and among almost all groups, the sales tax was by far the most popular way of raising increased revenue; the tax on earnings was the second most popular in seven cities; third in three cities. The number three choice in seven cities was the tax on automobile owners.

Why Did People Favor The Sales Tax?

Two obvious hypotheses are that it is paid in small bits at a time and that perhaps people felt that they have some control over what they buy and hence on the degree to which the tax affects them. We did not ask specifically for the reasons for peoples' preferences. Nonetheless, the important point is that the citizens of the ten cities have spoken more clearly about their preference than many observers would have expected.

HOW WOULD THE DATA BE SUMMARIZED?

It was not universally true that citizens thought local taxes were too high. There were only four cities of the ten in which there was a majority concerned about tax levels.

Second, an important element in the equation of demands for more services without further taxation was the perception of people not getting their

Table 5-26. Best Way of Raising Additional Tax Money, by Income

	Albuquerque	Atlanta	Baltimore	Boston	Denver	Kansas City, Kansas	Kansas City, Missouri	Milwaukee	Nashville	San Diego
Under $5,000										
Property Tax	14%	22%	21%	22%	15%	4%	7%	18%	23%	16%
Income Tax	20	16	10	19	16	27	28	21	15	18
Utilities Tax	15	13	12	11	15	6	6	8	9	10
Sales Tax	34	25	29	22	36	40	37	24	31	33
Car Owners' Tax	16	23	27	26	16	23	21	27	22	21
Other	1	1	1	*	1	*	1	2	*	2
Total	100%	100%	100%	100%	100%	100%	100%	100%	100%	100%
$5,000 to $9,999										
Property Tax	13%	17%	18%	8%	13%	7%	8%	7%	26%	18%
Income Tax	21	15	10	15	26	20	28	18	21	18
Utilities Tax	18	12	17	19	9	7	4	15	10	15
Sales Tax	39	40	36	43	35	53	47	34	28	40
Car Owners' Tax	8	15	19	13	17	13	13	23	15	8
Other	1	1	*	2	*	*	*	3	*	1
Total	100%	100%	100%	100%	100%	100%	100%	100%	100%	100%
$10,000 or More										
Property Tax	8%	7%	9%	13%	5%	6%	7%	3%	13%	10%
Income Tax	21	21	15	18	31	23	33	26	28	16
Utilities Tax	12	8	11	14	14	11	2	10	5	10
Sales Tax	53	57	48	48	42	53	51	34	35	55
Car Owners' Tax	6	7	12	4	8	6	6	25	19	7
Other	*	*	5	3	*	1	1	2	*	2
Total	100%	100%	100%	100%	100%	100%	100%	100%	100%	100%

*Less than 0.5 percent.

Table 5–27. Percent Who Chose Income Tax as Best Method of Raising Additional Tax Money, by Education

	Albuquerque	Atlanta	Baltimore	Boston	Denver	Kansas City, Kansas	Kansas City, Missouri	Milwaukee	Nashville	San Diego
Less than High School Graduate	15%	16%	11%	13%	19%	20%	25%	22%	17%	13%
High School Graduate	19%	18%	11%	16%	23%	18%	27%	17%	22%	17%
Any College	27%	19%	12%	22%	30%	42%	38%	31%	28%	18%

Table 5–28. Percent Who Chose Property Tax as Best Way to Raise Additional Tax Money, by Age and by Home Tenure

	Albuquerque	Atlanta	Baltimore	Boston	Denver	Kansas City, Kansas	Kansas City, Missouri	Milwaukee	Nashville	San Diego
Age										
Under 30 years	20%	21%	23%	21%	20%	7%	11%	12%	22%	24%
Over 30 years	7%	13%	14%	12%	7%	5%	6%	7%	18%	10%
Tenure										
Owns	6%	5%	4%	7%	6%	3%	5%	4%	13%	8%
Rents	20%	24%	26%	18%	18%	11%	13%	13%	29%	22%

money's worth for their taxes. This perception was most prevalent in cities and among groups within the cities where there was most clamor for more services.

Third, there were not any areas of service that many people were willing to cut back on. Parking control, freeways, and tax support of public transportation were the three areas for which there was the most willingness to reduce tax expenditures, but majority support for even these cutbacks was hard to come by.

Fourth, there was a very clear and widespread sentiment for raising money from sources other than property taxes. Taxing churches and schools, in some way, and using sales taxes rather than property taxes were widely supported ways of raising additional revenue.

NOTES TO CHAPTER FIVE

1. U. S. Bureau of the Census, Census of Governments, 1967.

Chapter Six

Housing

Housing is a concern of local general purpose governments in at least two respects. First, cities generally have responsibility for inspection of new house construction and inspection of all housing for fire and health hazards. Second, when the cost of housing people in cities becomes too great for residents to reasonably bear in their personal budgets, cities have traditionally sought solutions to this problem through provision of low income housing and other means.

This analysis does not recommend corrective procedures for the problems that exist. It does, however, present data on the cost and condition of housing, the way people feel about their housing, and their views on the role of city governments in housing.

HOW DOES HOUSING DIFFER BETWEEN THE TEN CITIES?

Some of these differences were presented in Chapter 3, but perhaps it is worth reviewing them here. One important difference was the rate at which houses were owned or rented. At one extreme was Boston, where less than 30 percent of the housing units were owner occupied. More typically, a city consisted of half renters and half home owners. However, in Albuquerque; Kansas City, Kansas; Kansas City, Missouri; and Nashville, over 60 percent of the houses and housing units were owner occupied.

Part of the differences between cities can be attributed to the kind of housing that existed in the city. For example, in Boston and Baltimore, only about 10 percent of all housing units were single-family, detached houses. In contrast, over 80 percent of the housing units in Albuquerque were in single-family structures, and over 70 percent of the housing units in Kansas City, Kansas; Kansas City, Missouri; Nashville; and San Diego were in single-family houses. To a considerable extent, the type of housing stock that exists in a community bears

88 *Citizen Attitudes Toward Local Government, Services, and Taxes*

a direct relationship to the likelihood of owner occupancy. The most common kind of house to own is a single-family house.

Was Ownership Evenly Distributed Among Different Groups in the Population?

There was clearly a significant relationship between income and home ownership (Table 6-1). In all cities except the two Kansas Cities, people with incomes over $10,000 were two or three times more likely to own a house than people with incomes under $5,000. In all cases, there was a direct relationship between income and the rate of home ownership.

How About The Blacks? Were They Under-Represented Among The Home Owners?

Overall, it was clear that there was a difference between blacks and whites in the rates of home ownership (Figure 6-1). For example, in Baltimore, 63 percent of the whites were home owners compared with only 31 percent of the blacks. In Kansas City, Kansas, 73 percent of the whites were home owners, but only 48 percent of the blacks owned their own homes. Only in Boston was there no difference between blacks and whites in this respect, and there the rates of ownership were comparatively low for both groups.

WHAT WERE THE RELATIVE COSTS OF OWNING AND RENTING A PLACE TO LIVE?

The monthly payments reported by homeowners for mortgage (where one existed), taxes, insurance, utilities, and maintenance were higher on the average than the gross rent (utilities included) reported by renters (Table 6-2). Such a comparison does not take into account differences in the size and facilities of owned and rented units, nor does it consider the tax benefits of home ownership. Even without these adjustments, however, housing costs were generally less of a burden to homeowners than to renters, when one considers the percentage of income spent on housing (Table 6-3).

One standard[1] for an appropriate amount to spend on housing is 25 percent or less—that is, anyone who is spending 25 percent or less of his gross income on housing is doing fairly well. Anyone who is spending more than 25 percent of his gross income on housing is spending too much. For all cities, homeowners reported spending the same or a lower proportion of their income on housing than did renters, even before their tax deductions for interest and property taxes. In three cities—Milwaukee; Kansas City, Kansas; and Kansas City, Missouri—there was virtually no difference between owners and renters in the percentage of their income that went into housing. And in Nashville, there was only a very small difference. In the rest, owners were clearly paying proportionately less than renters for housing.

Table 6–1. Percent Who Own Homes, by Income

	Albuquerque	Atlanta	Baltimore	Boston	Denver	Kansas City, Kansas	Kansas City, Missouri	Milwaukee	Nashville	San Diego
Less than $5,000	42%	21%	25%	13%	31%	60%	52%	25%	39%	38%
$5,000 to $9,999	65%	53%	38%	22%	52%	65%	69%	45%	57%	45%
$10,000 or More	86%	59%	68%	43%	77%	78%	80%	67%	83%	74%

Table 6–2. Total Monthly Payments for Housing, by Home Tenure and by City

	Albuquerque	Atlanta	Baltimore	Boston	Denver	Kansas City, Kansas	Kansas City, Missouri	Milwaukee	Nashville	San Diego
Homeowners										
Less than $80 per Month	16%	16%	21%	6%	11%	21%	9%	8%	14%	11%
$80 to $119	15%	10%	17%	10%	13%	14%	10%	18%	16%	9%
$120 to $159	29%	17%	30%	14%	28%	30%	21%	15%	25%	23%
$160 to $224	22%	23%	15%	25%	29%	20%	36%	29%	21%	28%
$225 or More	14%	26%	13%	34%	14%	12%	21%	28%	17%	24%
(N)	(307)	(211)	(232)	(125)	(188)	(128)	(261)	(207)	(274)	(289)
Renters										
Less than $80	30%	23%	15%	13%	17%	28%	19%	15%	27%	14%
$80 to $119	37%	29%	33%	19%	33%	22%	25%	23%	31%	24%
$120 to $159	24%	26%	34%	32%	31%	34%	28%	38%	27%	31%
$160 to $224	8%	14%	12%	26%	12%	15%	21%	16%	13%	21%
$225 or More	1%	7%	4%	8%	4%	1%	5%	6%	1%	9%
(N)	(144)	(256)	(265)	(371)	(163)	(65)	(116)	(231)	(144)	(212)

Note: "No response" data, 5 percent on the average, are not included in the table; therefore figures do not total 100 percent.

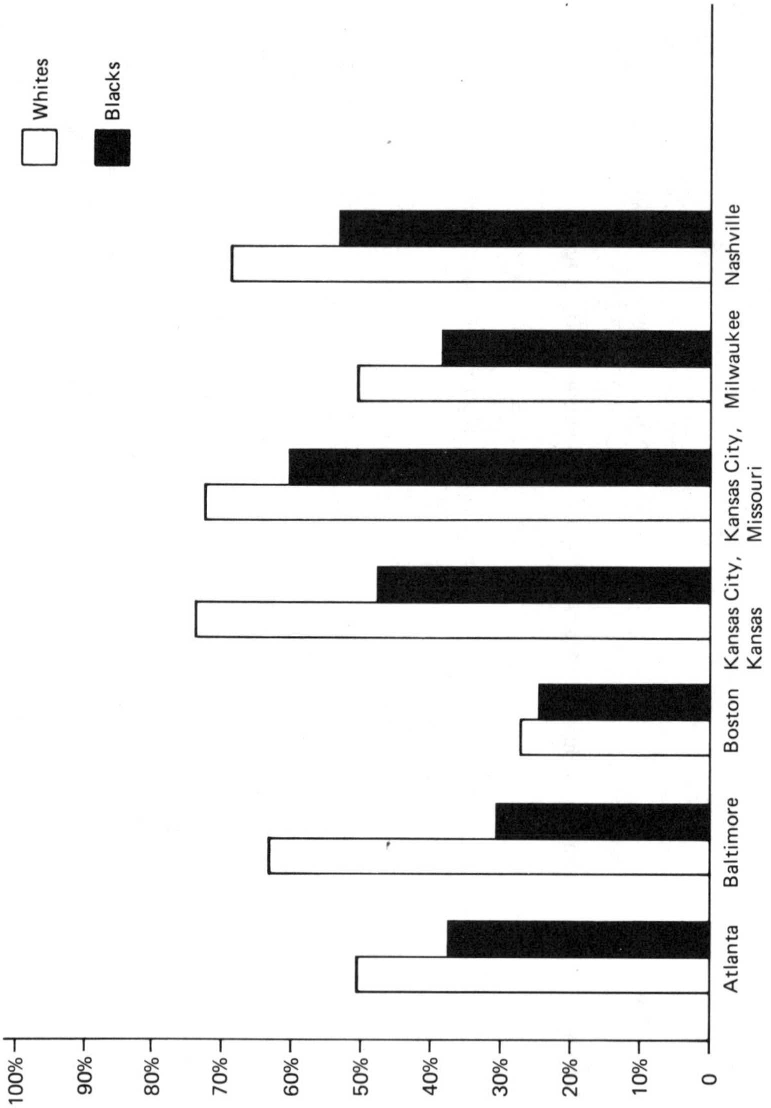

90 Citizen Attitudes Toward Local Government, Services, and Taxes

Figure 6—1. Percent Who Own Homes, by Race

Table 6-3. Cost of Housing as Percent of Total Annual Income, by Home Tenure

	Albuquerque	Atlanta	Baltimore	Boston	Denver	Kansas City, Kansas	Kansas City, Missouri	Milwaukee	Nashville	San Diego
Homeowners										
Less than 15% of Income	36%	35%	48%	31%	33%	24%	24%	20%	35%	39%
15% to 24%	41%	31%	35%	23%	37%	39%	40%	43%	33%	34%
25% to 34%	14%	12%	9%	15%	15%	19%	15%	18%	15%	14%
35% or More	9%	22%	8%	31%	15%	18%	21%	19%	17%	13%
Total	100%	100%	100%	100%	100%	100%	100%	100%	100%	100%
(N)	(280)	(193)	(214)	(108)	(171)	(123)	(248)	(193)	(223)	(266)
Renters										
Less than 15% of Income	23%	23%	25%	15%	24%	23%	19%	18%	26%	19%
15% to 24%	39%	32%	39%	30%	34%	39%	43%	39%	42%	37%
25% to 35%	10%	13%	15%	21%	18%	15%	16%	15%	14%	20%
35% or More	28%	32%	21%	34%	24%	23%	22%	28%	18%	24%
Total	100%	100%	100%	100%	100%	100%	100%	100%	100%	100%
(N)	(144)	(256)	(265)	(371)	(164)	(65)	(116)	(231)	(144)	(213)

How Was Income Related to Housing Costs?

In every city there was a direct, extremely strong relationship between family income and the percentage of income spent on housing: the poor spend a relatively large portion of their income on housing, the well-to-do spend a relatively small proportion.

In every city over half of those with incomes under $5,000 reported spending more than 25 percent of their income on housing (Table 6-4). In contrast, with the exception of Kansas City, Missouri, people with incomes over $10,000 were more likely than not to be spending less than 15 percent of their income on housing (Table 6-5).

These data mean that there is a very special double burden that poor people pay. First, because they are poor, they have less than $5,000 to spend. Second, they are clearly almost universally paying a disproportionate amount of their meager incomes for housing, which leaves a disproportionately small amount of money after housing to pay for food and other necessities. Even in the city where this was least true—Nashville—only 40 percent of persons with incomes under $5,000 were able to find housing for 25 percent of their income.

Were People With Low Incomes Simply Choosing to Live in Places That Were Too Expensive For Them?

Very consistently, those people living in housing in the poorest condition were also more likely than average to be paying more than a fourth of their incomes for housing (Figure 6-2). From 10 to 30 percent of the rental housing in cities was renting for less than $80 per month. Eighty dollars per month is more than a fourth of the income of anyone making less than $4,000 per year. Moreover, rental housing constituted generally less than half of the housing in a city. There was not, in short, very much housing available for the 20 to 30 percent of the population living on less than $5,000 per year.

Were People Unhappy About The Cost of Housing?

To an extent, but perhaps not as much as one might expect. When people were asked whether they thought they were paying too much for what they were getting or whether the cost of their housing was just about right, a substantial majority in every city said they thought the cost of their housing was just about right or at about fair market value (Figure 6-3). Indeed, only a minority of all those with incomes under $5,000 said they thought that the cost of their housing was "too much" (Table 6-6). People apparently have adjusted to the real cost of housing.

In most cities there was a significant relationship between income and saying that housing costs too much (Table 6-6). People with lower incomes were

Table 6-4. Percent Who Pay a Quarter or More of Their Family Income for Housing, by Income

	Albuquerque	Atlanta	Baltimore	Boston	Denver	Kansas City, Kansas	Kansas City, Missouri	Milwaukee	Nashville	San Diego
Less than $5,000	76%	77%	71%	90%	68%	67%	76%	80%	59%	81%
$5,000 to $9,999	23%	37%	24%	47%	35%	34%	43%	40%	39%	43%
$10,000 or More	6%	9%	5%	16%	7%	8%	9%	10%	12%	10%

Table 6-5. Percent of Citizens Who Spend Less Than 15 Percent for Housing of Total Family Income, by Income

	Albuquerque	Atlanta	Baltimore	Boston	Denver	Kansas City, Kansas	Kansas City, Missouri	Milwaukee	Nashville	San Diego
Less than $5,000	5%	5%	10%	2%	15%	9%	4%	2%	8%	4%
$5,000 to $9,999	26%	17%	25%	12%	16%	11%	14%	11%	16%	14%
$10,000 or More	52%	61%	64%	48%	61%	59%	39%	40%	59%	51%

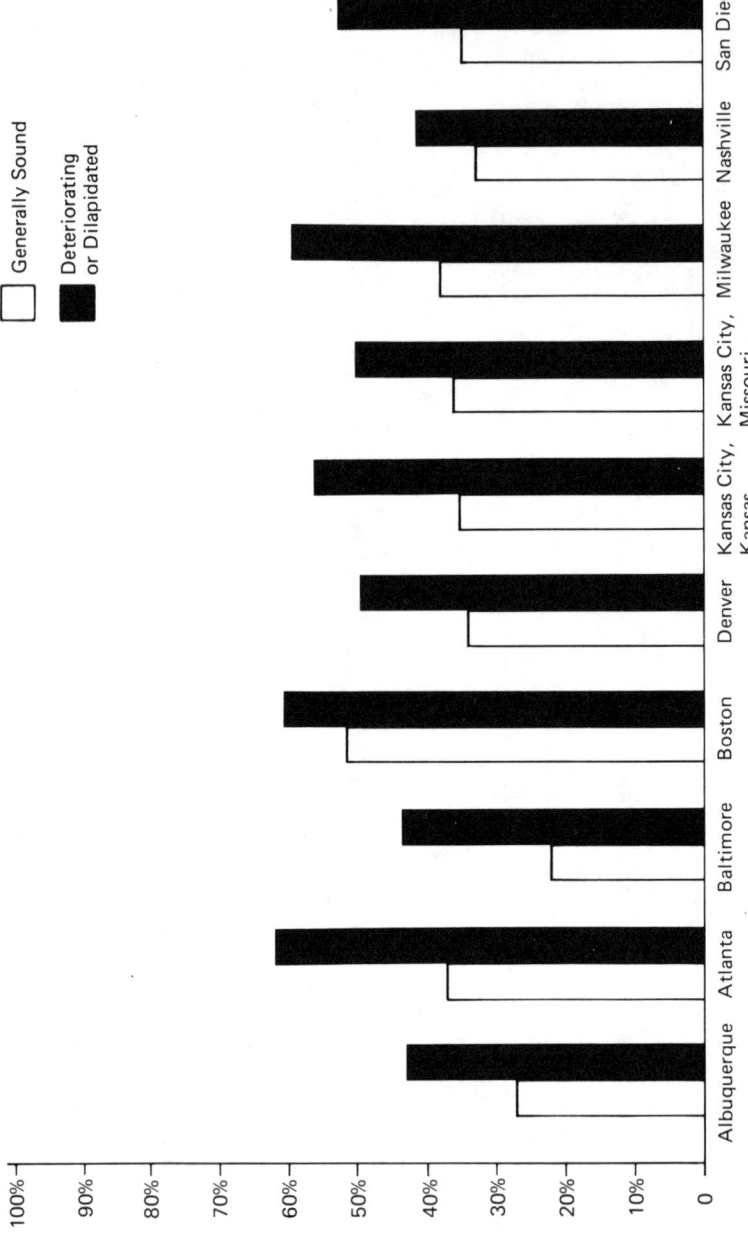

Figure 6–2. Percent Who Pay a Quarter or More of Annual Income for Housing, by Condition of Housing

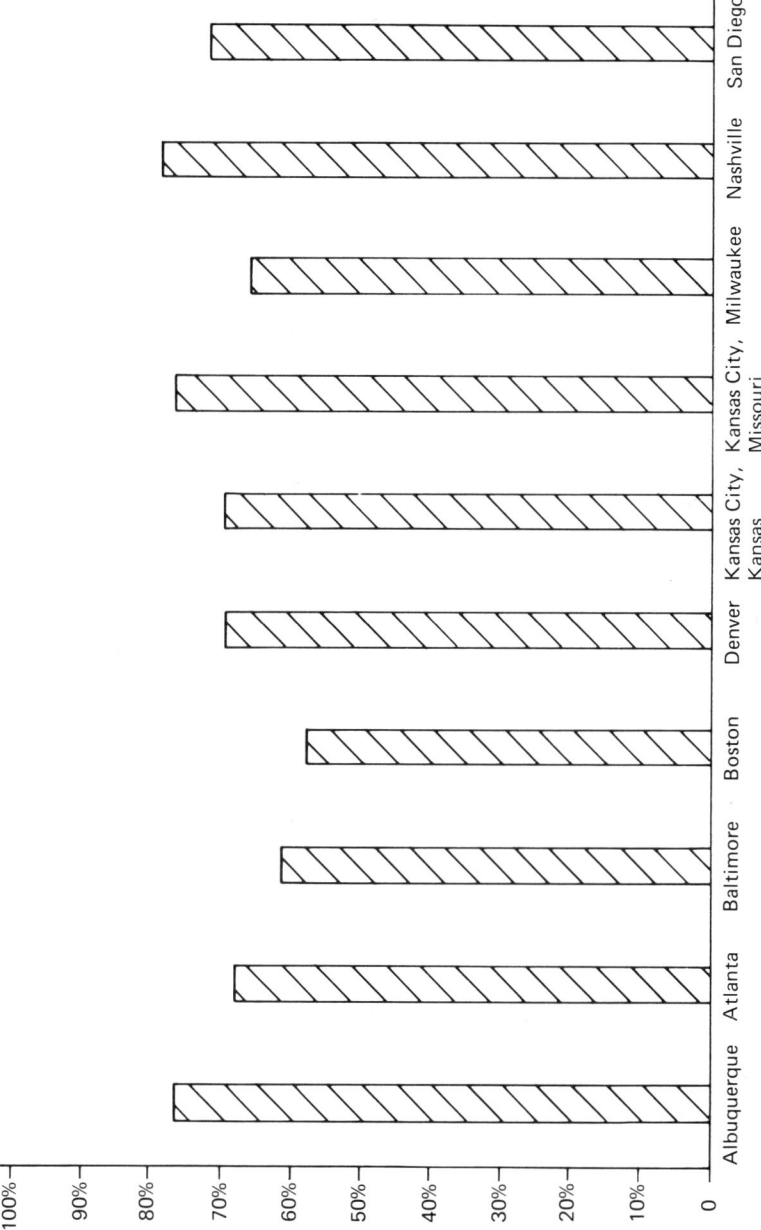

Figure 6-3. Percent Who Think Cost of Their Housing Is "About Right," by City

more likely to say that their housing did cost too much although there were two or three exceptions. Most notably, in Milwaukee the higher-income people tended to complain about their costs more than those with lower incomes, though not significantly so.

Were Racial Minorities More Likely to be Concerned About the Cost of Housing?

In four cities, blacks and whites were almost equally concerned about the cost of their housing (Figure 6-4). On the other hand, there were some cities where there were very substantial differences by race. For example, only 16 percent of the whites in Atlanta said they were paying too much for housing, compared with 47 percent of the blacks. Atlanta was the extreme in this respect, but in Milwaukee and Kansas City, Kansas, there were also substantial differences between blacks and whites.

Did Blacks Pay a Higher Percentage of Their Income for Housing?

Consistent with the lower than average incomes of minority groups, blacks generally reported paying a higher percentage of their incomes for housing than whites (Figure 6-5). This was not universally the case. In Baltimore and Boston, for example, there was virtually no difference between blacks and whites in the percentage of income they were paying for housing. However, in Atlanta, there was a large difference. Only 26 percent of the whites were spending more than a quarter of their income for housing, compared with 58 percent of the blacks. In Kansas City, Missouri, only a little more than a quarter of the whites were paying a quarter of their income for housing, compared with 61 percent of the blacks. Although more blacks in Kansas City, Missouri, paid more than 25 percent of their annual incomes for housing than in any other city, it was not a city where blacks were especially likely to express the view that they pay too much for housing. In five of the seven cities about which we can generalize, a majority of blacks reported paying a quarter or more of their incomes for housing. For whites, this was true in Boston only. Although there were a couple of exceptions, in more cities than not it appears that the cost of housing was more a problem for blacks than for whites.

OTHER THAN COSTS, WHAT PROBLEMS WERE THERE WITH HOUSING?

People were asked whether there were any serious reasons why their house or neighborhood was not a good place for them to live. The majority of people said "no" (Figure 6-6). On the average, only one in four persons said that there was a serious problem with his housing situation. Such responses were more prevalent

Housing 97

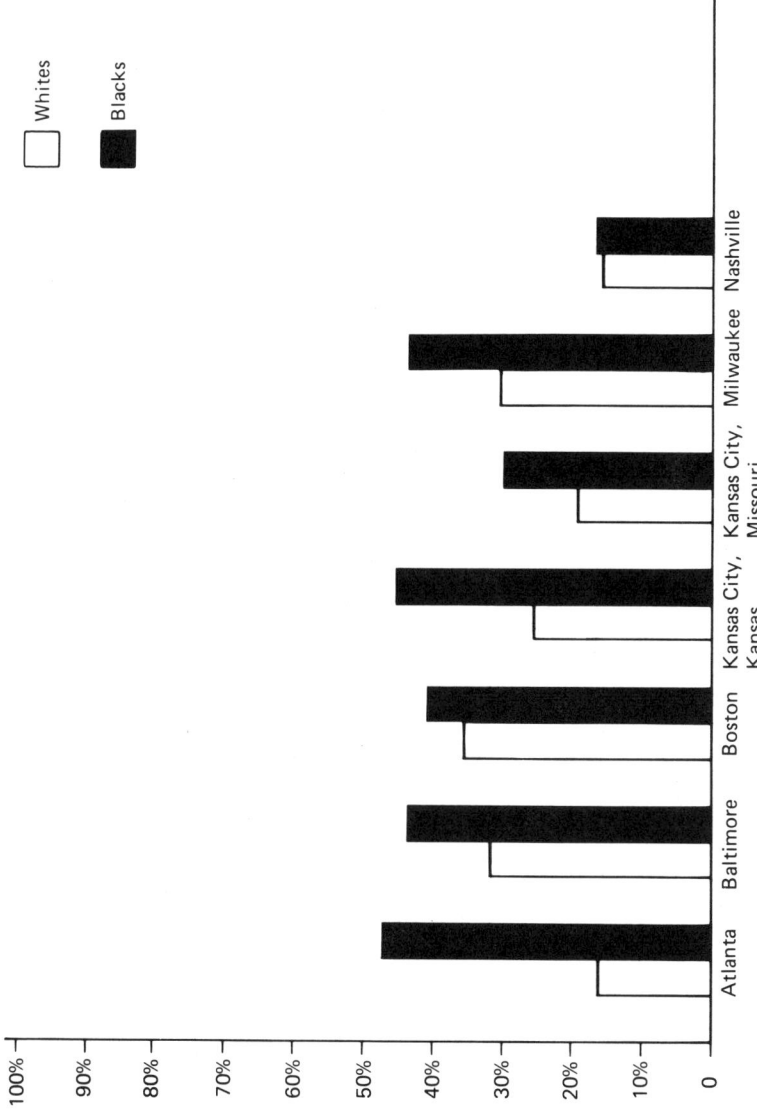

Figure 6-4. Percent Who Think They Pay Too Much for Housing, by Race

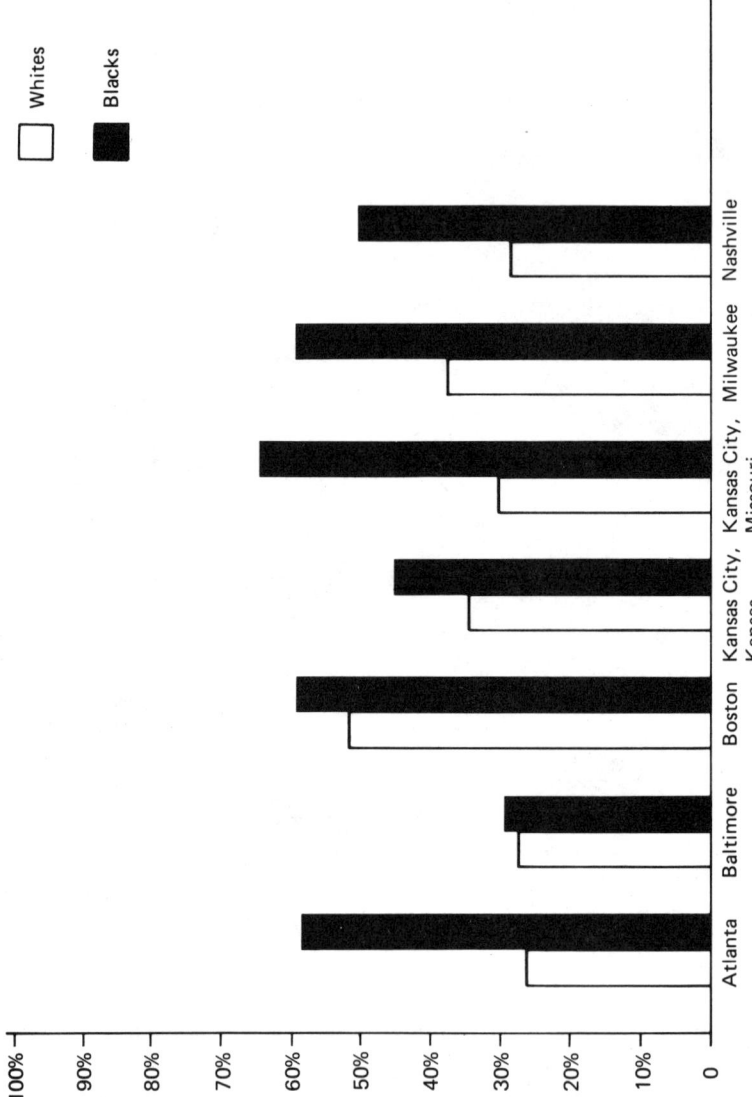

Figure 6-5. Percent Who Pay a Quarter or More of Annual Income for Housing, by Race

Housing 99

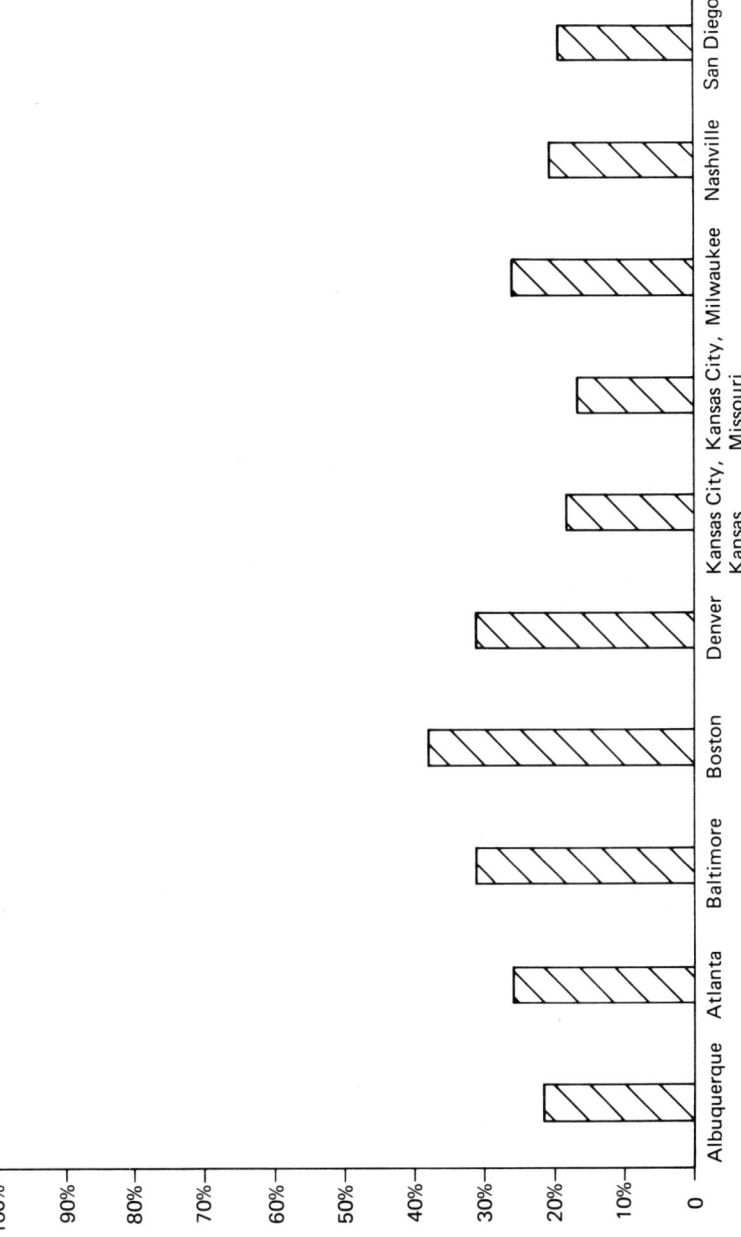

Figure 6-6. Percent Who Said There Was a Serious Problem with Their Housing, by City

Table 6-6. Percent Who Think They Pay Too Much for Housing, by Income

	Albuquerque	Atlanta	Baltimore	Boston	Denver	Kansas City, Kansas	Kansas City, Missouri	Milwaukee	Nashville	San Diego
Less than $5,000	30%	41%	45%	44%	27%	33%	20%	27%	14%	24%
$5,000 to $9,999	22%	29%	43%	39%	33%	35%	29%	33%	18%	32%
$10,000 or More	11%	20%	29%	31%	8%	21%	16%	36%	14%	15%

Table 6-7. Reason Why House or Neighborhood Is Not a Good Place to Live, by City

Response	Albuquerque	Atlanta	Baltimore	Boston	Denver	Kansas City, Kansas	Kansas City, Missouri	Milwaukee	Nashville	San Diego
Public Services	13%	6%	4%	3%	7%	9%	4%	2%	13%	4%
Physical Environment	32	32	21	24	35	25	30	32	29	45
Location	1	3	2	2	4	4	6	4	2	3
Neighborhood Composition	19	20	20	18	13	14	20	17	23	23
Safety	8	10	18	27	18	23	15	11	13	5
Bad for Children	9	7	5	5	4	9	6	6	10	11
Condition of House	7	13	22	13	12	14	13	15	6	5
Other House Problems	6	5	3	6	5	2	3	8	4	3
Financially Bad	3	3	3	2	2	*	1	4	*	1
Other General	2	1	2	*	*	*	2	1	*	*
Total	100%	100%	100%	100%	100%	100%	100%	100%	100%	100%
(N)	(99)	(116)	(148)	(185)	(108)	(35)	(62)	(111)	(84)	(98)

Note: Figures include only those respondents who said there was a serious problem, usually about 20 percent. Percentages are distributions of all codable responses.

*Less than 0.5 percent.

in Boston and to a lesser extent in Denver and Baltimore than in other cities in the study.

Most of those who said there was a problem focused on the characteristics of the neighborhood and the environment, not on the housing unit itself (Table 6–7). Only about one out of five responses mentioned anything about the particular housing unit. Generally, about 30 percent of the responses dealt with the character of the physical environment, its commercialism, or its run down condition, with another 15 percent concerned about safety and crime. Another 20 percent were critical of the composition of the neighborhood. The rest had complaints of all kinds, including city services, location, and other miscellaneous responses.

Were Some Groups More Likely to Have Complaints About Housing Than Others?

The most obvious expectation would be that the people who are well-to-do would have fewer complaints or problems with their housing than people with less money; but, in fact, there was not consistently a relationship between income and people saying that there was a serious problem with their housing (Table 6–8). Only in Baltimore and Albuquerque was there a relationship that was statistically significant. A similar lack of relationship was found when the answers to this question were tabulated by race (Table 6–9). Only in Boston was there a tendency for blacks to have more complaints than whites. In the other six cities, there was not a significant relationship.[2]

A slightly different picture emerged, however, from the responses of renters to a question about problems with the way houses are kept.[3] On the average, 20 to 25 percent of renters reported a problem that they considered serious (Figure 6–7). The rate was a bit lower than average in Nashville and San Diego, and much higher than average in Baltimore, where 45 percent of the renters reported a serious problem with the condition of their housing.

Because the question was asked only of renters, the number of sample cases in some categories was too small for reliability. However, when there were enough cases, it was fairly clear that blacks and those with low incomes were more likely than others to report a serious housing maintenance problem (Table 6–10 and 6–11). The same relationships appeared when the interviewer rating of the condition of each respondent's housing unit was tabulated by race and by income: housing units occupied by blacks were likely to be rated in less good condition than those occupied by whites; likewise, the housing of lower-income families was rated in less good condition than others (Table 6–12 and 6–13).

Thus, although race and income were not related to responses to the general question about serious problems with where people were living, they were fairly consistently related to the perceived level of maintenance and the rated condition of housing in which people live. However, in terms of the number of

Table 6-8. Percent Who Say There Is a Serious Problem with Their Housing, by Income

	Albuquerque	Atlanta	Baltimore	Boston	Denver	Kansas City, Kansas	Kansas City, Missouri	Milwaukee	Nashville	San Diego
Under $5,000	25%	29%	37%	35%	31%	18%	14%	24%	22%	21%
$5,000 to $9,999	25%	19%	33%	43%	35%	21%	20%	26%	22%	21%
$10,000 or More	16%	26%	20%	34%	26%	12%	16%	26%	18%	17%

Table 6-9. Percent Who Say There Is a Serious Problem with Their Housing, by Race

	Atlanta	Baltimore	Boston	Kansas City, Kansas	Kansas City, Missouri	Milwaukee	Nashville
White	25%	25%	34%	16%	16%	25%	20%
Black	25%	33%	47%	21%	16%	30%	18%
(N)	(244)	(253)	(357)	(65)	(114)	(225)	(141)

Housing 103

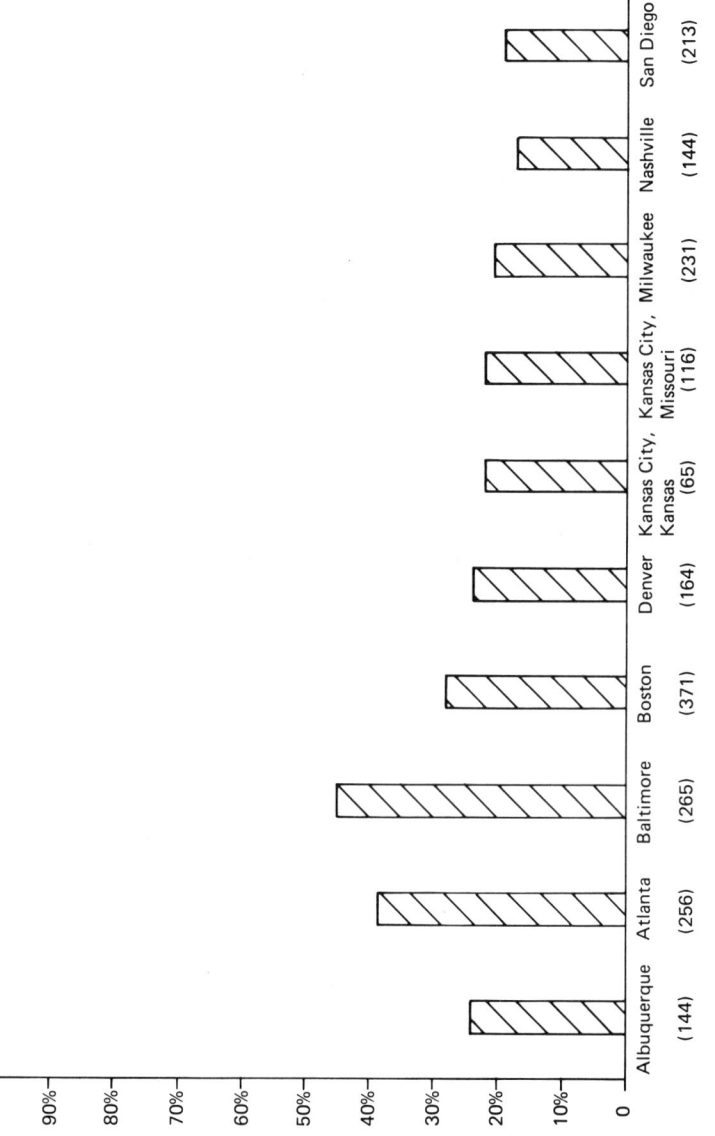

Note: This question was asked only of renters.

Figure 6-7. Percent of Renters Who say Their Housing Is Seriously in Need of Maintenance, by City

Table 6-10. Percent of Renters Who Say Their Housing Is Seriously in Need of Maintenance, by Race

	Albuquerque	Atlanta	Baltimore	Boston	Denver	Kansas City, Kansas	Kansas City, Missouri	Milwaukee	Nashville	San Diego
White (not Spanish)	*	12%	26%	15%	*	*	*	11%	*	*
Black	*	46%	48%	32%	*	*	*	*	*	*

Note: This question was asked only of renters.
*Too few cases to be reliable.

Table 6-11. Percent of Renters Who Say Their Housing Is Seriously in Need of Maintenance, by Income

	Albuquerque	Atlanta	Baltimore	Boston	Denver	Kansas City, Kansas	Kansas City, Missouri	Milwaukee	Nashville	San Diego
Less than $5,000	22%	41%	43%	24%	20%	*	17%	13%	16%	13%
$5,000 to $9,999	17%	24%	46%	20%	23%	*	23%	23%	13%	14%
$10,000 or More	*	16%	28%	12%	*	*	*	14%	*	3%

Note: This question was asked only of renters.
*Too few cases to be reliable.

Table 6-12. Percent of Housing Rated Dilapidated or Deteriorating, by Race

	Atlanta	Baltimore	Boston	Kansas City, Kansas	Kansas City, Missouri	Milwaukee	Nashville
White	6%	13%	13%	4%	6%	8%	9%
Black	21%	34%	23%	16%	8%	34%	17%

Note: Interviewer's rating of the following: Interviewer rating #5 (including definitions). We did not train the interviewers in housing inspection, therefore, this rating should only be taken as a rough index.

people affected, it appears that the cost of housing, more than the condition of housing, is the major housing problem for those with low incomes and for blacks.

DID PEOPLE THINK THAT LOCAL GOVERNMENT SHOULD PLAY A ROLE IN PROVIDING LOW-COST HOUSING?

People were asked whether they thought the local government should be responsible for having low-cost and moderate-cost housing built in the city (Table 6-14). Sixty to 90 percent of all people living in the cities said that the local government should take on that responsibility. These answers may not mean that people really cared whether the local, state, or federal government assumes the responsibility, but certainly they reflect substantial consensus about a need and that some level of government should be responsible for meeting that need.

Was It True That People Did Not Want Low-Cost Housing in Their Own Neighborhoods?

This attitude did not seem to prevail in most cities. We asked people how they would feel about having low-cost housing in their neighborhood, whether they thought it would be a good idea, whether they would just accept it, or whether they would be against it (Table 6-15). Only about one-fourth of the adults in most cities said they would be against low-cost housing in their neighborhood, and in the most resistant city—Atlanta—only 36 percent said they would be against it. This clearly does not mean that people wanted projects built in their own neighborhoods. It does indicate, however, that perhaps there was not the widespread resistance to building low-cost housing in neighborhoods that people might have anticipated.

Were All Segments of The Community Equally Willing to Have Low-Cost Housing in Their Neighborhoods?

The need for low-cost housing was much more acute for those with low incomes, and low-income housing would not represent as much of a change

Table 6-13. Percent of Housing Rated Dilapidated or Deteriorating, by Income

	Albuquerque	Atlanta	Baltimore	Boston	Denver	Kansas City, Kansas	Kansas City, Missouri	Milwaukee	Nashville	San Diego
Less than $5,000	18%	29%	53%	25%	24%	14%	11%	22%	26%	15%
$5,000 to $9,999	11%	9%	26%	18%	14%	9%	8%	10%	13%	7%
$10,000 or More	1%	2%	8%	5%	4%	2%	3%	3%	2%	1%

Note: Interviewer's rating of the following: Interviewer rating #5 (including definitions). We did not train the interviewers in housing inspection, therefore, this rating should only be taken as a rough index.

Table 6-14. Should Local Government Play a Role in Providing More Low- and Moderate-Cost Housing?

Response	Albuquerque	Atlanta	Baltimore	Boston	Denver	Kansas City, Kansas	Kansas City, Missouri	Milwaukee	Nashville	San Diego
Yes	66%	77%	87%	79%	65%	69%	60%	66%	76%	59%
No	32	19	13	16	26	27	36	30	20	39
Not Ascertained	2	4	*	5	9	4	4	4	4	2
Total	100%	100%	100%	100%	100%	100%	100%	100%	100%	100%
(N)	(471)	(469)	(500)	(507)	(357)	(193)	(383)	(443)	(426)	(517)

*Less than 0.5 percent.

in lower-income areas as it might mean for those in high-income areas. In every city, there was more support for low-income housing in an area of low-income people (Table 6–16). Nevertheless, the majority of those with incomes over $10,000 per year said they would accept the idea of low-income housing in their neighborhood, in every city except Atlanta. In Atlanta, 55 percent of those with incomes over $10,000, said they would be against low-cost housing in their neighborhood. There was no city in which the majority of whites said they would not accept low-income housing (Figure 6–8). Furthermore, when comparing renters and owners much the same pattern occurs (Figure 6–9). One would expect that renters would be the ones to benefit from low-income housing and that owners would be the ones who would be concerned about their property value. Nonetheless, with the exception of Atlanta, the majority of all home-owners in every city interviewed said they would accept low-income housing in their neighborhoods.

It is true that people's response to hypothetical interview questions may not be the same as their responses when they are faced with reality. Nevertheless, there was widespread acceptance of the idea that every city needs more low-cost housing, and there appeared to be only reasonably modest resistance in most segments of the population to the idea of low-cost housing nearby.

HOW HAS URBAN RENEWAL AFFECTED PEOPLE IN CITIES?

People were asked whether or not they personally had been affected by urban renewal. The percent saying they had been affected ranged from 2 percent in San Diego to 10 percent in Nashville (Table 6–17). The effects mentioned were both positive and negative. In those cities in which the most people had been moved by urban renewal, it appeared that blacks and those with low incomes were more likely than others to report having been moved (Table 6–18). This was clearly the case in Nashville. However, there were other cities in which the rate of being forced to move was no higher for blacks and those with low incomes than for others.

How Did People Feel About The Affects of Urban Renewal?

Respondents were asked whether they thought urban renewal had made their city a better place to live, a worse place to live, or had not made much difference (Table 6–19). Only a small percentage—less than 15 percent in any city, usually less than 10 percent—thought the overall impact of urban renewal had been negative.

How Did Different Population Segments Rate Urban Renewal?

Overall, blacks were as likely as whites to say urban renewal had made their city a better place to live (Figure 6–10), and there was one in which

108 Citizen Attitudes Toward Local Government, Services, and Taxes

Table 6–15. Attitude Toward Low-Cost Housing in Citizen's Neighborhood, by City

Response	Albuquerque	Atlanta	Baltimore	Boston	Denver	Kansas City, Kansas	Kansas City, Missouri	Milwaukee	Nashville	San Diego
Good Idea	35%	28%	35%	55%	32%	37%	32%	35%	26%	27%
Accept It	35	33	36	23	40	35	33	41	37	39
Against It	29	36	29	18	22	26	33	21	34	32
Not Ascertained	1	3	*	4	6	2	2	3	3	2
Total	100%	100%	100%	100%	100%	100%	100%	100%	100%	100%
(N)	(471)	(469)	(500)	(507)	(357)	(193)	(383)	(443)	(426)	(517)

*Less than 0.5 percent.

Table 6–16. Percent Who Would Accept or Favor Low-Income Housing in Their Own Neighborhood, by Income

	Albuquerque	Atlanta	Baltimore	Boston	Denver	Kansas City, Kansas	Kansas City, Missouri	Milwaukee	Nashville	San Diego
Less than $5,000	87%	87%	87%	89%	85%	82%	74%	86%	80%	73%
$5,000 to $9,999	72%	68%	77%	85%	78%	80%	66%	81%	74%	76%
$10,000 or More	63%	45%	59%	69%	66%	60%	61%	74%	55%	60%

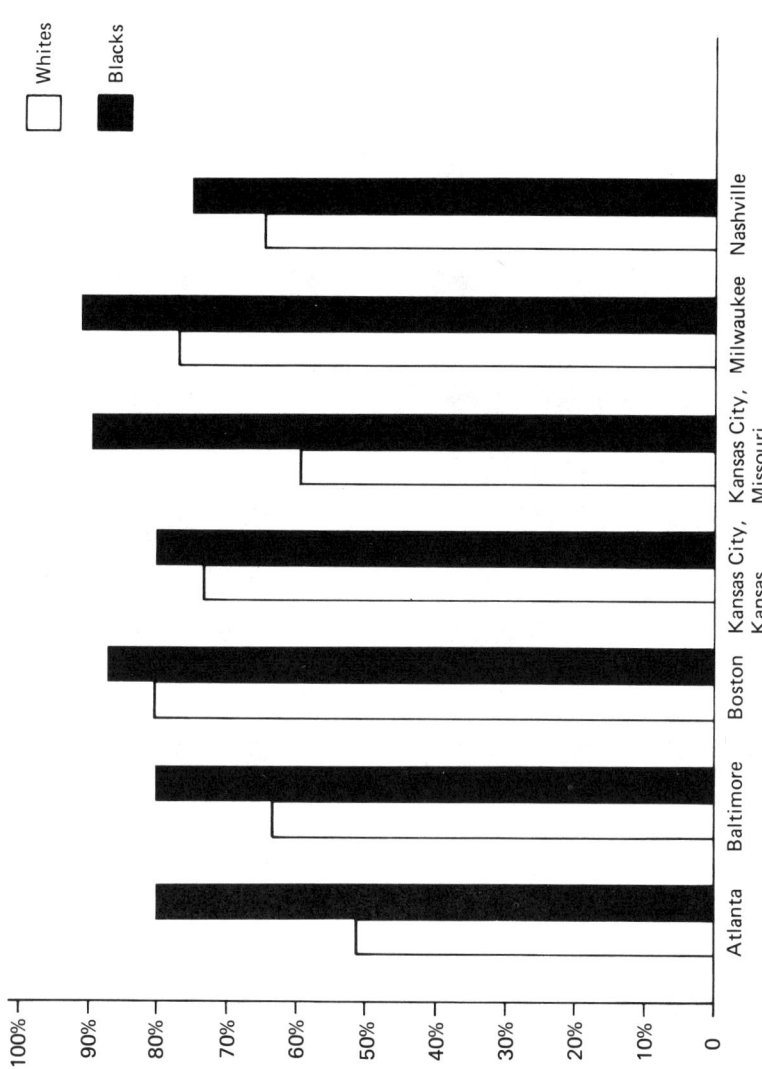

Figure 6–8. Percent Who Would Accept or Favor Low-Income Housing in Their Own Neighborhood, by Race

110 Citizen Attitudes Toward Local Government, Services, and Taxes

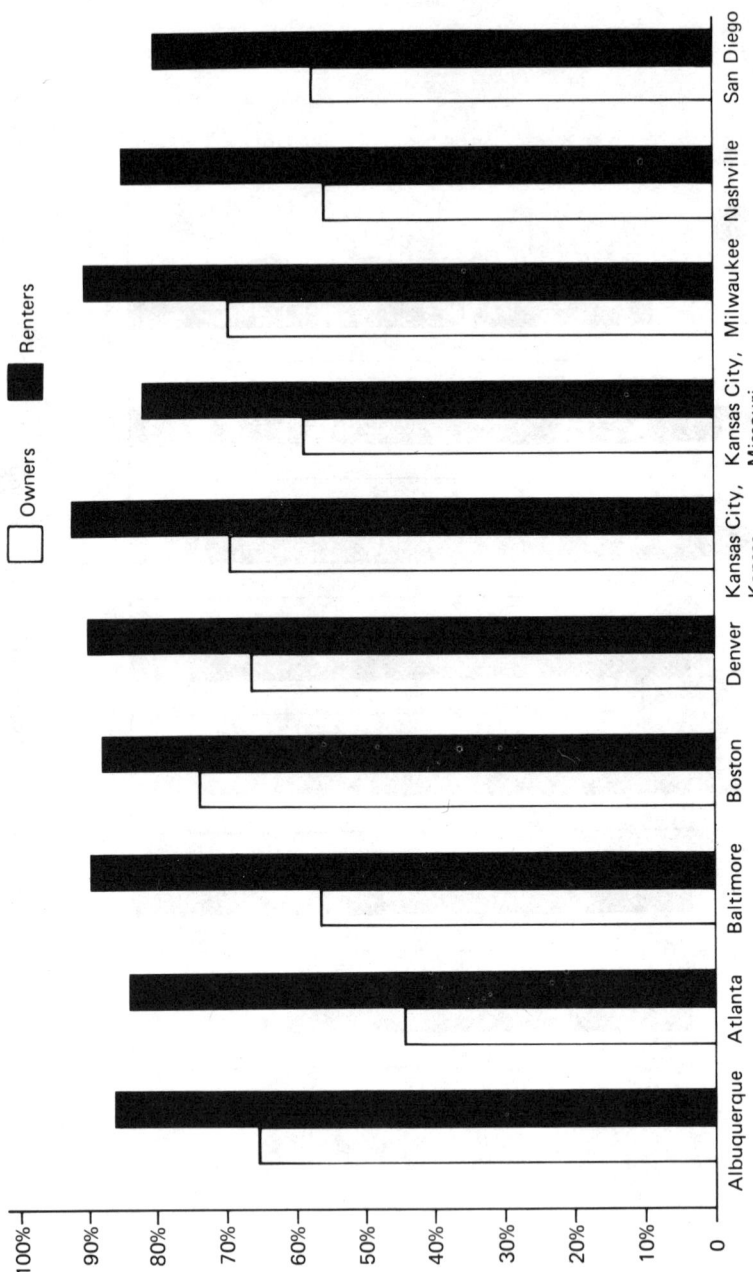

Figure 6–9. Percent Who Would Accept or Favor Low-Income Housing in Their Own Neighborhood, by Home Tenure

Table 6–17. Percent Who Say They Have Been Personally Affected by Urban Renewal, by City

Response	Albuquerque	Atlanta	Baltimore	Boston	Denver	Kansas City, Kansas	Kansas City, Missouri	Milwaukee	Nashville	San Diego
Yes	5%	9%	7%	10%	6%	9%	7%	8%	10%	2%
No	95%	91%	93%	90%	94%	91%	93%	92%	90%	98%
Total	100%	100%	100%	100%	100%	100%	100%	100%	100%	100%
(N)	(471)	(469)	(500)	(507)	(357)	(193)	(383)	(443)	(426)	(517)

Table 6–18. Percent Forced to Move by Urban Renewal, by Race and by Income

	Albuquerque	Atlanta	Baltimore	Boston	Denver	Kansas City, Kansas	Kansas City, Missouri	Milwaukee	Nashville	San Diego
Race										
White		1%	*	1%	*	2%	1%	2%	4%	
Black		3%	2%	8%		*	4%	7%	15%	
Income										
Under $5,000	1%	5%	2%	1%	*	1%	1%	4%	9%	*
$5,000 to $9,999	1%	*	1%	4%	1%	2%	1%	3%	9%	*
$10,000 or More	*	1%	*	2%	1%	2%	2%	1%	1%	*

*Less than 0.5 percent.

112 Citizen Attitudes Toward Local Government, Services, and Taxes

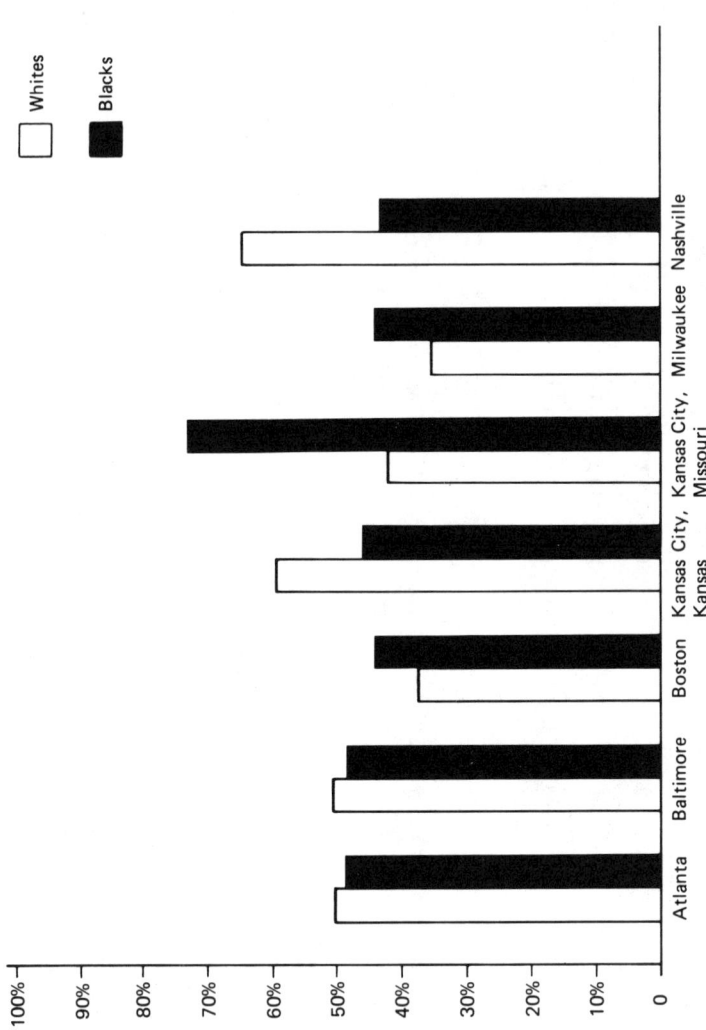

Note: People who had not heard of urban renewal were excluded from this table, which ranged from 10 to 38 percent (see Table 6-19).

Figure 6-10. Percent Who Say Urban Renewal Has Made Their City a Better Place to Live, by Race

blacks were more favorable than whites. People in the lower-income categories (which included many aged) were less familiar with urban renewal than others in many cities. Among those who knew about urban renewal, lower-income people's responses were mixed; in three cities, poor people were more positive about the affects of urban renewal than wealthier people, and in four cities the opposite was the case (Table 6-20).

WHAT OTHER ROLES DID CITIZENS FEEL THE LOCAL GOVERNMENT SHOULD PLAY IN RELATION TO HOUSING?

People were asked: "How well do you think local agencies do in inspecting houses and getting owners and landlords to make needed repairs?" Less than 38 percent of the citizens in any city said that the city government does "very well" or "well enough" (Table 6-21). The majority ratings were "not too well" and "not well at all."

This perception was not most prevalent among the poor people, who were most likely to suffer from deficiencies in their housing and more likely to live in neighborhoods where housing problems were prevalent. On the contrary, in most cities there was a significant relationship in the other direction—that is, both better-educated people and people with higher incomes were more likely to think that the job that the local agencies were doing in inspecting housing was less than it should be (Tables 6-22 and 6-23). Blacks, however, were generally more likely to see a problem in housing inspection than whites, and renters were generally more likely to see a problem with housing inspection than home owners (Figures 6-11 and 6-12).

Thus there was fairly widespread consensus among the populations in most cities that more could be done in the field of inspection. Furthermore, the people most likely to have this perception included those people with incomes over $10,000, the college educated, the blacks, and the renters.

Did People Really Want More Code Enforcement?

"Inspecting houses and having owners clean up houses that are run down or have rats or other health hazards" was one of only two items for which a majority of people in all cities expressed the view that the city should be spending more money (Chapter 4).

Did Different Segments of The Population Favor Spending More for Code Enforcement?

There was very little relationship between either education or income and thinking that more money should be spent on inspecting houses (Tables 6-24

Table 6–19. Effect of Urban Renewal on the City as a Place to Live, by City

	Albuquerque	Atlanta	Baltimore	Boston	Denver	Kansas City, Kansas	Kansas City, Missouri	Milwaukee	Nashville	San Diego
Better	31%	49%	49%	37%	53%	55%	49%	36%	61%	22%
Worse	2	6	10	15	2	6	4	7	7	3
No Difference	41	24	31	32	34	28	34	38	22	37
Not Heard of Urban Renewal	26	21	10	16	11	11	13	19	10	38
Total	100%	100%	100%	100%	100%	100%	100%	100%	100%	100%
(N)	(413)	(438)	(491)	(468)	(313)	(186)	(363)	(423)	(385)	(448)

Table 6–20. Percent Who Say Urban Renewal Has Made Their City a Better Place to Live, by Income

	Albuquerque	Atlanta	Baltimore	Boston	Denver	Kansas City, Kansas	Kansas City, Missouri	Milwaukee	Nashville	San Diego
Less than $5,000	51%	62%	47%	44%	56%	50%	64%	43%	55%	43%
$5,000 to $9,999	45%	62%	53%	44%	56%	70%	59%	41%	66%	40%
$10,000 or More	31%	64%	59%	46%	65%	60%	48%	48%	75%	33%

Note: People who had not heard of urban renewal were excluded from this table.

Table 6-21. How Well Do Local Agencies Do in Inspecting Houses and Effecting Needed Repairs?

Response	Albuquerque	Atlanta	Baltimore	Boston	Denver	Kansas City, Kansas	Kansas City, Missouri	Milwaukee	Nashville	San Diego
Very Well	6%	14%	8%	7%	5%	10%	6%	13%	10%	7%
Well Enough	16	20	23	20	21	25	21	24	22	28
Not too Well	26	31	37	27	33	32	35	31	25	26
Not Well at All	28	23	29	30	19	22	25	20	17	16
Not Ascertained	24	12	3	16	22	11	13	12	26	23
Total	100%	100%	100%	100%	100%	100%	100%	100%	100%	100%
(N)	(471)	(469)	(500)	(507)	(357)	(193)	(383)	(443)	(426)	(517)

Table 6-22. Percent* Who Say Local Agencies Enforce Housing Inspection Code "Not Too Well" or "Not Well at All, by Income

	Albuquerque	Atlanta	Baltimore	Boston	Denver	Kansas City, Kansas	Kansas City, Missouri	Milwaukee	Nashville	San Diego
Less than $5,000	63%	50%	67%	65%	59%	61%	60%	48%	48%	51%
$5,000 to $9,999	65%	61%	64%	70%	72%	67%	72%	61%	59%	54%
$10,000 or More	75%	74%	68%	73%	71%	58%	73%	60%	63%	55%

*Percentages based only on those answering question. An average of about 15 percent of the responses were "not ascertained."

116 Citizen Attitudes Toward Local Government, Services, and Taxes

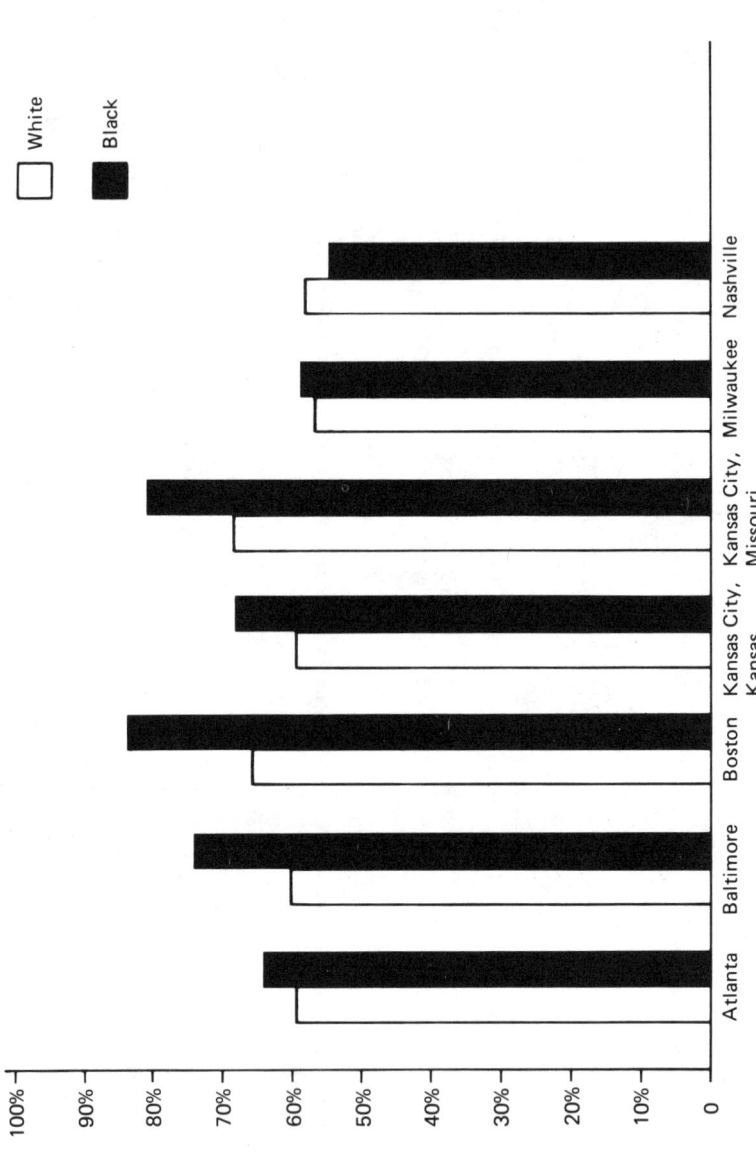

Figure 6-11. Percent* Who Say Local Agencies Enforce Housing Inspection Code "Not Too Well" or "Not Well at All," by Race

*Percentages based only on those answering question. An average of about 15 percent of the responses were "not ascertained."

Housing 117

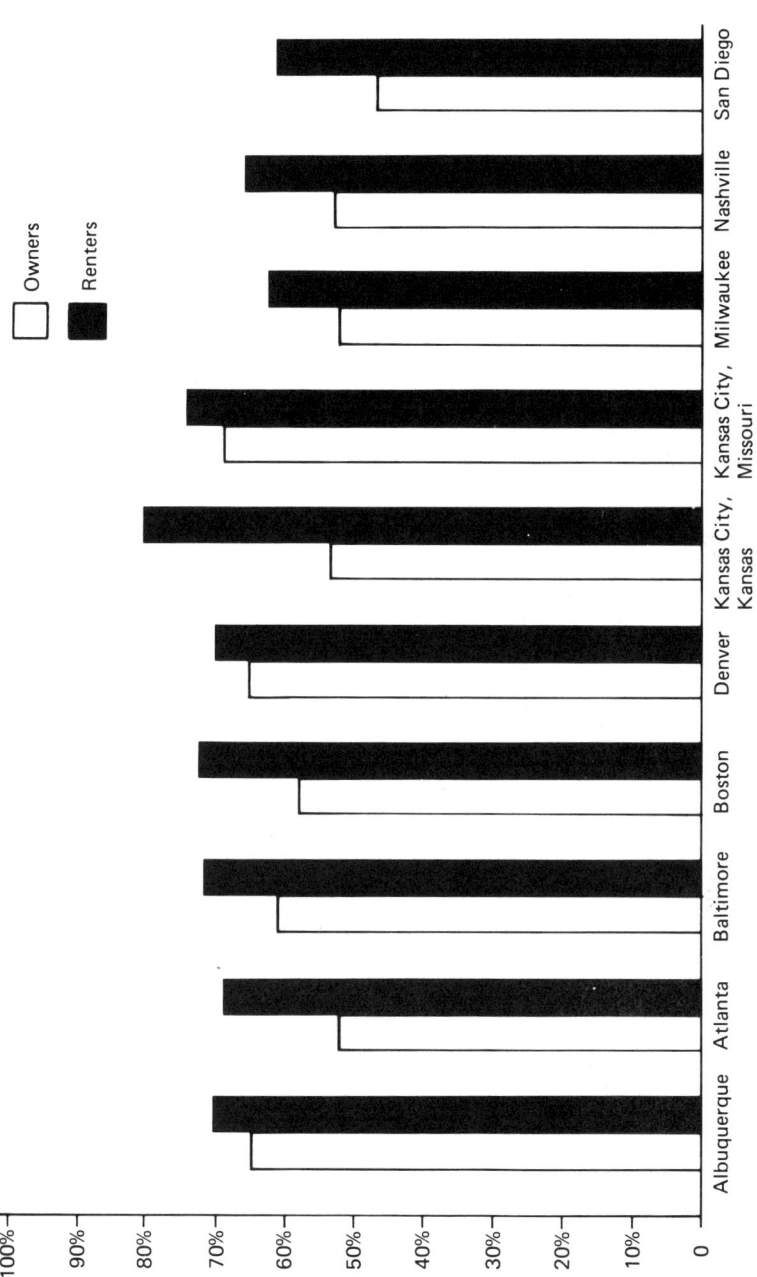

Figure 6–12. Percent* Who Say Local Agencies Enforce Housing Inspection Code "Not Too Well" or "Not Well at All," by Home Tenure

*Percentages based only on those answering question. An average of about 15 percent of the responses were "not ascertained."

Table 6-23. Percent* Who Say Local Agencies Enforce Housing Inspection Code "Not Too Well" or "Not Well at All," by Education

	Albuquerque	Atlanta	Baltimore	Boston	Denver	Kansas City, Kansas	Kansas City, Missouri	Milwaukee	Nashville	San Diego
Less than High School Graduate	59%	53%	65%	60%	54%	56%	54%	49%	48%	42%
High School Graduate	70%	63%	69%	70%	67%	65%	75%	60%	57%	56%
Any College	71%	68%	67%	76%	76%	73%	77%	70%	72%	57%

*Percentages based only on those answering question. An average of about 15 percent of the responses were "not ascertained."

Table 6-24. Percent Who Want More Money Spent on Housing Inspection, by Education

	Albuquerque	Atlanta	Baltimore	Boston	Denver	Kansas City, Kansas	Kansas City, Missouri	Milwaukee	Nashville	San Diego
Less than High School Graduate	58%	75%	81%	75%	71%	69%	71%	61%	63%	56%
High School Graduate	61%	68%	68%	72%	62%	70%	63%	64%	60%	62%
Any College	56%	70%	66%	76%	64%	70%	70%	65%	63%	58%

and 6—25). There was a clear trend in most cities for renters to want to spend more money in this area than home owners, and for blacks to want to spend money in this area more than whites (Figures 6—13 and 6—14). Nonetheless, the majority of all home owners who answered the question in all cities were in favor of spending more money on housing inspection. Thus, while there were some differences in the amount of emphasis that some groups would put on this service, it was an activity for which all segments in all cities favored an increase in city performance.

HOW CAN THE HOUSING DATA BE SUMMARIZED?

Basically, there were three ways in which housing was an issue for people. With respect to costs, it would appear that there was not enough housing in most cities that people with the lowest incomes could afford. Most people who lived in cities with incomes under $5,000 spent more than one-third of their income on housing—well beyond the accepted standard of an appropriate amount to spend on housing.

With respect to condition, between 6 and 25 percent of the housing in the cities was rated by interviewers as in need of substantial repairs. Between 20 and 25 percent of the renters in most cities said they had relatively serious maintenance problem that had not been taken care of. The older cities such as Baltimore and Boston tended to have higher rates of problems with housing conditions.

The two standard government interventions in the housing situation, low-cost public housing and urban renewal, both seemed to have reasonable public support and acceptance. There was general consensus from most people that there was a need for more low and moderate cost housing in the city and that the local government should take the initiative in establishing these. There also was generally only minority resistance to the idea of having low-cost housing in peoples' neighborhoods, even among the better educated and wealthier.

Urban renewal has often been opposed by the poor and the blacks. It was clear, however, that in some cities these groups perceived themselves as beneficiaries of urban renewal. There were examples of cities in which substantial portions of the population have been forced to move as a result of urban renewal, and in those cities, the blacks and the poor were particularly likely to have been forced to move. There were other cities in which the negative consequences to citizens were minimal, however, while the benefits to citizens, particularly the blacks, were most evident.

Interest in upgrading neighborhoods took another form in citizens' support for enforcing standards of property maintenance and care and was widespread in all cities and among all segments of the population. Such an approach penalizes only those who fail to maintain their property at an adequate level,

Table 6–25. Percent Who Want More Money Spent on Housing Inspection, by Income

	Albuquerque	Atlanta	Baltimore	Boston	Denver	Kansas City, Kansas	Kansas City, Missouri	Milwaukee	Nashville	San Diego
Less than $5,000	60%	73%	78%	73%	65%	66%	76%	67%	75%	62%
$5,000 to $9,999	59%	75%	75%	76%	62%	77%	67%	63%	58%	59%
$10,000 or More	57%	68%	69%	73%	67%	61%	63%	60%	62%	59%

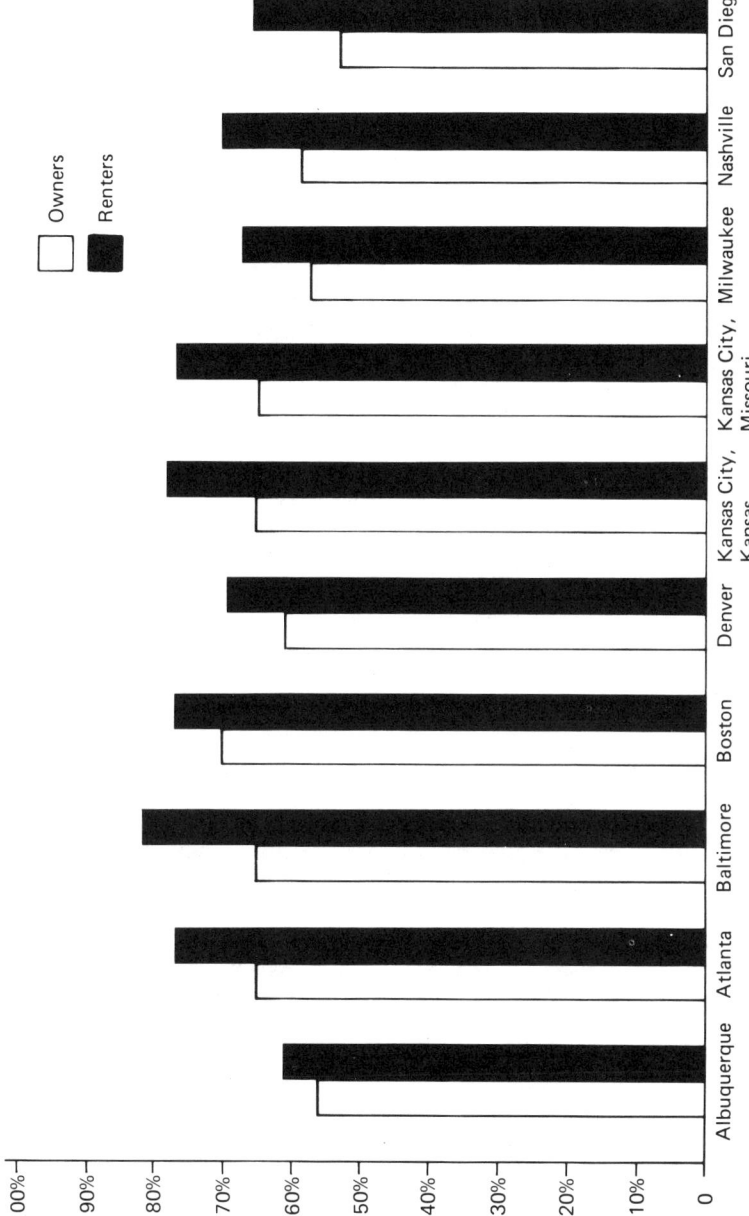

Figure 6-13. Percent Who Want to Spend More Money on Housing Inspection, by Home Tenure

122 Citizen Attitudes Toward Local Government, Services, and Taxes

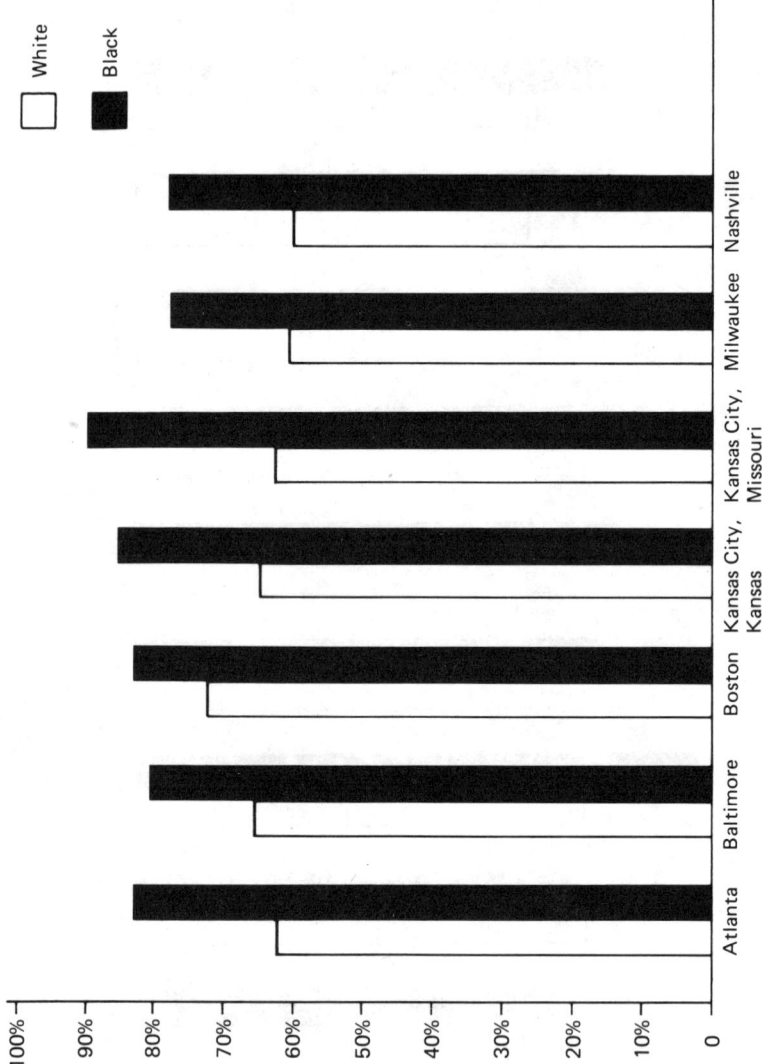

Figure 6–14. Percent Who Want to Spend More Money on Housing Inspection, by Race

which may account for the breadth of support for code enforcement. Such a program does little or nothing to alleviate the problem of housing costs. It is, however, a direct attack on sub-standard conditions in rental housing particularly, and it directly responds to the concern for quality of the neighborhood and environment, which is widespread.

NOTES TO CHAPTER SIX

1. Twenty-five percent is the standard used by most departments of the federal government.
2. This question was "Are there any serious ways that this house or this neighborhood is not a good place for you (and your family) to live?"
3. This question was "In some neighborhoods people tell us about problems with the way houses are kept—things like dangerous floors, poor heating, bad wiring, toilets that don't work, rats, and other things. Do you have any problems like that here now in this (house/building)?"

Chapter Seven

Transportation

In all cities, there are two transportation systems that are partially financed out of public funds. The first is a system of streets maintained and built with public funds, which receives its greatest use from private cars. The other system, often utilizing the same public streets, includes drivers and equipment that are often partially supported by public funds. In only one of the ten cities in this survey, Boston, was there a rapid transit system. In the other cities, the mass transportation system consisted of buses. In only one of the cities, Milwaukee, was there private ownership of the bus system.

An issue of continuing major concern in cities is the role that buses and other forms of mass transportation play *vis-à-vis* cars. The decisions made by local governments—whether dealing with minor details of traffic control or major investments in mass transit—greatly influence the trends of the general public toward use of private or public transportation.

In this project, we have attempted to measure the extent to which different segments of the population relied on the public transportation system, and their interest in increased use of public transportation systems. The issues of tax support for public transportation and improvement of driving conditions were also examined.

HOW DID MOST PEOPLE GET AROUND IN CITIES?

Most people said they used cars to get around in cities. In all but two of the cities, at least eight out of ten families owned a car, and similar numbers reported that the car was the way they most often got around the city (Figure 7–1 and Table 7–1). In Albuquerque and San Diego, in excess of 90 percent of the population interviewed said they relied solely or mainly on a car for transportation.

Baltimore and Boston citizens reported notably less reliance on cars.

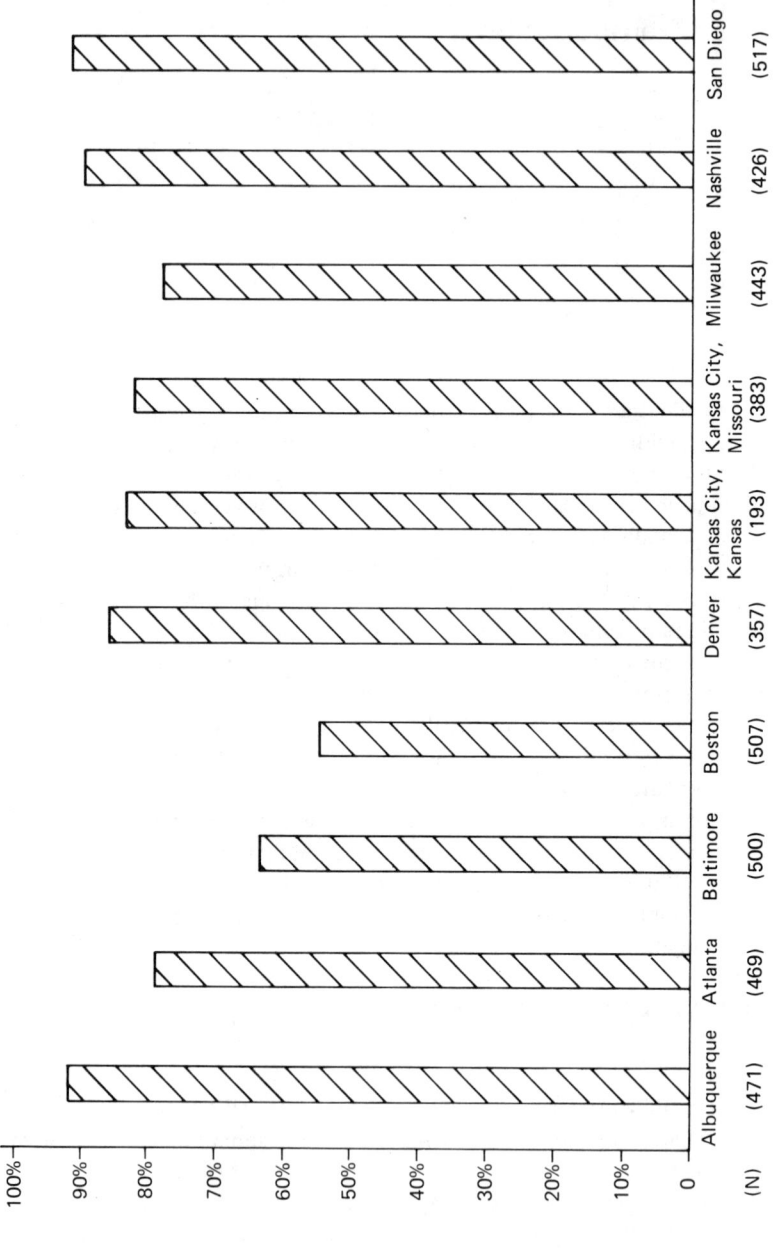

Figure 7-1. Percent Who Own a Car, by City

In Baltimore, only a little over 60 percent of the population owned a car; and only 59 percent mentioned a car as a main way of getting around the city. In Boston, only a little more than 50 percent of the population owned a car and less than 40 percent mentioned a car as a main way of getting around the city.

Were Cars Owned Equally By All Segments of The Population?

The aged and those with incomes under $5,000 were considerably less likely to own cars than others in the city (Table 7-2). In five of the cities, 50 percent or more of those with low incomes did not own a car. In four cities, about 50 percent or more of those 65 and older did not own a car. Although the pattern was the same in all cities, differences between cities were substantial.

To What Extent Did People Use Mass Transportation?

In about five cities, less than 20 percent of the people mentioned public transportation as a main method of getting around the city (Table 7-1). In three other cities, the figure was between 20 and 30 percent of the population. There were only two cities—Baltimore and Boston—in which close to half of the people reported primary reliance on mass transportation.

The preceeding figures relate to the question of "What sorts of transportation do you most often use?" Another index comes from a question about how frequently "you or anyone in your family uses a bus or trolley" (Table 7-3). In six cities, roughly half the population said they "never" use public transportation. The range of that figure went from 70 percent in Albuquerque to about 40 percent in Denver. In these cities it can truly be said that the public transportation system was provided for a minority of the population.

In contrast, there were four cities in which half or more said they used the public transportation to some extent. At the low end of this group falls Milwaukee and Atlanta, where around one-half the families used it at least once a week. In those two cities, a fourth of the population used public transportation almost every day. The other two cities—Baltimore and Boston, the two high-user cities—reported roughly 40 percent of the population using the public transportation system almost every day and 60 or 70 percent of the population using public transportation at least once a week.[1]

How Did Car Ownership Relate to Use of Public Transportation?

First, it was clear that rates of car ownership in a city were inversely related to the rates of use of public transportation—that is, there were more cars in cities in which use of public transit was low, and vice versa. It was particularly noteworthy that over half those with incomes under $5,000 per year owned a car in five of the six cities in which public transit use was lowest; and half or

Table 7-1. Type of Transportation Used Most Often, by City

Response	Albuquerque	Atlanta	Baltimore	Boston	Denver	Kansas City, Kansas	Kansas City, Missouri	Milwaukee	Nashville	San Diego
Car or Truck	90%	72%	59%	39%	81%	86%	81%	72%	90%	91%
Bus, Trolley, Subway	10	30	47	64	18	13	20	29	11	9
Walking	5	4	7	14	9	6	6	8	2	3
Other	2	7	15	12	5	5	4	3	2	3
(N)	(471)	(469)	(500)	(507)	(357)	(193)	(383)	(443)	(426)	(517)

Note: Figures are the percentage of the population in each city giving each type of response. Because some people gave no codable response and others more than one, percentages do not add to 100 percent.

Table 7-2. Percent Who Own a Car, by Income and by Age

	Albuquerque	Atlanta	Baltimore	Boston	Denver	Kansas City, Kansas	Kansas City, Missouri	Milwaukee	Nashville	San Diego
Income										
Less than $5,000	68%	47%	17%	28%	66%	58%	41%	39%	56%	61%
$5,000 to $9,999	95	85	61	59	88	91	86	88	93	96
$10,000 or More	99	98	93	81	98	98	99	94	100	99
Age										
Less than 30 Years	92%	83%	63%	58%	87%	91%	86%	86%	94%	96%
30 to 44 Years	96	81	69	65	93	87	92	86	94	97
45 to 64 Years	90	76	67	54	79	87	85	82	89	89
65 Years or Older	64	60	31	30	64	57	50	42	58	59

Table 7-3. How Often Public Transportation Is Used, by City

Response	Albuquerque	Atlanta	Baltimore	Boston	Denver	Kansas City, Kansas	Kansas City, Missouri	Milwaukee	Nashville	San Diego
Almost Every Day	3%	27%	40%	40%	10%	9%	14%	23%	9%	5%
Once or Few Times a Week	5	8	14	21	9	5	5	15	6	6
Less Often	18	26	19	21	32	25	30	39	22	25
Never	70	34	21	7	44	57	46	16	60	59
Not Ascertained	1	*	*	1	1	*	*	*	*	*
Total	100%	100%	100%	100%	100%	100%	100%	100%	100%	100%
(N)	(471)	(469)	(500)	(507)	(357)	(193)	(383)	(443)	(426)	(517)

*Less than 0.5 percent.

more of the aged owned cars in all six of those cities. There undoubtedly is a circular relationship: high car ownership reduced use of public transportation, which in turn limited the frequency and extensiveness of transit service, which in turn made it more difficult to rely on public transportation and more necessary for people to own a car.

Table 7-4 divides the population into four basic patterns of transportation for a family:

1. A family relies on a car and seldom or never uses public transportation.
2. A family does not rely on a car, and members get around on public transportation.
3. A family most often relies on a car but also regularly relies (once a week or more) on public transportation as well. Such patterns might characterize a family in which public transit was used to commute to work, or in which the children relied on public transit to get to school.
4. A family does not rely on a car and seldom (less than once a week) uses public transportation.

Only 5 to 10 percent of the population reported getting along without relying on cars and without public transportation at least once a week. Most people required regular transportation in one of these ways. However, up to 30 percent of the aged—those over 65—reported such a "low transportation" pattern.

The pattern of relying solely on cars and seldom or never using public lic transportation, characterized 70 percent or more of the families in San Diego; Albuquerque; Kansas City, Kansas; and Nashville and close to 60 percent of families in Denver and Kansas City, Missouri. However, only 40 percent in Atlanta, about 20 percent in Milwaukee and Baltimore, and 6 percent in Boston reported sole reliance on cars, unsupplemented by at least weekly use of public transportation.

Only a third of car-owning families in Baltimore and Milwaukee, and a tenth in Boston, did not report at least weekly use of public transportation (Tables 7-5 and 7-6). However, of course the pattern of reliance on cars, with little or no use of public transit, was highly related to income in all cities as it was to car ownership (Table 7-4).

Except in Boston, it was very uncommon for a family with an income over $10,000 to report sole reliance on public transportation to get around the city. In Baltimore and Milwaukee, the rates were 11 and 16 percent respectively; in other cities they were less than 5 percent. However, the pattern of people in this income bracket frequently included supplementing car travel with at least weekly public transit. In Baltimore and Milwaukee, this was the most common pattern.

Basically what emerged was that in the cities where a larger percentage of the population used public transit, people with lower incomes were likely

Table 7-4. Pattern of Car and Transit Use, by Income

	Albuquerque	Atlanta	Baltimore	Boston	Denver	Kansas City, Kansas	Kansas City, Missouri	Milwaukee	Nashville	San Diego
[a]*Car Reliant*										
Less than $5,000	53%	24%	7%	5%	31%	51%	30%	10%	42%	46%
$5,000 to $9,999	86	35	19	5	64	77	60	22	75	81
$10,000 or More	94	65	30	14	74	82	81	40	92	87
[b]*Public Transit Reliant*										
Less than $5,000	20	50	60	69	29	23	39	48	32	26
$5,000 to $9,999	4	26	44	61	12	5	13	35	8	3
$10,000 or More	—	4	12	48	5	3	2	16		2
[c]*Car & Public Transit Users*										
Less than $5,000	11	12	8	12	12	9	4	17	12	10
$5,000 to $9,999	8	33	30	29	21	15	23	43	16	15
$10,000 or More	4	30	55	28	20	15	17	43	8	10
[d]*Non-Travelers*										
Less than $5,000	16	14	25	14	28	17	27	25	14	18
$5,000 to $9,999	2	6	7	5	3	3	4		1	1
$10,000 or More	2	1	3	10	1			1		1

[a]Reports relying on car as a main way to get around city, and seldom or never using public transit.
[b]Does not report relying on car as a main way to get around city and uses public transit at least once a week.
[c]Reports relying on car as a main way to get around city and using public transit at least once a week.
[d]Does not report relying on car as a main way to get around city and uses public transit less than once a week.

Table 7-5. Percent Who Use Public Transportation at Least Once a Week, by Number of Cars Owned

Number of Cars	Albuquerque	Atlanta	Baltimore	Boston	Denver	Kansas City, Kansas	Kansas City, Missouri	Milwaukee	Nashville	San Diego
0	35%	75%	77%	83%	55%	47%	61%	69%	56%	61%
1	12	34	54	65	21	12	24	40	16	13
2	6	24	38	50	14	11	6	33	8	7

Table 7-6. Percent Who Ride Public Transportation Almost Every Day, by Number of Cars Owned

Number of Cars	Albuquerque	Atlanta	Baltimore	Boston	Denver	Kansas City, Kansas	Kansas City, Missouri	Milwaukee	Nashville	San Diego
0	8%	55%	59%	48%	21%	18%	33%	34%	38%	16%
1	3	22	33	35	10	6	14	21	9	5
2	3	16	19	29	6	8	3	16	3	2

to rely solely on public transportation, and people with higher incomes often used public transit to supplement cars. In cities with less used public transit, the high-income people relied solely on cars, while the majority of low-income people either managed to buy cars or arranged their lives so they did not have to use any kind of transportation at all.

WHO USED THE PUBLIC TRANSPORTATION SYSTEM?

To some extent there were common answers to this question in all cities. People with low incomes used public transportation more than others; blacks used it more than whites in those cities in which there are substantial black populations; the aged relied on public transportation more than those who are younger; and, as we have seen, people without cars used public transportation more than people with cars (Table 7–7).

Once again, for any given group—those with high incomes, whites, young people—the order of use across cities was fairly constant: Boston and Baltimore highest, then Atlanta and Milwaukee, then the rest. There was also a fairly constant ordering within each city.

There may be a tendency for differences in use of public transportation by race to be less pronounced in those cities in which overall use is highest. For example, blacks and whites did not differ significantly in Milwaukee and Boston. It was very clear that a distinctive aspect of ridership in Baltimore and Boston was the high rate at which people with incomes $10,000 or higher used public transportation. In most cities, however, there were not very many people who could comfortably afford cars who relied on public transportation.

How Did People Feel About Using Public Transportation?

People were asked whether they thought cities should work harder to improve their public transportation or work harder to make it easier for people to drive. Admittedly, in many of these 10 cities, it was already quite easy to drive. Thus, the answers may in part have reflected the fact that there was no further attention required to make driving easy. Nonetheless, it is significant that in eight of the ten cities, a majority of the people interviewed said they wanted the city to work harder to improve public transportation—despite the fact that in only one of those cities did the majority of the people interviewed rely mainly on public transportation as a way of getting around the city (Table 7–8).

It should also be noted that in five of the ten cities there was no relationship between wanting to improve public transportation and income (Table 7–9). In eight cities a majority of those with $10,000 incomes said they wanted more emphasis on public transportation; even though the low-income people were considerably more dependent on public transportation,

Table 7-7. Percent Who Mention Public Transportation as Type Transportation Most Often Used, by Income, Race, and Age

	Albuquerque	Atlanta	Baltimore	Boston	Denver	Kansas City, Kansas	Kansas City, Missouri	Milwaukee	Nashville	San Diego
Income										
Less than $5,000	25%	50%	63%	79%	39%	30%	48%	51%	34%	29%
$5,000 to $9,999	7	32	52	61	13	9	20	27	9	4
$10,000 or More	2	11	32	49	5	2	5	16	1	3
Race										
Whites		14%	36%	63%		7%	16%	28%	7%	
Blacks		50	57	68		27	34	36	29	
Age										
Less than 30 Years	7%	25%	48%	57%	12%	11%	9%	18%	8%	4%
30 to 44 Years	6	33	42	56	10	13	15	18	7	5
45 to 64 Years	10	31	46	71	22	9	17	32	12	9
65 Years or Older	27	37	61	75	41	24	51	56	24	35

Table 7-8. Should City Improve Public Transportation or Make Driving Easier?

Response	Albuquerque	Atlanta	Baltimore	Boston	Denver	Kansas City, Kansas	Kansas City, Missouri	Milwaukee	Nashville	San Diego
Make Driving Easier	48%	35%	27%	20%	24%	44%	38%	32%	58%	34%
Improve Public Transportation	41	55	69	74	69	51	58	60	37	59
Not Ascertained	11	10	4	6	7	5	4	8	5	7
Total	100%	100%	100%	100%	100%	100%	100%	100%	100%	100%
(N)	(471)	(469)	(500)	(507)	(357)	(193)	(383)	(443)	(426)	(517)

Table 7-9. Percent Who Say City Should Improve Public Transportation Rather Than Making Driving Easier by Income, Race, and Car Ownership

Income	Albuquerque	Atlanta	Baltimore	Boston	Denver	Kansas City, Kansas	Kansas City, Missouri	Milwaukee	Nashville	San Diego
Less than $5,000	52%	67%	78%	84%	81%	69%	74%	81%	56%	62%
$5,000 to $9,999	38	57	73	78	72	58	63	64	36	61
$10,000 or More	48	67	66	80	82	46	51	62	38	68
Race										
Whites		60%	69%	82%		57%	61%	70%	37%	
Blacks		65	73	71		56	66	58	54	
Car Ownership										
Owns car	43%	60%	64%	80%	74%	53%	56%	57%	36%	63%
Does Not Own Car	68	69	81	82	86	83	81	90	69	83

Table 7-10. Response of Those Who Never Use Public Transportation to "Should City Improve Public Transportation or Make Driving Easier?"

	Albuquerque	Atlanta	Baltimore	Boston	Denver	Kansas City, Kansas	Kansas City, Missouri	Milwaukee	Nashville	San Diego
Make Driving Easier	57%	42%	44%	45%	31%	45%	56%	54%	65%	43%
Improve Public Transportation	43	58	56	55	69	55	44	46	35	57
Total	100%	100%	100%	100%	100%	100%	100%	100%	100%	100%
(N)	(329)	(159)	(105)	(36)	(155)	(111)	(174)	(73)	(253)	(308)

there was considerable support among high-income people for improved public transportation.

Blacks and whites did not differ consistently in their view of whether public transportation should be improved (Table 7-9). As a matter of fact, there was only one city—Nashville—in which blacks and whites differed significantly in the expected direction—that is, where whites were more concerned with driving and blacks were more concerned with public transportation. In fact, in the two other cities in which blacks and whites differed—Milwaukee and Boston—the blacks were less in favor of improved public transportation.

In six of the ten cities, a majority of those people who said they never use public transportation said cities should improve public transportation more than they should improve driving facilities (Table 7-10). In eight of the ten cities, a majority of those who owned cars thought more emphasis should be given to improving public transportation facilities (Table 7-9). In only two cities— Albuquerque and Nashville—could one say that there was a substantial portion of the population that was not particularly interested in better public transportation. In those cities, of course, those people who did not own cars and those people who were poor were very much in favor of increased transportation, but there were substantial groups among the wealthier and those with cars who apparently were mainly interested in driving. In the other cities, however, one could say there is broad based support for increased public transportation systems, both among users and among those who were not users.

To What Extent Was Transportation A Racial Related Issue?

It was a race-related issue in that, in all cities in which there was a substantial black population, blacks were less likely than whites to own cars. It was a race-related issue in that, in most cities in which blacks were a substantial portion of the population, blacks were more likely than whites to rely on the public transportation system to get around the city. Transportation was not a race-related issue, however, in that there was generally equal support among blacks and whites for improving public transportation.

Was Public Transportation An Issue of The Poor and Aged?

First, while the rate of owning cars varied greatly from city-to-city, people with incomes under $5,000 were in all cases less likely than people with incomes over $10,000 to own cars, usually much less likely, although in Denver and Albuquerque as many as 70 per cent of those with incomes under $5,000 did own cars. In general, those cities where the public transportation system was used least were those in which the poor were most likely to own a car.

Consistent with the rate of owning cars, there was a very high correlation between income and the likelihood that the person cited public transportation as the main way of getting around the city. To cite some specific examples, in Baltimore, 63 percent of those who had incomes under $5,000 cited the bus as their main way of getting around the city, compared with 30 percent of those with incomes of $10,000 or higher. In Milwaukee, about 50 percent of those with incomes under $5,000 cited the bus as a way of getting around the city compared with only 15 percent of those with incomes over $10,000.

There was a similar relationship for the aged. The aged owned cars less than younger people, although a larger percentage of them owned cars in those cities where public transportation usage was lowest. Reliance on public transportation was more frequently mentioned by the aged as well.

There were also differences in the rates at which people are concerned with improving public transportation. In at least five of the ten cities, people with lower incomes were significantly more concerned with improving public transportation than people with incomes over $10,000. In the other five cities, there was no particular difference by income.

WOULD MORE PEOPLE RIDE THE PUBLIC TRANSPORTATION SYSTEM IF IT WERE IMPROVED?

We asked those people who did not already use public transportation daily whether changes in the system would increase their use of it, and many of them— from one-fifth to one-half of the population—said "yes" (Table 7–11). Almost 40 percent of the people in Kansas City, Missouri, Milwaukee; and San Diego, and 54 percent in Denver, said that changes in the public transportation system would increase their usage. On the other hand, with present and potential users combined, less than 50 percent of the people in Albuquerque; Kansas City, Kansas; Nashville; and San Diego would use public transportation even if it were changed.

It should not be forgotten that some cities include less urbanized areas than others. Undoubtedly rates of public transportation usage are always lower on a metropolitan area-wide basis than in the central city. Rates of use in Albuquerque and Nashville were no doubt lower than in other cities at least in part because the outlying areas are incorporated in the city and hence part of the sample population.

It is noteworthy that the people who said "yes" included a good representation from among people whose incomes were over $10,000 in most cities (Table 7–12). When there were differences by race, whites were more likely than blacks to say that improved public transportation would increase their use. These figures, of course, reflect the fact that those with low incomes and blacks were generally more likely already to be using public transportation daily. They indicate, however, that people in all segments of society at least thought they might be in the market for public transportation.

Table 7-11. Would Changes in Public Transportation Increase Usage?

Response	Albuquerque	Atlanta	Baltimore	Boston	Denver	Kansas City, Kansas	Kansas City, Missouri	Milwaukee	Nashville	San Diego
Yes	31%	26%	22%	26%	54%	30%	38%	37%	26%	38%
No	62	44	34	29	34	48	45	36	62	56
Uses Daily	4	29	43	43	9	10	13	24	11	5
Not Ascertained	3	1	1	2	3	12	4	3	1	1
Total	100%	100%	100%	100%	100%	100%	100%	100%	100%	100%
(N)	(471)	(469)	(500)	(507)	(357)	(193)	(383)	(443)	(426)	(517)

Table 7-12. Percent Who Say Changes in Public Transportation Would Increase Usage, by Income and by Race

	Albuquerque	Atlanta	Baltimore	Boston	Denver	Kansas City, Kansas	Kansas City, Missouri	Milwaukee	Nashville	San Diego
Income										
Less than $5,000	28%	15%	22%	30%	64%	41%	34%	51%	23%	32%
$5,000 to $9,999	30	27	20	24	56	35	37	40	24	37
$10,000 or More	36	37	26	26	56	33	46	32	32	42
Race										
Whites		32%	27%	26%		38%	43%	43%	28%	
Blacks		20	18	23		35	27	21	24	

What Sorts of Changes Did People Say Would Increase Usage?

The answers to this question were many and varied a lot from city-to-city. One answer, however, stood out in nine out of the ten cities—more frequent scheduling (Table 7–13). Most of the systems were bus systems. More frequent bus schedules accounted for 60 percent of the changes or suggestions for improvement in the Baltimore system. It also accounted for roughly one-third of all the responses in Albuquerque; Boston; Kansas City, Missouri; Milwaukee; Nashville; and San Diego.

The second most prevalent issue mentioned was cost. However, this response was not equally distributed in all cities. There were three cities in which the cost of public transportation was cited by as many as one-third or more of the people who thought they might increase their utilization of the system: the two Kansas Cities and Milwaukee. In San Diego, Denver, and Boston, about one-fifth of potential users mentioned cost as an issue; it was seldom mentioned by people in other cities.

There has been serious discussion among transportation experts about the extent to which more attractive, faster, well-planned, and economically feasible transportation would increase ridership in areas where use is now low. A key problem with a bus system is running a sufficient number of buses to minimize waiting time and at the same time not running more buses at more expense than the amount of use justifies. These data indicate that users as well as planners see scheduling and costs as the key issues in making public transportation more attractive. They do not, however, help us to understand how to provide better transportation in downtown areas at reasonable cost. Some of the answers that were seldom mentioned as things that would improve or increase the use of public transportation should be noted. Very few people mentioned anything about the condition of buses, the quality of stations, or the equipment in general. Another change one might have expected was faster service—getting people more quickly from one place to another. Only in one city—Atlanta—was this mentioned as a factor by as many as one-fourth of those people who thought they might ride the bus more if the service were better.

Although this does not mean that providing a more attractive environment or installing an effective rapid transit system in a city would not be a popular step or attract new riders, it does suggest that, possibly because people do not see it as realistic, such changes were not what people were anticipating when they said they were potential users.

WHAT DID PEOPLE SAY ABOUT FINANCING PUBLIC TRANSPORTATION?

We asked people: "Do you think tax money should be used to help support the public transportation system, or do you think that fares should be high enough

Table 7-13. Type of Improvement Mentioned to Increase Usage of Public Transportation, by City

	Albuquerque	Atlanta	Baltimore	Boston	Denver	Kansas City, Kansas	Kansas City, Missouri	Milwaukee	Nashville	San Diego
Better Scheduling	37%	18%	58%	33%	33%	12%	31%	29%	40%	32%
Cost	13	10	8	19	23	35	38	43	5	23
Extend Services	35	57	15	24	37	48	25	22	47	39
Ambience, Newer Facilities	7	7	10	16	1	3	2	3	6	2
Safety & Crime	*	3	7	7	*	1	1	1	*	1
Other	8	5	2	1	6	1	3	2	2	3
Total	100%	100%	100%	100%	100%	100%	100%	100%	100%	100%
(N)	(146)	(122)	(110)	(132)	(193)	(58)	(146)	(164)	(111)	(196)

Note: Figures are based on responses of only those people who did not already use public transportation daily and who said changes would increase their usage—about 30 percent on the average. The figures are weighted for the number of adults and are based on all codable responses, which included up to three responses per interview.
*Less than 0.5 percent.

to pay for the whole cost of the system?" Tax support for public transportation is an example of the community as a whole supporting a service for a minority of the population. This was the case in every city but Boston and Baltimore, where public transportation served a majority of the population. Thus, perhaps it is not surprising that a majority of the citizens were willing to support public transportation with tax money in only five of the ten cities studied (Table 7–14). In five other cities, a majority of respondents were against tax support of public transportation. In three cities—Kansas City, Kansas; Milwaukee; and Nashville—the margins in favor of fares paying the entire cost of public transportation were substantial.

It might be expected that the people in those cities where public transportation was used most would also be most willing to support the system with tax money, but this was not always the case. Just under 50 percent of Baltimore citizens supported the use of tax monies for public transportation. On the other hand in some cities where reported use was quite low—Albuquerque, Denver, and San Diego—a majority were in favor of tax monies supporting public transportation.

Similarly within cities it was not clear that users were those most in favor of supporting the system with tax money. For example, there was virtually no association between income and willingness to use tax money to support public transportation, despite the fact that there was a clear relationship between income and the use of the system (Table 7–15).

In all but two cities, those respondents who had attended college were significantly more likely to say that tax money should be used to support the system than those respondents who had not graduated from high school (Table 7–16). One may guess that this pattern reflects the sophistication of the college respondents: knowledge of the fact that most public transportation systems have to be supported by tax money, if fares are to be at all reasonable. Since college people use public transportation systems less than others, it is unlikely that they were expressing mere self-interest.

It is likely then that the simple fact of understanding the economics of public transportation was one factor in endorsing tax support of public transportation. It was also clear that there was widespread feeling that a public transit system should be self-supporting. The aspirations of the public for better public transportation together with the sentiment for a self-supporting system may well be incompatible in most cities, unless the area to be served is very narrowly defined. Furthermore, whether or not a majority in a city wants or needs public transportation, there remains the question of how best to serve that 10 to 30 percent of the population that does not own a car—the poor and the aged in particular.

Transportation 143

Table 7-14. Percent Who Say Tax Money Should Help Support Public Transportation

Response	Albuquerque	Atlanta	Baltimore	Boston	Denver	Kansas City, Kansas	Kansas City, Missouri	Milwaukee	Nashville	San Diego
Tax Money Used	53%	54%	48%	53%	60%	37%	46%	39%	37%	54%
Fares Pay Cost	40	40	51	36	28	58	47	51	58	40
Not Ascertained	7	6	1	11	12	5	7	10	5	6
Total	100%	100%	100%	100%	100%	100%	100%	100%	100%	100%
(N)	(471)	(469)	(500)	(507)	(357)	(193)	(383)	(443)	(426)	(517)

Table 7-15. Percent Who Say Tax Money Should Help Support Public Transportation, by Income

	Albuquerque	Atlanta	Baltimore	Boston	Denver	Kansas City, Kansas	Kansas City, Missouri	Milwaukee	Nashville	San Diego
Less than $5,000	52%	57%	42%	69%	73%	38%	47%	44%	42%	54%
$5,000 to $9,999	52	58	47	59	70	40	51	43	43	54
$10,000 or More	63	61	53	57	69	35	49	48	35	59

Table 7-16. Percent Who Say Tax Money Should Help Support Public Transportation, by Education

Education	Albuquerque	Atlanta	Baltimore	Boston	Denver	Kansas City, Kansas	Kansas City, Missouri	Milwaukee	Nashville	San Diego
Less than High School Graduation	49%	48%	49%	54%	59%	30%	41%	41%	38%	45%
High School Graduate	50	55	46	57	73	35	43	43	32	52
Any College	68	71	48	75	74	67	65	59	47	66

Table 7-17. Percent Who Want Type of Change to Make Driving Easier, by City

	Albuquerque	Atlanta	Baltimore	Boston	Denver	Kansas City, Kansas	Kansas City, Missouri	Milwaukee	Nashville	San Diego
Street System	43%	29%	28%	18%	22%	41%	40%	22%	56%	21%
Traffic Control	32	25	24	21	22	29	35	23	24	21
Parking	9	7	18	24	15	9	14	16	13	14
Lower Costs	2	1	6	7	1	3	5	3	3	2
Environment, Safety	2	1	1	2	*	*	*	1	2	1
Reduce Number Cars	8	26	17	25	20	13	18	16	12	13
(N)	(471)	(469)	(500)	(498)	(351)	(191)	(379)	(431)	(424)	(516)

Note: Percentages are based on all codable responses, up to three responses per interview. Because miscellaneous and uncodable responses are omitted, percentages do not add to 100 percent.
*Less than 0.5 percent.

WHAT ABOUT THOSE PEOPLE WHO WANTED TO MAKE IT EASIER TO DRIVE?

People were asked what should be done, if anything, to make driving easier in the city. Roughly 75 percent of the respondents had some constructive comment to make (Table 7-17). The most common responses had something to do with fixing or improving the street system itself. These included such actions as fixing potholes, improving the road surface, widening the streets, and constructing new roads, but not freeways. Such responses were particularly prominent in Albuquerque and the two Kansas Cities. They were somewhat less prevalent than average in San Diego, Milwaukee, and Boston.

Improvement of traffic lights or traffic arrangements such as one way streets and rotaries was perhaps second in frequency of mention. Such comments were distinctively high in Kansas City, Missouri, and Albuquerque, but less prevalent in Boston and San Diego. The other general issue which received some comment was parking. This problem was mentioned more often in Boston than anywhere else.

There was a scattering of responses aimed at reducing the number of cars on the roads. Such suggestions included better public transportation so people would not drive, limiting traffic, staggering work hours, restricting cars coming into the city, and restricting the number of cars that people could own. Such sentiments were particularly prominent in Boston and Denver. However, in no city were such responses given by more than 10 percent of the population.

HOW WOULD THE DATA BE SUMMARIZED?

The people who were most concerned about improving driving conditions were those people who relied primarily on cars. In all but one of the ten cities, the majority of the people relied on the car as their main way of getting around the city. There was some expressed interest in all cities—indeed considerable interest in most cities—in improving mass transportation. It seems reasonable to say that there appeared to be a potential market for more public transportation and that this market would include more people of higher incomes than the survey found among current users. It was not clear that public transportation necessarily needed to continue to service primarily the poor.

Nonetheless, the sentiment was clearly for a parallel system in most cities: an improved public system operating alongside an effective car transport system. In general, there was not widespread antagonism to the car, though there was general feeling that there had been a sufficient investment made in freeways and other types of road construction. Traffic regulation, maintaining the streets that now exist, and, in some cities, parking were cited as steps that would make driving easier. The majority of people, it would appear, were planning to continue to drive, at least as one of the ways they get around the city. The role of public transportation would, within the immediate future, be primarily a supplement to car transportation in most cities. It is the extent to which it would supplement cars that seemed to be at issue.

NOTES TO CHAPTER SEVEN

1. These figures mean that at least someone in the family was said to use the public transportation system every day, not every member of the family.

Chapter Eight

Law and Order

The need for effective and equal enforcement of law has become, probably more than ever, an issue of national concern and political importance. Time and again, the issues of crime and law and order are cited publicly as major problems in our nation's cities, and they continue as a core problem to city governments and officials.

In this chapter, an analysis is presented of the extent to which people really are experiencing problems with respect to safety and at people's views of police and the way they are doing their job.

WERE PEOPLE IN CITIES AFRAID?

As an index of the sense of security people felt, we asked how safe they felt walking alone in their neighborhood streets at night (Table 8-1). In San Diego and Albuquerque, more than 75 percent of all people said they felt "very safe" or "pretty safe" on their neighborhood streets alone at night, while in contrast, in Baltimore and Boston, less than half the people said they felt "very safe" or "pretty safe" alone at night on their neighborhood streets. It is clear that fear varies a lot from city-to-city. But even in the cities where people felt safest—San Diego and Albuquerque—close to one in five adults said they felt "pretty unsafe" or "very unsafe."

Did Different Segments of the Population Feel More Afraid Than Others?

The patterns in this respect were clear in every city, no matter what the average level of felt safety was. Less-educated people were more afraid than better educated people (Table 8-2). Poor people were more afraid than those with higher incomes (Table 8-3). Blacks were more afraid than whites (Figure 8-1). Women were more afraid than men (Figure 8-2). And people over

Table 8-1. How Safe People Feel in Their Neighborhoods Alone at Night, by City

Response	Albuquerque	Atlanta	Baltimore	Boston	Denver	Kansas City, Kansas	Kansas City, Missouri	Milwaukee	Nashville	San Diego
Very Safe	31%	16%	9%	11%	15%	10%	16%	25%	18%	29%
Pretty Safe	45	38	33	33	44	43	37	41	41	47
Pretty Unsafe	13	18	23	19	14	17	17	17	16	11
Very Unsafe	9	24	34	35	23	29	30	16	21	10
Not Ascertained	2	4	1	2	4	1	*	1	4	3
Total	100%	100%	100%	100%	100%	100%	100%	100%	100%	100%
(N)	(471)	(469)	(500)	(507)	(357)	(193)	(383)	(443)	(426)	(517)

*Less than 0.5 percent.

Table 8-2. Percent Who Say They Feel "Very Safe" or "Pretty Safe" in Their Neighborhoods Alone at Night, by Education

	Albuquerque	Atlanta	Baltimore	Boston	Denver	Kansas City, Kansas	Kansas City, Missouri	Milwaukee	Nashville	San Diego
Less than High School Graduation	54%	40%	30%	31%	46%	44%	32%	55%	44%	58%
High School Graduation	75	55	43	41	55	60	56	65	66	75
Any College	88	71	60	59	66	57	61	75	76	82

65 were more afraid than younger people (Table 8-4). With only minor exceptions, each one of these relationships holds up significantly in every city.

Did People Think They Live in High Crime Areas?

People generally felt there was less crime in their own neighborhoods than there is in other parts of the city (Table 8-5). There was a slight tendency in some cities for the poor and the blacks to be more likely than others to think they lived in higher crime areas (Table 8-6 and Figure 8-3). Even among those groups, however, only small minorities (usually less than 10 percent) reported that perception. Most people said that their own neighborhoods were safer than others. It seems likely that the familiarity with one's own neighborhood is a major factor in making one feel safer there. Yet despite that tendency, a very large number of people do not feel safe on the streets at night in their own neighborhood.

WHAT TYPES OF CRIMES ARE PEOPLE CONCERNED ABOUT?

People were asked to say which of the following problems they thought they should be given most attention by city government: prostitution; gambling, making book, numbers; breaking into houses, burglary; robbing people on the street; stealing cars; demonstrations in the streets; selling drugs, dope; speeding, reckless driving (Table 8-7). Prostitution and gambling, two types of crimes that may pose little threat to non-participants, were almost never cited as significant problems for the government to work on. Similarly, stealing cars and demonstrations in the streets were not cited very often as major problems. Car theft—one of the most prevalent crimes—was cited by only 10 percent or less in every city as one of the two most important crimes to work on. Demonstrations in the streets were not mentioned by more than 10 percent in any city except Milwaukee, where there was a history of demonstrations at the time of the study.

Somewhere in the middle, as a concern, was speeding or reckless driving. On the average, about 20 percent of the people cited this as one of the major two problems for the city to work on. In Nashville, one in three persons cited this as a major problem. The fact that control of driving was more often cited as a problem than control of gambling or car theft may suggest that people's concern about law and order is more a concern about personal well-being than a generalized concern with morality or law enforcement.

The three most frequently cited problems on the list were drug sales, burglary, and robbing people on the streets. More than half the adults in every city in the study cited drug sale as one of the two major law and order problems in the city; and in some cities as many as 75 or 80 percent of the population cited this as a major problem. Burglary was cited by about 45 percent of all

Table 8–3. Percent Who Say They Feel "Very Safe" or "Pretty Safe" in Their Neighborhoods Alone at Night, by Income

	Albuquerque	Atlanta	Baltimore	Boston	Denver	Kansas City, Kansas	Kansas City, Missouri	Milwaukee	Nashville	San Diego
Less than $5,000	55%	30%	28%	33%	41%	38%	23%	42%	42%	57%
$5,000 to $9,999	74	56	37	44	57	51	45	68	60	76
$10,000 or More	90	71	54	53	76	65	73	77	74	83

Table 8–4. Percent Who Say They Feel "Very Safe" or "Pretty Safe" in Their Neighborhoods Alone at Night, by Age

	Albuquerque	Atlanta	Baltimore	Boston	Denver	Kansas City, Kansas	Kansas City, Missouri	Milwaukee	Nashville	San Diego
Less than 30 Years	79%	58%	43%	60%	65%	55%	63%	67%	74%	82%
30 to 44 Years	80	61	45	48	67	60	59	83	62	75
45 to 64 Years	75	47	41	34	48	54	48	56	58	75
65 Years or More	51	23	26	16	35	36	26	40	42	46

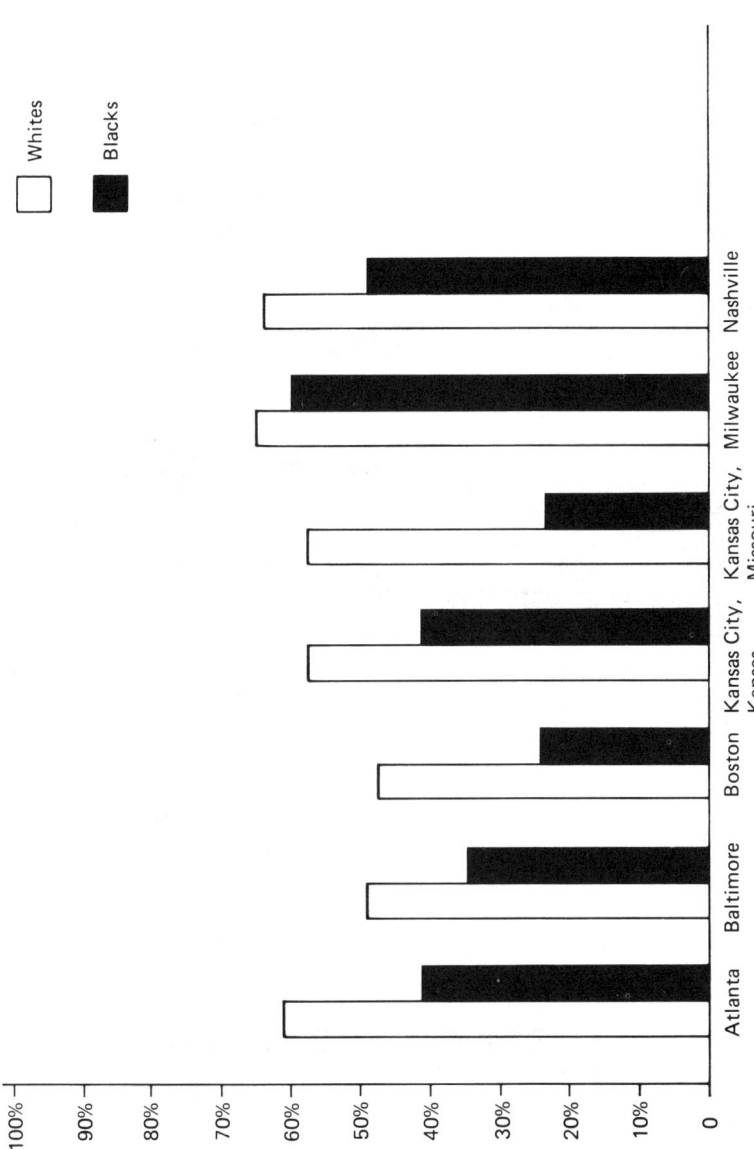

Figure 8-1. Percent Who Say They Feel "Very Safe" or "Pretty Safe" in Their Neighborhoods Alone at Night, by Race

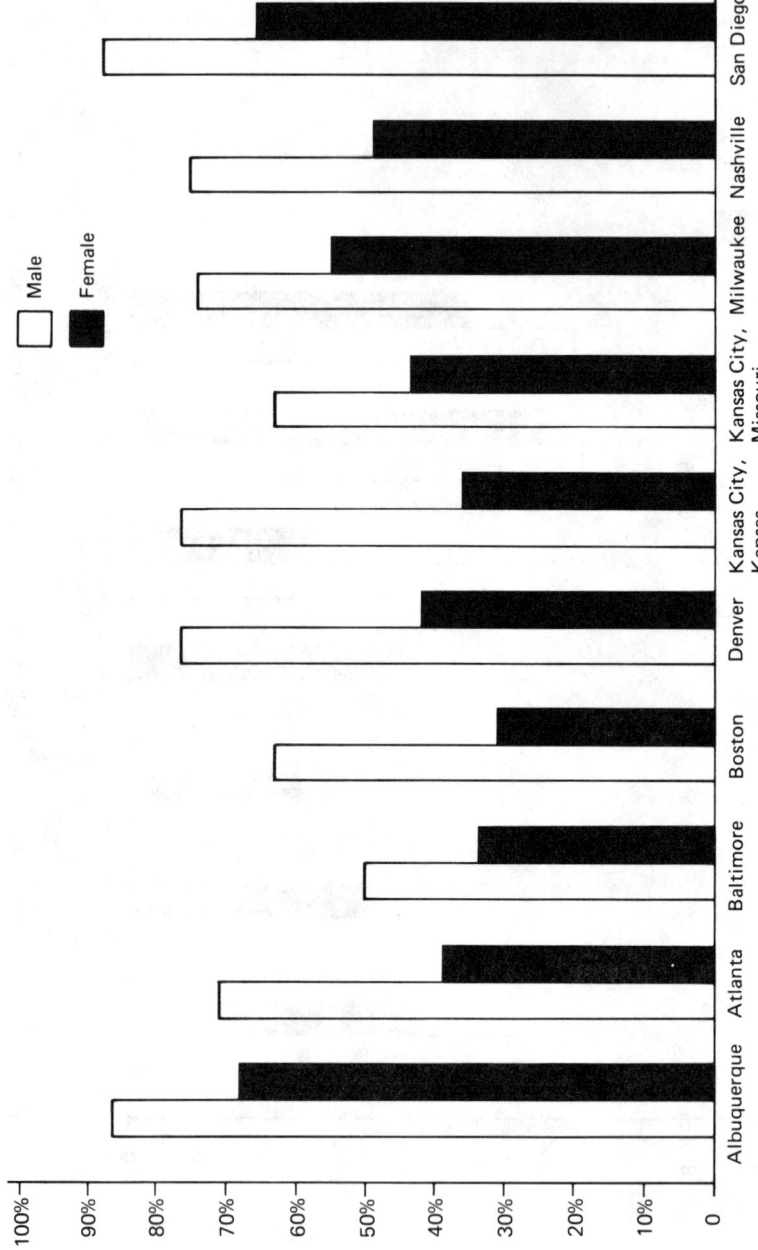

Figure 8-2. Percent Who Say They Feel "Very Safe" or "Pretty Safe" in Their Neighborhoods Alone at Night, by Sex

Table 8-5. How Citizens Feel About the Relative Amount of Crime in Own Neighborhoods, by City

Response	Albuquerque	Atlanta	Baltimore	Boston	Denver	Kansas City, Kansas	Kansas City, Missouri	Milwaukee	Nashville	San Diego
More Crime	4%	3%	9%	13%	5%	3%	5%	4%	3%	3%
Less Crime	64	66	47	42	56	74	73	66	64	66
Same Amount	29	28	43	40	34	23	21	29	31	27
Not Ascertained	3	3	1	5	5	*	1	1	2	4
Total	100%	100%	100%	100%	100%	100%	100%	100%	100%	100%
(N)	(471)	(469)	(500)	(507)	(357)	(193)	(383)	(443)	(426)	(517)

*Less than 0.5 percent.

Table 8-6. Percent Who Feel There Is More Crime in Their Neighborhood Than Rest of City by Income

	Albuquerque	Atlanta	Baltimore	Boston	Denver	Kansas City, Kansas	Kansas City, Missouri	Milwaukee	Nashville	San Diego
Less than $5,000	7%	7%	19%	19%	14%	5%	10%	10%	6%	4%
$5,000 to $9,999	4	1	9	15	5	5	6	6	4	3
$10,000 or More	2	3	4	11	3	2	2	3	1	3

154 Citizen Attitudes Toward Local Government, Services, and Taxes

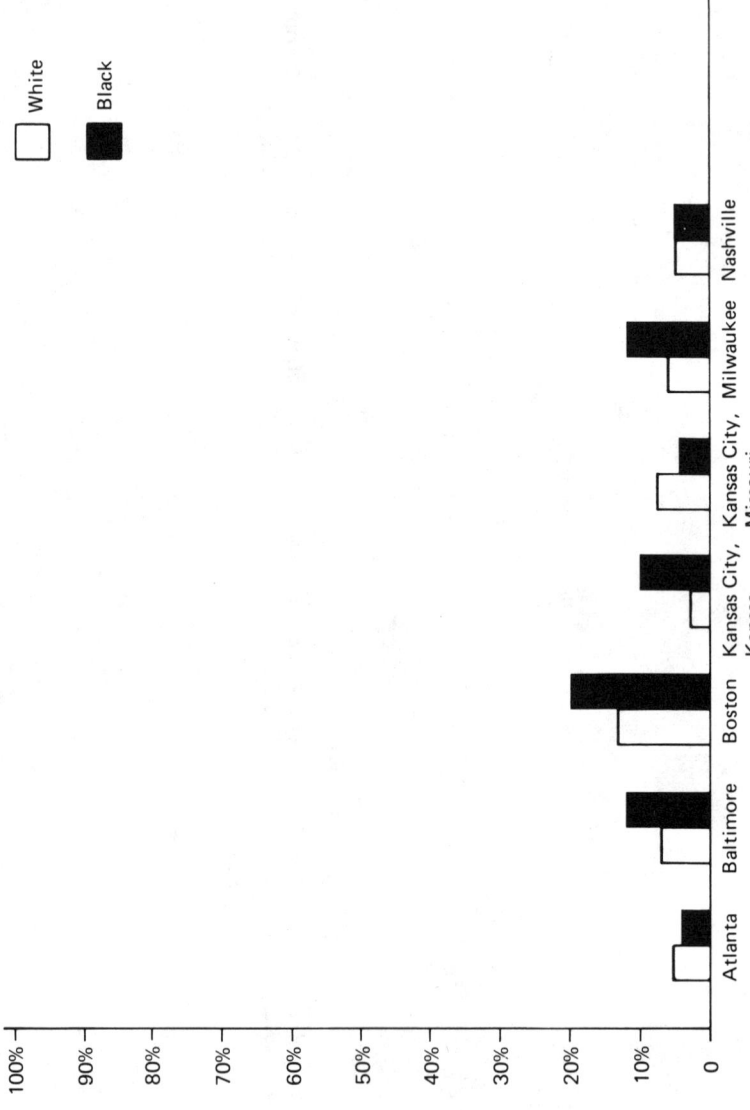

Figure 8-3. Percent Who Feel There Is More Crime in Their Neighborhood Than Rest of City, by Race

Table 8-7. Percent of People Who Chose Problem as Important for City Government to Work On, by City

	Albuquerque	Atlanta	Baltimore	Boston	Denver	Kansas City, Kansas	Kansas City, Missouri	Milwaukee	Nashville	San Diego
Prostitution	2%	6%	3%	5%	3%	3%	6%	4%	1%	2%
Gambling	2	8	6	6	4	6	2	3	4	3
Burglary	72	44	36	39	46	43	53	38	48	45
Robbing on Street	9	37	61	49	28	50	51	38	22	18
Stealing Cars	6	7	3	11	7	9	5	6	9	4
Demonstrations	4	6	5	8	9	11	10	21	8	11
Selling Drugs	76	67	77	61	64	56	59	65	69	83
Speeding	24	20	7	12	23	21	12	22	33	30
Not Ascertained	5	5	2	9	16	1	2	3	6	4

Note: Figures total 200 percent because people were asked for both first and second priorities.

people. The pattern was fairly even across all cities with one exception: in Albuquerque, about 75 percent of the population was concerned with burglary.

Concern about robbing people on the streets, however, was much less even. In cities where people reported feeling safer, such as in San Diego and Albuquerque, there was very little concern with robbing people on the streets. In both of those cities, there was at least twice as much mention of speeding drivers as of robbing people. On the other hand, in those cities where there was a considerable amount of fear reported, such as in Baltimore, Boston and the two Kansas Cities, concern about people being robbed in the streets was correspondingly high, running 50 percent and above in each city. Robbery, of course, is the one prevalent crime in which the individual himself is present and possibly in danger; in most other crimes against private victims, it is property that is threatened, and the individual himself is often absent.

Did People's Fears Correspond With Reality?

We asked people whether they or anyone living with them had been the victim of a crime during the year preceding the interview. Such an approach, while perhaps not yielding perfect rates, has been shown to be better than police records at measuring the rates of such crimes as burglaries and robberies, many of which are not reported to the police and do not appear on official records (Table 8-8).

Burglary is the crime of unlawful entry to commit a felony or theft. The figures presented include attempted burglary, even when no theft occurred. Reported burglary rates were relatively constant across cities at around 12 burglaries per 100 households. Nashville and Kansas City, Kansas, were lower than the other cities, while the rates in Albuquerque and Denver may be slightly higher than others.

Robbery takes place in the presence of the victim and involves taking something of value from him by force or threat of force. Pocket picking and purse snatching were excluded from this category. The rates in all cities range from 3 to 5 per 100 households. The range is sufficiently small and the rates so low that it is not possible to say reliably what differences exist between cities in this respect.

The other crime that threatens the individual himself, rather than just his property, is assault, with or without a weapon. These crimes are the ones that one would think would be most directly related to fear, particularly fear of walking the streets. The possibly misleading aspect of the data is that assaults commonly come from family members or from people known to the victim, while presumably the key issue in fear is the threat of being accosted by a stranger. With this reservation, one can combine reported assaults, robberies, and purse snatching (a non-index crime that does involve confrontation) and arrive at some index of the danger rate in each city. It appears that the citizens of Albu-

Table 8-8. Number of Crimes Against Household Members in Past Year per 100 Households, by City

Crime	Albu-querque	Atlanta	Baltimore	Boston	Denver	Kansas City, Kansas	Kansas City, Missouri	Milwaukee	Nashville	San Diego
Burglary*	15	12	12	13	14	9	13	11	8	11
Car Theft	4	4	5	9	5	4	4	3	2	2
Theft from Cars	7	4	2	3	7	5	5	5	6	6
Total Crimes Against Property	26	20	19	25	26	18	22	19	16	19
Pocket Picked, Purse Snatched	1	3	3	8	2	3	2	2	2	1
Assaults	1	5	2	4	3	3	3	4	3	1
Robbery (Armed or Not)	3	4	5	5	5	4	5	5	4	4
Total Crimes Against Persons	5	12	10	17	10	10	10	11	9	6

*Included attempted burglary.

querque and San Diego were responding realistically when they said they felt safe. Rates of crimes involving the victim personally appear to be lower there than elsewhere. Similarly, the higher than average rate of fear reported in Boston corresponds with a higher reported rate of crime of this kind. However, one is struck by the fact that the rates were all in the range of 9 to 12 per 100 households, except in Albuquerque, San Diego, and Boston. The relatively high level of concern about robbery expressed in the two Kansas Cities and Baltimore compared with the lower level of concern in Atlanta and Milwaukee is difficult to explain on the basis of the actual rates of victimization. Obviously, in addition to the actual commission of crimes against persons, there are other factors that help make people more or less afraid and more or less concerned about being robbed.

There are, of course, many more crimes against property, when the victim is not present, than crimes directly involving the victim himself. One can combine burglaries, car thefts, and thefts off of and out of cars into an index that roughly reflects the likelihood of any household having something stolen or threatened when he is not present. Thefts from mailboxes were excluded from this index.

Rates for this index ranged from 16 per 100 households in Nashville to 26 per 100 households in Albuquerque and Denver. While there was some consistency between these rates and the rate of crime against persons, it was far from perfect. Furthermore, while these figures may help slightly to explain why people feel safer in Nashville and Milwaukee, they do little to explain the fear in Baltimore

How Did These Rates Compare With Official Police Records?

We shall not attempt a definitive answer to this question; but some comparisons may be useful. As noted earlier, one source of discrepancy between survey and police estimates of crime is that far from all crimes are reported to police. Another is that people may have difficulty in placing events exactly in a one-year period—a necessity for computing rates accurately.[1]

The crime that is most often reported to police is car theft;[2] and for this crime the rates derived from the survey data were very comparable to the rates from police records.[3] In only one of the ten cities do the two estimates differ by as much as 1 per 100 households. The correspondence between burglary rates estimated from the survey and from police records is lower. From 3 to 10 times as many burglaries and attempted burglaries were reported in interviews as one would expect from police records (Table 8-9).

The ordering of burglary rates among the cities was fairly similar using the two sources; but perhaps it is worth noting the three cities in which there was a much higher than average discrepancy between interview estimates and police estimates. Police records in Boston, Milwaukee, and San Diego indicate

Table 8-9. Burglary and Car Theft Rates oer 100 Households from Citizen Attitude Survey and Police Records, by City

City	Burglaries per 100 Households		Car Thefts per 100 Households	
	CAS	UCR[a]	CAS	UCR[b]
Albuquerque	15	5	4	2
Atlanta	12	2	4	3
Baltimore	12	4	5	4
Boston	13	3	9	8
Denver	14	3	5	4
Kansas City, Kansas	9	4	4	3
Kansas City, Missouri	13	5	4	4
Milwaukee	11	1	3	2
Nashville	8	2	2	2
San Diego	11	1	2	2

[a]Residential burglaries for this period were provided by the Director of the Federal Bureau of Investigation.
[b]Number of crimes reported in *Uniform Crime Reports–1969* (Washington: U. S. Department of Justice, 1969) divided by the number of occupied housing units in each city.

burglaries in 3, 1, and 1 households per 100, respectively, in 1969. Interview-based estimates yield figures of 13, 11, and 11. These differences were significantly higher than one can account for by the non-reporting of crimes to police.[4] Since the data collection procedures in each city were comparable, it may be that record-keeping policies and procedures in each city affect the similarity of survey and record estimates.

In any case, one can see that survey data did yield estimates of burglary rates quite different from police records—but rather similar estimates of car theft rates. For crimes such as murder, survey data are not useful and police data are probably very accurate. For some of the less serious and more prevalent types of crimes, however, survey data can provide a valuable supplement to other available sources for estimates of rates.

HOW DID PEOPLE RATE THEIR POLICE FORCE?

We asked people to rate their police as "very good," "good enough," "not so good," or "not good at all." About 40 percent of the people in San Diego and Milwaukee rated their police "very good." But in most cities, the figure was somewhere around 25 percent. However, the majority of people rated the police either "very good" or "good enough"—70 percent in most cities (Table 8-10).

The cities can roughly be divided into two groups in terms of citizen rating of police protection. Among the more positive cities are San Diego, Milwaukee, the two Kansas Cities, Denver, and Albuquerque. In each of these cities, 75 percent or more rated the police as "very good" or "good enough." On the

Table 8–10. Rating of Police Protection in Neighborhood, by City

Response	Albuquerque	Atlanta	Baltimore	Boston	Denver	Kansas City, Kansas	Kansas City, Missouri	Milwaukee	Nashville	San Diego
Very Good	32%	22%	19%	20%	31%	28%	28%	39%	20%	41%
Good Enough	45	42	41	37	43	48	46	44	44	46
Not So Good	14	25	30	25	15	20	19	10	23	7
Not Good at All	5	6	10	13	5	3	3	5	6	2
Not Ascertained	4	5	*	5	6	1	4	2	7	4
Total	100%	100%	100%	100%	100%	100%	100%	100%	100%	100%
(N)	(471)	(469)	(500)	(507)	(357)	(193)	(383)	(443)	(426)	(517)

*Less than 0.5 percent.

other hand, in Nashville, Boston, Baltimore, and Atlanta, the figure tended to be around 60 percent. Overall, however, probably the most important point is that the majority of citizens in most cities were moderately to very positive about their police.

How Did Different Segments of the Population Feel About Police?

By income and education, there were not consistent differences in the way police were rated (Tables 8-11 and 8-12). There were three cities in which those with incomes over $10,000 were significantly more positive than those with lower incomes. There was one city in which the college educated and high school graduate populations were significantly more positive than those who had not finished high school. Although the differences were all in the same direction, no association was the most common pattern.

However, the picture was quite different when we compared the responses of blacks and whites (Figure 8-4). In all seven cities in which there were significant black populations, blacks were more critical of the police than whites. The size of the difference varied somewhat from city-to-city; but in all cases, the differences were statistically significant.

There was also a tendency for people between 18 and 30 years old to be more critical of the police than older people (Table 8-13). In at least five of the ten cities, people aged 65 and older rated the police more favorably than younger adults. However, the relationships to age were not nearly as significant or consistent as the differences between blacks and whites in their ratings of police.

Did The Differences Relate to Perceptions of The Quality of Police Service or Police-Community Relations?

We had two different questions to get at these two dimensions. In one question, we asked how quickly the police come when someone in the neighborhood calls for help. Another question asked how the police treat people in the neighborhood. On both of these questions, blacks differed from whites significantly.

In all cities, more people thought that the police come "right away" than thought they "take a while" when they are called for help (Table 8-14). However, there were significant differences between cities. In Boston and Atlanta, almost the same number of people said the police take a while to come as said they come right away. Of the four cities that were rated somewhat lower by citizens in terms of general police protection in the neighborhood, three of them— Atlanta, Boston and Nashville—tended to be below average with respect to citizen perception of police responsiveness. The two most highly rated police depart-

Table 8-11. Percent Who Rate Police Protection in Their Neighborhoods "Very Good" or "Good Enough," by Income

	Albuquerque	Atlanta	Baltimore	Boston	Denver	Kansas City, Kansas	Kansas City, Missouri	Milwaukee	Nashville	San Diego
Less than $5,000	76%	59%	58%	59%	72%	75%	76%	82%	66%	88%
$5,000 to $9,999	78	67	64	56	77	80	78	86	73	88
$10,000 or More	88	71	62	59	86	73	79	87	67	91

Table 8-12. Percent Who Rate Police Protection in Their Neighborhoods "Very Good" or "Good Enough," by Education

	Albuquerque	Atlanta	Baltimore	Boston	Denver	Kansas City, Kansas	Kansas City, Missouri	Milwaukee	Nashville	San Diego
Less than High School	82%	58%	61%	59%	83%	73%	74%	82%	70%	86%
High School Graduation	83	72	60	57	75	80	81	90	71	87
Any College	79	73	69	59	79	75	77	82	69	92

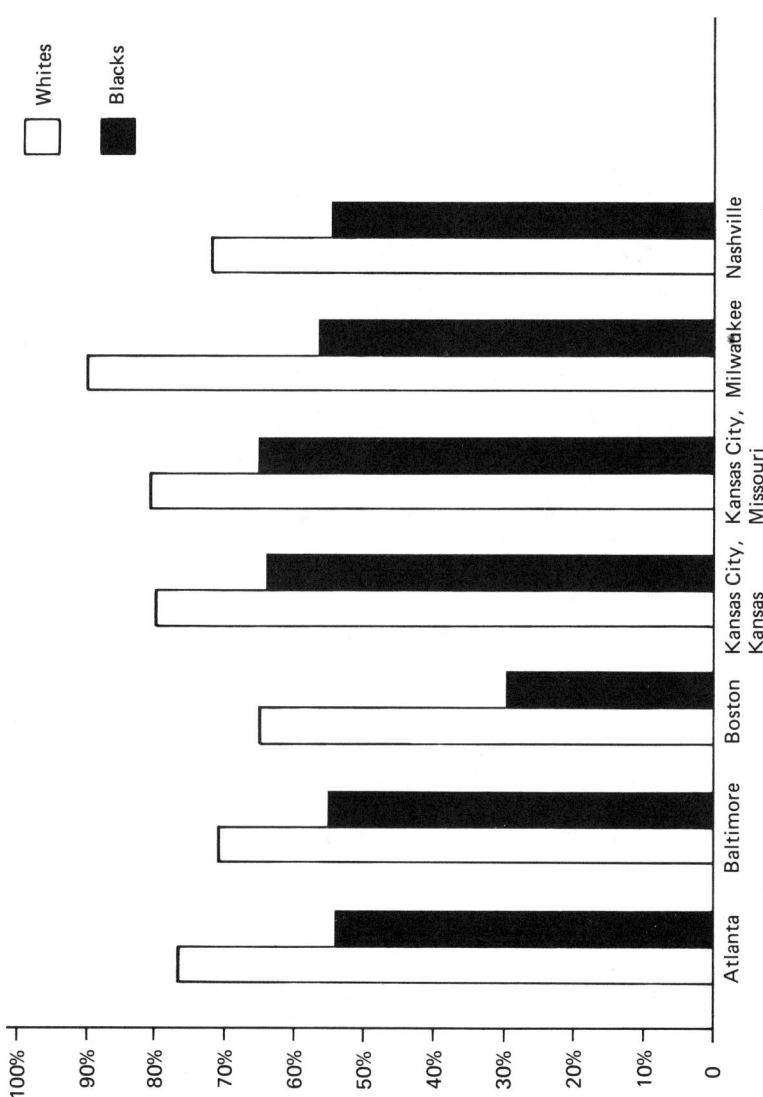

Figure 8-4. Percent Who Rate Police Protection in Their Neighborhoods "Very Good" or "Good Enough," by Race

164 Citizen Attitudes Toward Local Government, Services, and Taxes

Table 8-13. Percent Who Rate Police Protection in Their Neighborhoods "Very Good" or "Good Enough," by Age

	Albuquerque	Atlanta	Baltimore	Boston	Denver	Kansas City, Kansas	Kansas City, Missouri	Milwaukee	Nashville	San Diego
Less than 30 Years	71%	63%	59%	55%	75%	63%	76%	77%	68%	90%
30 to 44 Years	80	66	61	54	76	80	76	86	67	85
45 to 64 Years	86	69	62	61	80	81	79	89	72	90
65 Years or More	88	78	72	63	90	84	85	88	71	91

Table 8-14. People's Perception of Amount of Time for Police to Answer Calls, by City

Response	Albuquerque	Atlanta	Baltimore	Boston	Denver	Kansas City, Kansas	Kansas City, Missouri	Milwaukee	Nashville	San Diego
Come Right Away	57%	41%	62%	43%	53%	61%	60%	60%	50%	65%
Take a While	22	36	35	41	23	24	22	25	25	15
Not Ascertained	21	23	3	16	24	15	18	15	25	20
Total	100%	100%	100%	100%	100%	100%	100%	100%	100%	100%
(N)	(471)	(469)	(500)	(507)	(357)	(193)	(383)	(443)	(426)	(517)

ments—San Diego and Milwaukee—were also rated high with respect to police responding to calls.

Within cities, more low-income people said police did not come quickly than did people having higher incomes (Table 8-15). This relationship held in six of the ten cities. In the other four, there was little or no such relationship. These differences do not compare in clarity or magnitude with the differences between blacks and whaites (Figure 8-5). In all cities, blacks were significantly less likely to say that police come right away when they are called for help. The differences ranged from about 18 percentage points in Kansas City, Missouri, to almost 40 percentage points in Nashville. Whether or not it was an accurate perception, a majority of blacks in all cities but Kansas City, Missouri, and Baltimore said police did not respond quickly to calls. Blacks apparently did not think they were getting the same service.

How About Community Relationships?

There appeared to be general satisfaction with the way the police treated people (Table 8-16). In the most critical city in this respect—Baltimore—only 20 percent of the residents rated the way the police treat the people (them and their neighbors) to be "not so good" or "not good at all." The incidence of such ratings varied between 5 percent and 20 percent. While it is not technically appropriate to compare the incidence of response to two different ordinal scales, the overall impression from the data is that slow response by police was a more prevalent citizen perception than problems in the area of community relations.

How About Differences Among Segments of the Population of Cities?

There was a significant difference between blacks and whites in the way people rated the way they and their neighbors were treated by the police (Figure 8-6). Nonetheless it was notable that in every city, more than half the blacks rated the way the police treated them as either "very good" or "good enough." In fact only in Boston did this figure drop below 60 percent. There was even one city, Kansas City, Missouri, where almost half the blacks gave the police a "very good" rating—which is about the same rating the whites gave the police in Baltimore and Nashville—and was considerably better than the whites gave the police in Boston.

Older people tended to give the police somewhat higher ratings than people under 30 in all cities (Table 8-17). On the average, 80 percent of those people under 30 rated the police "very good" or "good enough" compared to 94 percent of those over 65.

WHAT WERE THE IMPLICATIONS OF THE DATA?

We probably did not adequately measure the feelings of young people about police, because we interviewed only those 18 and older who lived in households

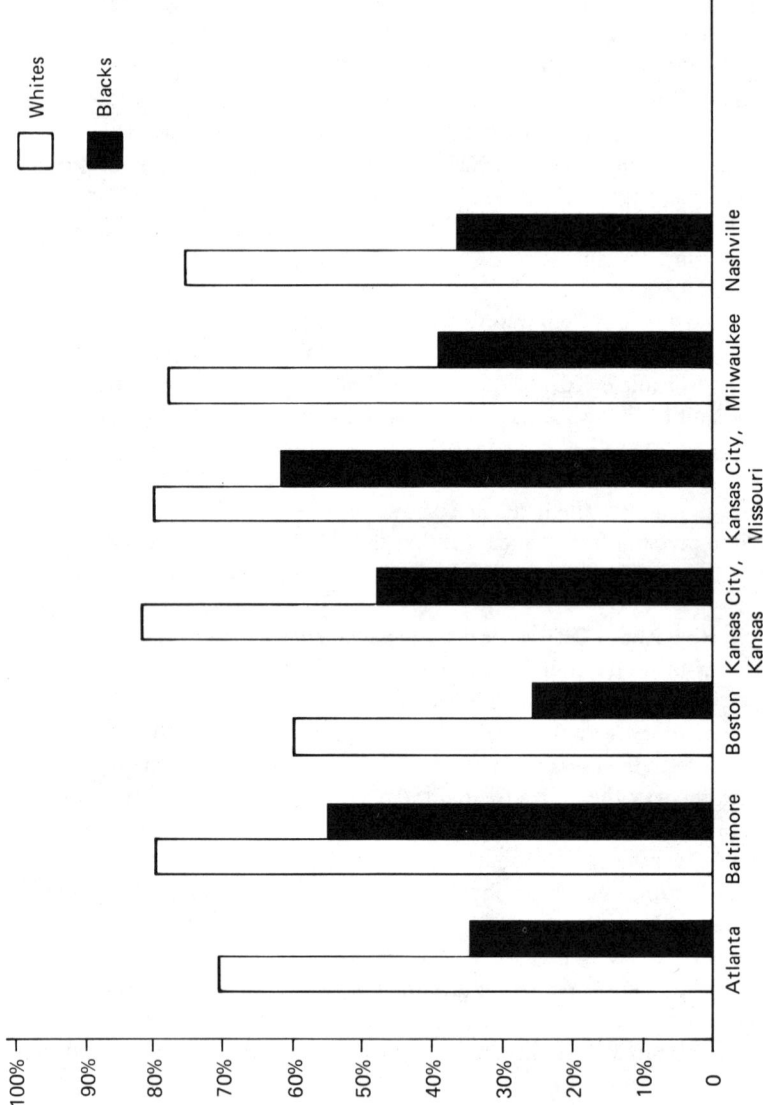

Figure 8–5. Percent Who Say Police Come Right Away, by Race

Table 8-15. Percent Who Say Police Respond to Calls Quickly, by Income

	Albuquerque	Atlanta	Baltimore	Boston	Denver	Kansas City, Kansas	Kansas City, Missouri	Milwaukee	Nashville	San Diego
Less than $5,000	64%	44%	61%	51%	62%	74%	69%	72%	58%	88%
$5,000 to $9,999	75	51	65	53	68	75	72	69	72	79
$10,000 or More	81	63	72	54	79	65	79	72	72	82

Table 8-16. Rating of Way Police Treat People in Neighborhood, by City

Response	Albuquerque	Atlanta	Baltimore	Boston	Denver	Kansas City, Kansas	Kansas City, Missouri	Milwaukee	Nashville	San Diego
Very Good	47%	37%	30%	29%	44%	44%	50%	52%	40%	51%
Good Enough	34	38	48	44	29	42	35	32	41	34
Not So Good	6	7	16	12	8	7	3	5	6	4
Not Good at All	2	5	5	6	4	2	3	4	2	3
Not Ascertained	11	13	1	9	15	5	9	7	11	8
Total	100%	100%	100%	100%	100%	100%	100%	100%	100%	100%
(N)	(471)	(469)	(500)	(507)	(357)	(193)	(383)	(443)	(426)	(517)

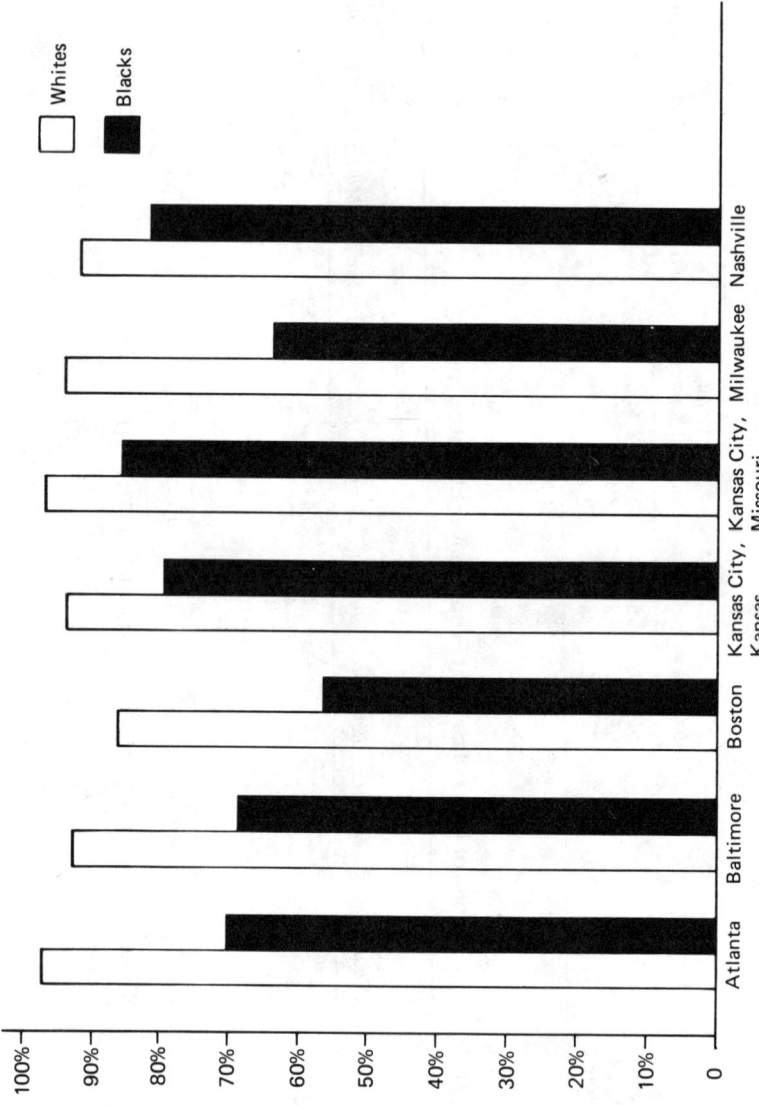

Figure 8–6. Percent Who Say Police Treat People "Very Good" or "Good Enough," by Race

Table 8-17. Percent Who Say Police Treat People "Very Good" or "Good Enough" by Age

	Albuquerque	Atlanta	Baltimore	Boston	Denver	Kansas City, Kansas	Kansas City, Missouri	Milwaukee	Nashville	San Diego
Less than 30 Years	82%	77%	72%	65%	76%	85%	93%	82%	87%	81%
30 to 64 Years	93	88	82	85	88	91	95	93	91	97
65 Years or More	93	95	91	91	97	94	96	91	96	95

170 Citizen Attitudes Toward Local Government, Services, and Taxes

other than dormitories. So we have less to say about police relations with youth. Among the population interviewed, however, the most obvious issue with respect to citizen attitudes toward the police was the feelings of the blacks in cities. Although one perhaps should not minimize the problem of how blacks thought they were treated by police, the perception that police did not respond quickly to calls for help seemed more important. It was particularly important because improving the quality of individual interactions between police and citizens is difficult and, at best, will take a long time. However, reducing police response time is a management problem that can be solved.

One should not forget that blacks reported a higher level of fear walking the streets than whites. They were as supportive of stronger police patrols as whites. It is reasonable to think that what the blacks wanted from police was protection and help. We do not know the extent to which the perceptions of the blacks were accurate, that response time was slower in black areas. To the extent that they were correct and this can be changed, or they were not correct but the image can be changed, there is reason to think that we will be working directly on the problem of why blacks were less satisfied with police than whites.

NOTES TO CHAPTER EIGHT

1. Another problem that affects comparisons is that the survey data are population based (i.e., the figures are the number of those in a city's population that were victims, regardless of where the crime occurred), whereas the police figures are area based (the number of crimes occurring in the city, regardless of where the victim lived). We can correct the survey data to eliminate crimes occurring outside the city, but we cannot calculate the police figures to crimes against residents. This issue probably affects burglary comparisons very little (as burglary takes place at the person's residence) but could definitely affect robbery and car theft figures, where the crime often occurs away from home.
2. When we asked people who experienced a car theft whether or not it had been reported to the police, about 90 percent said it had.
3. Figures used are from *Uniform Crime Reports–1969,* Washington: U. S. Department of Justice, 1969. Residential burglary rates were kindly provided by the Director of the Federal Bureau of Investigation. The year for which respondents were reporting in the Citizen Attitude Survey included about 6 or 7 months in 1970 and 5 or 6 months of 1969. Hence the periods do not exactly correspond.
4. About three-fourths of the burglaries reported to interviewers were said by respondents to have been reported to the police. However, we do not know the rate at which a formal police report was filled out.

Chapter Nine

Teaching the Children

Schools are the most costly of local government activities. Although they are often directly operated by units of government other than the city itself, citizen satisfaction or dissatisfaction with their schools is a significant factor affecting their attitudes toward local services.

Through the decade of the 1960s, increased emphasis was placed on the quality of education in this country. It is, however, impossible to compare citizen satisfaction with schools in 1970 with earlier periods since there are no comparable data from earlier periods. What has been done here is to describe the situation in 1970: who uses the schools; what is the general level of satisfaction of the cities' residents with their schools; what are the differences in the way various segments of the city populations felt; and what changes do they see as desirable in the delivery of education.

TO WHAT EXTENT DID CITY RESIDENTS RELY ON THE PUBLIC SCHOOLS?

Less than half of the population in most cities had children. Of those families with school age children, 80 percent or more relied solely on the public schools in seven out of ten cities (Table 9–1). In Boston, Milwaukee, and Denver, the rates were between 55 and 75 percent. Nevertheless, this meant only 30 to 40 percent of the total population had children using the public schools at any given time (Figure 9–1). In Boston, only 1 in 5 families had a child in the public schools or a pre-school child who was about to attend public school. Thus, the public school system was like the transportation system in that a majority of the population was supporting a service for the minority. It differed from public transportation, importantly, in that most people either will have or have had children in public school at some time.

171

Table 9-1. Type of School Families Send Children to, by City

School	Albuquerque	Atlanta	Baltimore	Boston	Denver	Kansas City, Kansas	Kansas City, Missouri	Milwaukee	Nashville	San Diego
Public Only	81%	80%	81%	55%	73%	79%	83%	70%	81%	81%
Public and Private	3	3	*	2	3	*	1	1	1	2
Public and Parochial	2	1	1	5	4	4	3	5	1	2
Private Only	4	10	4	4	7	2	1	3	8	3
Parochial Only	6	1	5	23	8	9	6	16	7	7
Public and Other	*	1	1	1	*	*	2	*	1	*
Other	4	4	8	10	5	6	4	5	1	5
Total	100%	100%	100%	100%	100%	100%	100%	100%	100%	100%
(N)	(229)	(185)	(230)	(159)	(166)	(82)	(171)	(184)	(194)	(218)

Note: Figures are based only on families with school age children, plus those with children 3 to 5 who were asked where children would most likely go to school.
*Less than 0.5 percent.

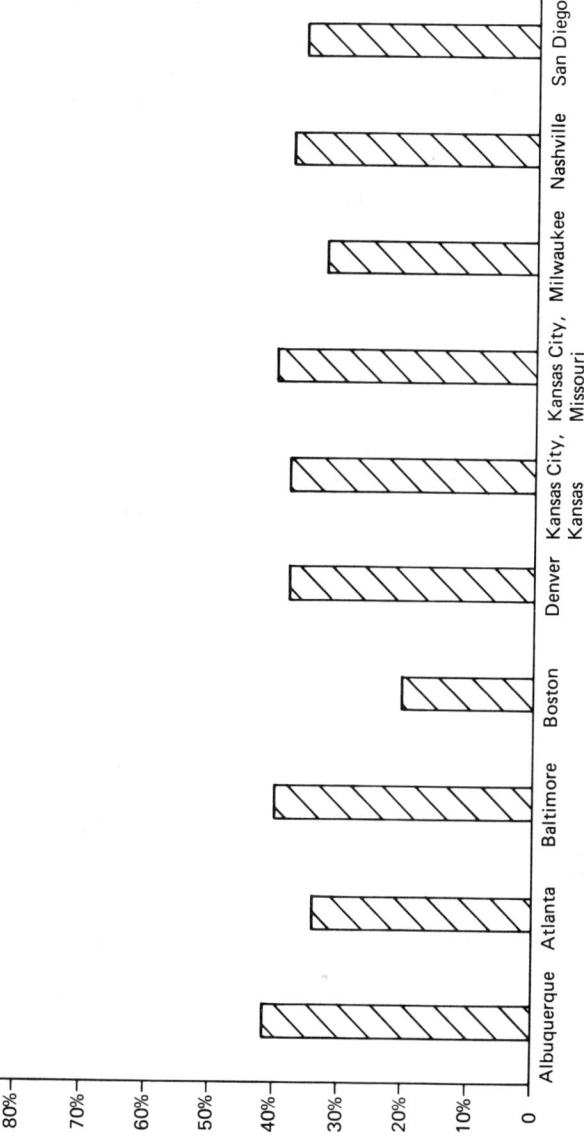

Figure 9-1. Percent of Households Using the Public Schools, by City

Note: Figures are based on all households in city.

How Many People Used Parochial Schools?

There were only two cities in the study in which more than 12 percent relied on parochial schools either wholly or in combination with public schools (Table 9–1). In Milwaukee, a little over 20 percent of the families with school age children used parochial schools to some extent. In Boston, almost 30 percent of these families relied on parochial schools. This was not by chance, of course; Boston and Milwaukee were the two cities in the sample in which a majority of the families were Catholic. Boston was about 60 percent Catholic and Milwaukee about 50 percent Catholic. Even in these two cities, however, a substantial majority—60 percent in Boston and 70 percent in Milwaukee—relied to some extent on the public schools (Table 9–2). In every city for which we could make reliable estimates, a majority of Catholic families relied at least in part on the public schools.

How Did People Feel About Helping to Support Parochial Schools With Public Money?

Catholics clearly supported such a policy in every city; only a minority of the white Protestants in any city said they supported such a policy. The blacks varied from city-to-city in whether a majority favored public help to church-supported schools (Table 9–3). In the two cities in which there were the largest Catholic populations and the most reliance on parochial schools—Boston and Milwaukee—a modest majority of all residents said they would favor such support (Table 9–4). In Kansas City, Kansas, where only 20 percent of the population was Catholic, there was also a majority. This majority resulted from 90 percent of the Catholics there being in favor of such support plus 40 percent of the white Protestants and 70 percent of the blacks. In Baltimore, the citizens were split about in half with respect to tax help for church-supported schools. In the other cities, a majority would not favor such a policy.

Table 9–2. Type of School Catholic Families Send Children to, by City

Response	Albuquerque	Baltimore	Boston	Denver	Milwaukee	San Diego
Public Only	77%	62%	48%	55%	61%	84%
Parochial Only	11	16	29	17	21	12
Public and Other	7	6	11	14	10	3
Other	5	16	12	14	8	1
Total	100%	100%	100%	100%	100%	100%
(N)	(103)	(50)	(105)	(51)	(96)	(69)

Note: There were too few Catholic families with school age children in the samples for the other four cities to make reliable estimates.

Table 9–3. Percent Who Support Public Funding for Parochial Schools, by Religion and by Race

	Albuquerque	Atlanta	Baltimore	Boston	Denver	Kansas City, Missouri	Milwaukee	Nashville	San Diego
White Catholic	62%		67%	68%	75%	77%	69%		52%
White Protestant	23		45	37	30	36	41		25
Black	*		45	52	*	53	53		*

*Too few cases.

Table 9–4. Should Tax Money Go to Support Parochial Schools?

Response	Albuquerque	Atlanta	Baltimore	Boston	Denver	Kansas City, Kansas	Kansas City, Missouri	Milwaukee	Nashville	San Diego
Yes	38%	35%	51%	57%	40%	55%	45%	56%	34%	32%
No	62	65	49	43	60	45	55	44	66	68
Total	100%	100%	100%	100%	100%	100%	100%	100%	100%	100%
(N)	(471)	(469)	(500)	(507)	(357)	(193)	(383)	(443)	(426)	(517)

HOW DID PEOPLE IN CENTRAL CITIES FEEL ABOUT THEIR SCHOOL SYSTEMS?

It is difficult to use survey data to estimate the absolute level of satisfaction of people. We are on firmer ground discussing differences between groups or between cities. Nonetheless, it is useful to get some sense of the extent to which schools are seen as a problem area.

When we asked people to rate the quality of education children received in their neighborhood schools, the clearly dominant answers were "very good" or "good enough" (Table 9–5). Except in Boston and Baltimore, less than a quarter of the people in the cities rated their schools as low as "not so good" or "not good at all"; another 10 to 20 percent said they did not know enough about the schools to make a judgment. When we asked people about city problems or about services and facilities that should be improved in their neighborhoods, only about 10 percent of the responses were related to schools. However, when we asked about a list of specific service areas, a majority of the people in seven cities said that more should be spent on schools. Furthermore, when we asked people to select the three most important areas for increased effort from a list of 16 services, "public schools" was among the most cited items in nine of the ten cities. (See Chapter 4.)

Thus, we are faced with the situation that relatively few people said the schools were not good or cited them as a major problem. However, there was the feeling that more money should be spent on schools; and on the average, about one-third of the cities' populations considered schools one of the three most important areas for increased effort.

The question is whether schools were a problem area, or just a service for which there was a relatively high level of support for continuing improvement. It is the author's feeling that there was not widespread concern in most cities that schools were a problem, in the sense of being a markedly inadequate service, but that there was sentiment in some cities that they could and should be improved. This tenuous conclusion was based on the fact that more people describe the schools as "good enough" than as "very good" in all cities but Milwaukee. It was also based on the fact that, except in Boston, a majority (up to 85 percent) of those who chose schools as an important area for increased effort rated their schools as "very good" or "good enough" (Figure 9–2).

Did People With Children Feel The Same Way About Schools As People Who Did Not Have Children?

There were no significant differences in the rating of the schools between people with children in the school system and people who had no children (Figure 9–3). In some cities, however, there was a difference between those families that used public schools and those whose children went to parochial or

Table 9-5. Quality of Education in Neighborhood Schools, by City

Response	Albuquerque	Atlanta	Baltimore	Boston	Denver	Kansas City, Kansas	Kansas City, Missouri	Milwaukee	Nashville	San Diego
Very Good	30%	28%	26%	14%	27%	31%	31%	36%	30%	31%
Good Enough	33	36	46	35	34	47	35	32	39	33
Not So Good	17	16	22	23	17	10	18	16	17	18
Not Good at All	6	3	4	10	3	4	4	4	3	4
Not Ascertained	14	17	2	18	19	8	12	12	11	14
Total	100%	100%	100%	100%	100%	100%	100%	100%	100%	100%
(N)	(471)	(469)	(500)	(507)	(357)	(193)	(383)	(443)	(426)	(517)

178 Citizen Attitudes Toward Local Government, Services, and Taxes

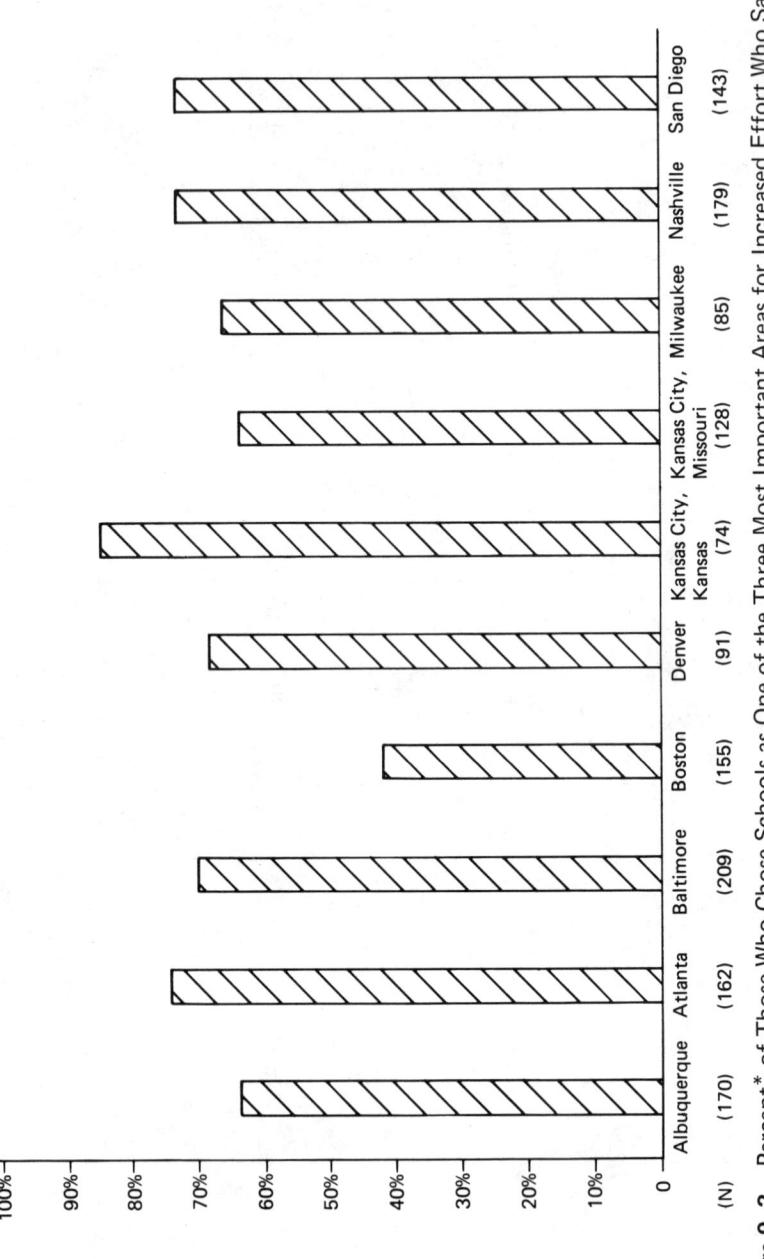

Figure 9-2. Percent* of Those Who Chose Schools as One of the Three Most Important Areas for Increased Effort Who Said the Quality of Education in Their Schools Was "Good Enough" or "Very Good," by City

*Percentages exclude "not ascertained" responses, ranging from 2 to 18 percent.

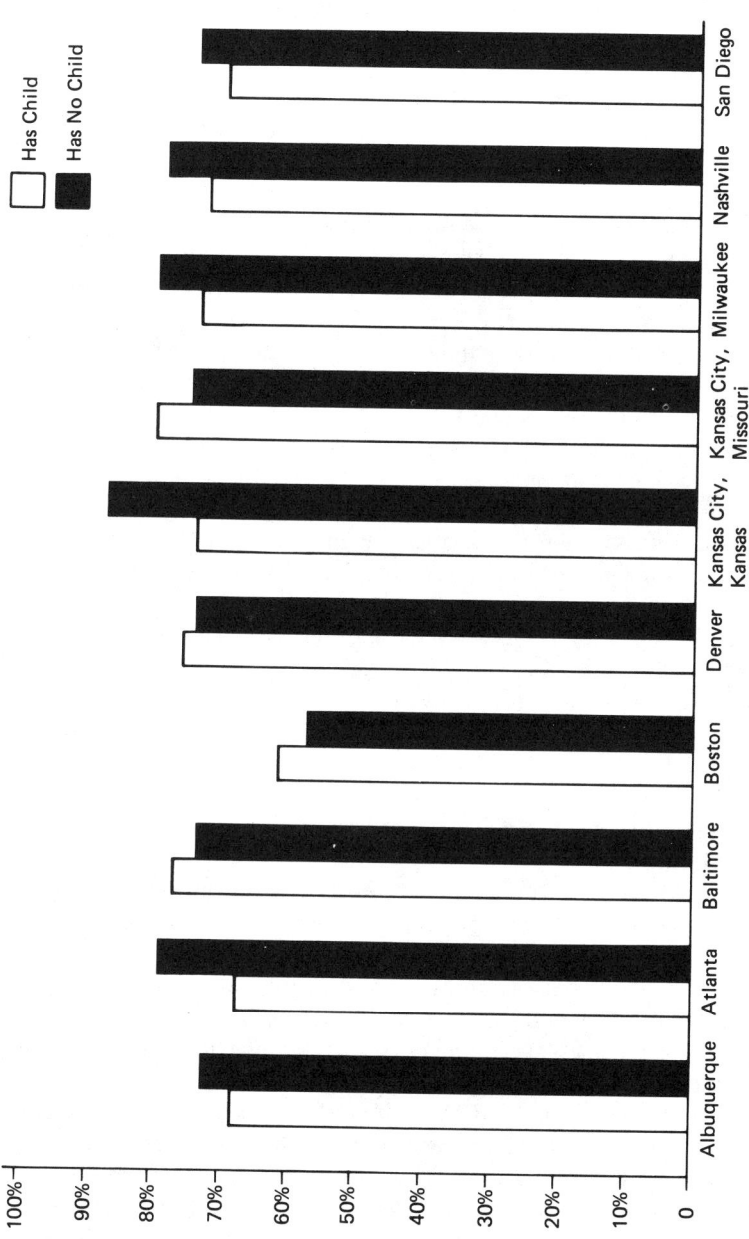

Figure 9–3. Percent* Rating Quality of Neighborhood School as "Very Good" or "Good Enough," by Population with School Age Children vs. Population without Children

*Percentages exclude "not ascertained" responses ranging from 2 to 18 percent.

private schools (Figure 9-4). It is predictable that those who opted away from the public schools would be more critical of them. Perhaps the surprising aspect of the data is that the differences were not larger or more consistent.

Did Different Population Segments Differ in Their View of the Schools?

We asked people whether their neighborhood schools were better, the same, or worse than schools in the rest of the city. In every city with a substantial black population, blacks were more likely than whites to say that the schools in their areas were not as good as in the rest of the city (Figure 9-5). The extent of the difference between blacks and whites varied from city-to-city. In Atlanta, Baltimore, and Nashville, differences were modest, but significant. In Boston, the two Kansas Cities, and Milwaukee, differences in this respect were more marked. Well over half the blacks in Boston thought their neighborhood schools were not as good as the other schools in the city, compared with only one-fourth of the whites in Boston. In the two Kansas Cities and Milwaukee, 30 to 40 percent of the blacks thought their neighborhood schools were not as good as the other schools in the city, compared to less than 10 percent of the whites.

We also asked people to rate the education children receive in their neighborhood schools (Figure 9-6). In several cities, for example, Atlanta and Baltimore, there were no differences between blacks and whites in their ratings of the schools in their neighborhoods, even though blacks tended to report that their schools were inferior to those in the rest of the city. The same pattern tended to occur in the two Kansas Cities, though there the blacks also tended to rate the schools slightly lower than the whites. In Milwaukee, and even more so in Boston, however, blacks and whites differed significantly in their ratings of the schools.

Did The Same Differences Exist by Income?

There were only three cities in which there was any notable association between income and the rating people gave to their neighborhood schools (Table 9-6). In two of those cities, the relationship was opposite from that which one would anticipate. In both Boston and Kansas City, Kansas, those with higher incomes were more likely to rate their schools low. Denver was the only city in which there was a notable association in the expected direction: higher income people rated their schools better than lower income people.

There was a slight but noticeable tendency for people who had been to college to be more critical of schools than those who had not finished high school (Table 9-7). It may be a reasonable hypothesis that those people who had been to college and expected college for their children also expected more from the public schools. Although the association between education and the rating of the schools was significant in only one city—Boston—the recurrent slight tend-

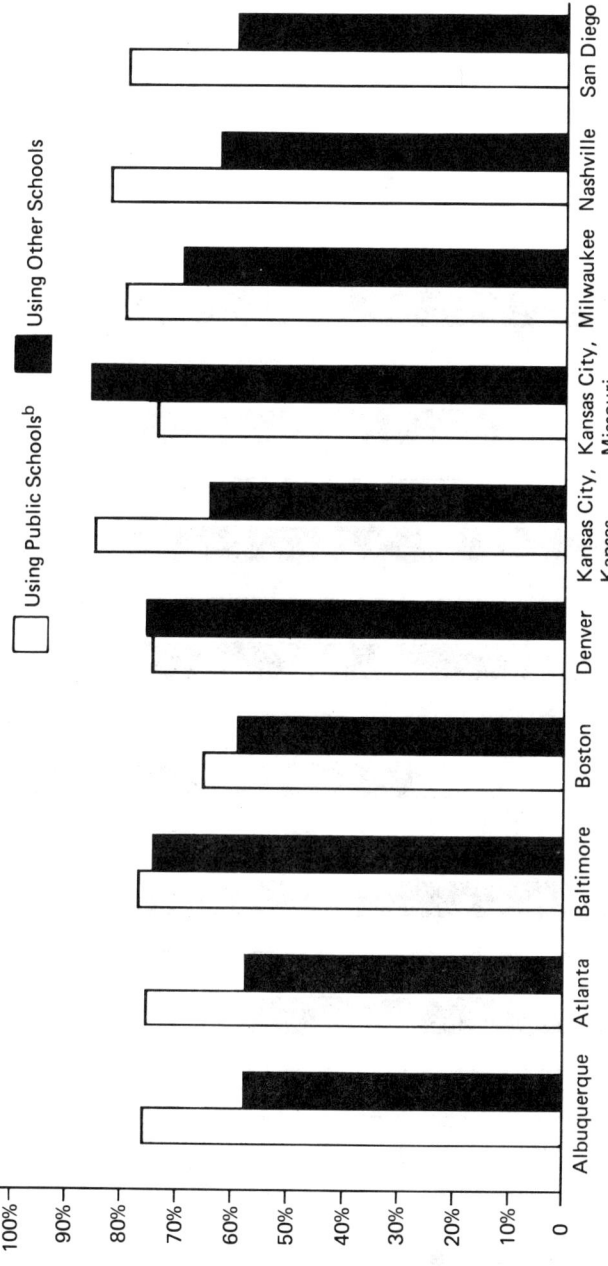

Figure 9–4. Percent* Who Rate Quality of Neighborhood Schools as "Very Good" or "Good Enough," by Families Using Public Schools vs. Families Using Other Schools[a]

[a]Figures for "other" schools include parochial and private schools.
[b]Figures for public schools include some families who are sending their children both to public and private or parochial schools.

*Percentages exclude "not ascertained" responses ranging from 2 to 18 percent.

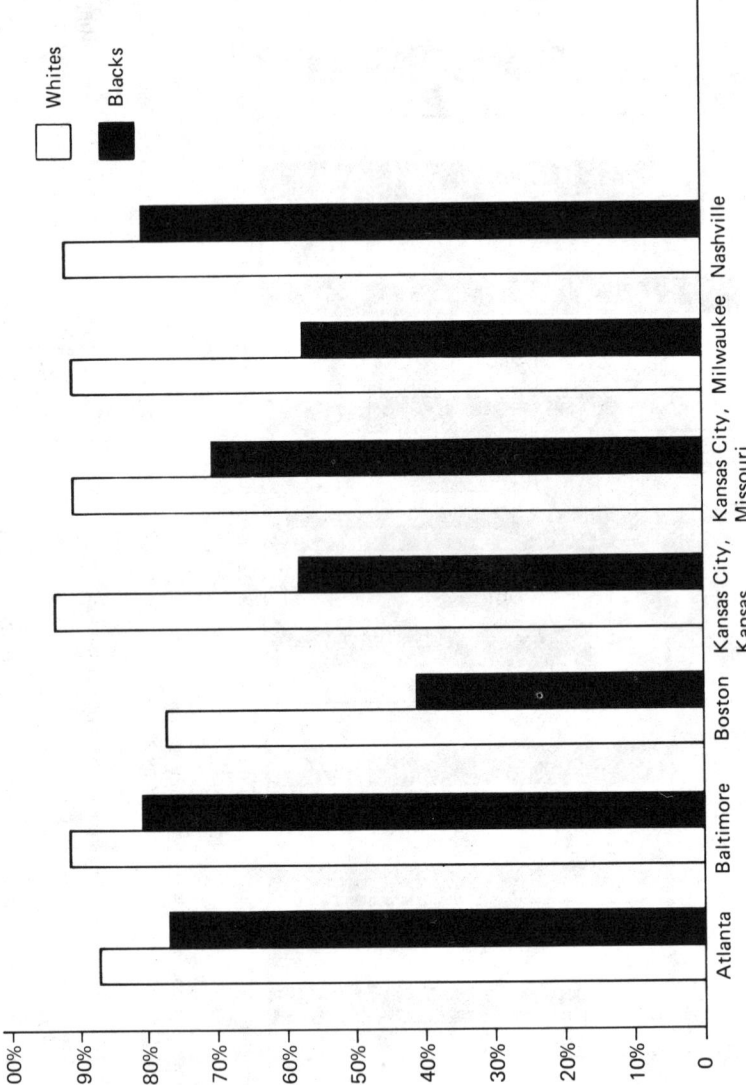

Figure 9–5. Percent Who Say Neighborhood Schools Are "Better" or "Same" as Rest of City, by Race

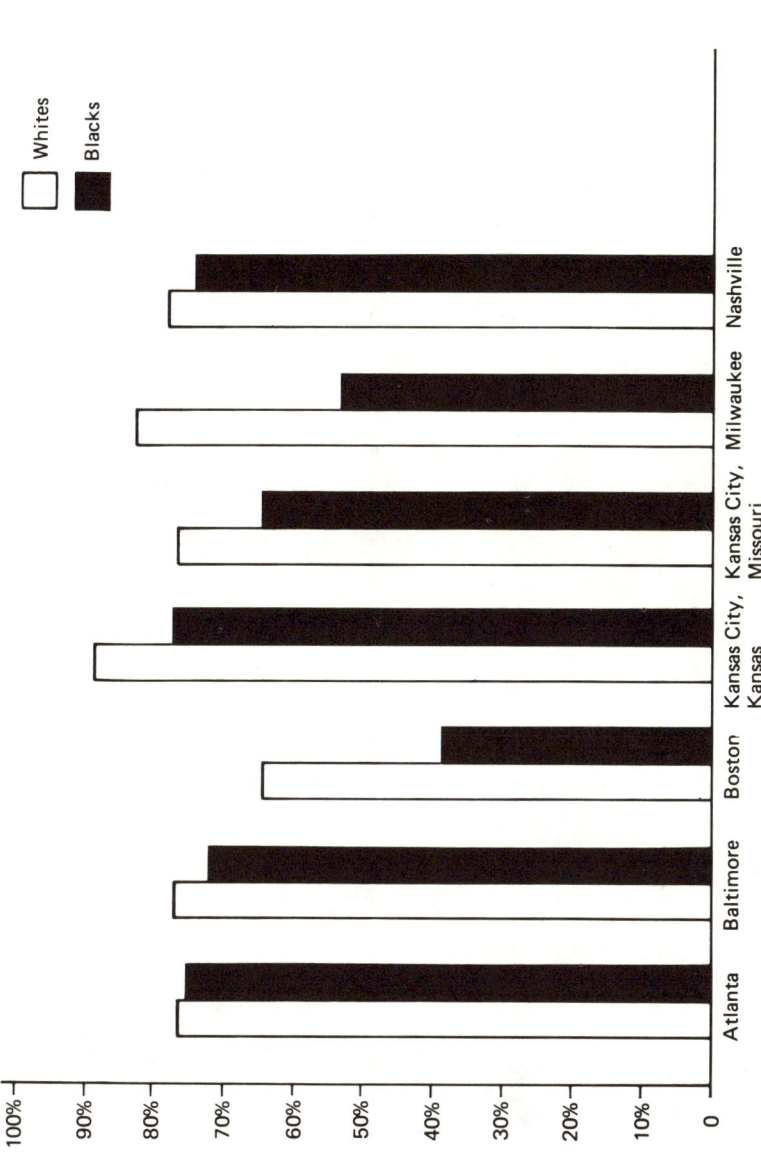

Figure 9–6. Percent Who Say Quality of Education in Neighborhood Schools Is "Very Good" or "Good Enough," by Race

Table 9-6. Percent* Who Say Education in Neighborhood Schools Is "Very Good" or "Good Enough," by Income

	Albuquerque	Atlanta	Baltimore	Boston	Denver	Kansas City, Kansas	Kansas City, Missouri	Milwaukee	Nashville	San Diego
Less than $5,000	69%	76%	64%	65%	72%	94%	73%	81%	78%	74%
$5,000 to $9,999	77	82	80	56	69	80	76	73	79	77
$10,000 or More	73	67	72	52	82	79	73	81	76	74

*Percentages exclude "not ascertained" responses ranging from 2 to 18 percent.

Table 9-7. Percent* Who Say Education in Neighborhood Schools Is "Very Good" or "Good Enough," by Education

	Albuquerque	Atlanta	Baltimore	Boston	Denver	Kansas City, Kansas	Kansas City, Missouri	Milwaukee	Nashville	San Diego
Less than High School Graduate	78%	78%	73%	72%	79%	88%	79%	76%	80%	76%
High School Graduate	74	77	75	59	71	86	72	81	77	72
Any College	69	71	76	39	72	72	74	76	75	77

*Percentages exclude "not ascertained" responses ranging from 2 to 18 percent.

ency in most cities suggests that better educated people may have been more critical.

There is no way from these data to say how some objective evaluation procedure would rate the schools in low-income areas. When people were rating schools, they evaluated them by their own criteria. We can say that people in low-income areas were as satisfied with their schools as people in high-income areas. Insofar as schools in low-income areas were less adequate, they were inadequate in ways that were not salient to people living in the areas.

WHAT CHANGES DID PEOPLE WANT IN THEIR SCHOOL SYSTEMS?

When we asked people in what ways, if any, their schools could be improved, roughly one-fourth of them had no suggestions whatsoever. Of those people who did have suggestions, patterns pretty much followed what one would expect: bigger or better buildings and more or better teachers (Table 9-8). An issue that came up in all cities to some extent, which might not have been expected, was one about controlling or disciplining students. Two issues that seldom came up that might have been expected were changes in the curriculum or courses and changes in the role the parents play in the school system.

When we asked people specifically what courses, if any, people thought should be taught, which were not then taught in the schools, roughly 70 percent had no suggestions (Table 9-9). From 4 to 10 percent suggested that sex education would be a useful addition to the school curriculum; up to 6 percent mentioned vocational studies. Up to 8 percent suggested that black studies should be added. Among blacks, the highest response came from Milwaukee, where 13 percent of the blacks said black studies should be added (Table 9-10). In most other cities with significant black populations, the rate was about 10 percent. No other type of addition was mentioned by more than 5 percent of the total population of any city.

Although there was no single type of course change or curriculum addition that 10 percent of the total population of a city mentioned, this figure does not indicate the amount of support a proposed curriculum change might receive. It does indicate that there were not large numbers of people for whom a major concern was adding any given course to the curriculum.

What About Community Control?

When we asked people whether or not parents had the right amount of say in their school systems, between 17 and 33 percent of the adults said that parents had not had the right amount of involvement in school policy (Table 9-11). The rate of such sentiment was highest in Boston, lowest in Kansas City, Kansas.

When we asked people what changes should be made so that parents

Table 9-8. Ways Cited to Improve Neighborhood Schools, by City

	Albuquerque	Atlanta	Baltimore	Boston	Denver	Kansas City, Kansas	Kansas City, Missouri	Milwaukee	Nashville	San Diego
More or Better Facilities	13%	15%	34%	29%	16%	20%	15%	11%	16%	13%
More or Better Staff	33	29	32	31	23	25	28	23	31	25
Curriculum Changes	13	9	8	8	12	5	9	11	10	19
School–Community Relations	11	6	5	3	4	3	5	2	5	2
Non-Educational Issues	10	12	12	15	18	21	18	13	13	17
Financial Issues	8	5	1	3	3	6	9	1	7	3
Other	2	*	1	1	*	*	*	1	1	1
(N)	(471)	(469)	(500)	(507)	(357)	(193)	(383)	(443)	(426)	(517)

Note: Figures are weighted for the number of adults. Figures are the percentages of people giving each response. Responses do not total 100 percent because some people mentioned more than one way while others did not respond in any way.
*Less than 0.5 percent.

Table 9-9. Percent Who Want Selected Additional Courses Taught in Schools, by City

Course	Albuquerque	Atlanta	Baltimore	Boston	Denver	Kansas City, Kansas	Kansas City, Missouri	Milwaukee	Nashville	San Diego
Black Studies	1%	2%	8%	4%	3%	3%	2%	2%	2%	1%
Sex Education	4	7	5	8	5	4	4	4	10	4
No Additional Courses	67	69	74	66	73	80	80	74	64	78
(N)	(471)	(469)	(500)	(507)	(357)	(193)	(383)	(443)	(426)	(517)

Note: Figures are weighted for the number of adults are the percentages of people giving each response. Responses do not total 100 percent because some people mentioned more than one type of additional course, while others did not respond in any way; and miscellaneous responses are omitted.

Table 9-10. Percent of Blacks Who Mention Black Studies as Course Which Should Be Taught in Public Schools, by City

	Atlanta	Baltimore	Boston	Kansas City, Kansas	Kansas City, Missouri	Milwaukee	San Diego
Percent of Blacks Who Mention Black Studies	4%	12%	11%	9%	9%	13%	12%

Table 9-11. Do Parents Have Enough Say in School Policy?

Response	Albuquerque	Atlanta	Baltimore	Boston	Denver	Kansas City, Kansas	Kansas City, Missouri	Milwaukee	Nashville	San Diego
Right Amount	55%	52%	67%	39%	47%	57%	51%	50%	59%	53%
Not Right Amount	23	27	28	33	29	17	19	21	21	22
Not Ascertained	22	21	5	28	24	26	30	29	20	25
Total	100%	100%	100%	100%	100%	100%	100%	100%	100%	100%
(N)	(471)	(469)	(500)	(507)	(357)	(193)	(383)	(443)	(426)	(517)

could have more say, the answers were quite traditional (Table 9-12). By far the most prevalent response in all cities was the encouragement of direct parent-school communication on an informal basis. The second most prevalent response in most cities laid the burden squarely on the parents themselves: parents should take more initiative and more interest in the schools in order to have more influence. The third most common response was to strengthen the PTA or PTO.

Establishing a neighborhood school committee or a parents' organization outside of the standard PTO was a minor response in all the cities, even among those who wanted more parent involvement in the schools. The most support for this idea came from Denver, where about 25 percent of those who wanted more say (only 7 percent of the total population) suggested neighborhood school committees or parent organizations. Typically, only 2 or 3 percent of the total population expressed this view—less than 10 percent of all responses.

Thus, whatever the merits of neighborhood school committees, the population as a whole in these cities was not very concerned about neighborhood control of schools in 1970; and those people who were concerned about community and parent involvement in schools saw the traditional forms of direct parent-teacher discussion and parent-school discussion as the main ways of accomplishing this.

Were Blacks More Concerned About Community Control Than Whites?

In four of the seven cities in which we had enough blacks to generalize about, the blacks were less likely than whites to say that parents have enough say in school policy (Figure 9-7). In the other three cities, there was no difference between blacks and whites in this respect.

WHAT ABOUT THE PROBLEM OF RACIAL INTEGRATION OF SCHOOLS?

We asked people how much of a problem racial integration of schools had been in their cities. There appeared to be no consistent relationship between the location or racial composition of the cities and how serious the problem of school integration was said to be (Figure 9-8). Citizens of northern cities no less than southern cities, of cities with relatively small black populations no less than those with larger ones, saw school integration as a serious problem. (Figure 9-9). The two cities in which a majority of adults labeled the problem as "serious" were Kansas City, Missouri, and Denver—neither really a southern city—with black populations of 21 and 7 percent, respectively. The problem was seen as least serious in Albuquerque; San Diego; Nashville; and Kansas City, Kansas. Blacks and whites in all seven cities with significant black populations were almost identical in the rate at which they thought school integration was a serious problem. Where they differed sharply, however, was in their perception of how to

Table 9-12. Ways in Which Parents Should Have More Say for Those Who Want More Say, by City

Response	Albuquerque	Atlanta	Baltimore	Boston	Denver	Kansas City, Kansas	Kansas City, Missouri	Milwaukee	Nashville	San Diego
More Individual Interest	26%	34%	26%	21%	36%	20%	15%	26%	16%	26%
Strong PTA–PTO	24	17	19	14	8	20	19	11	7	19
Neighborhood School Committee	9	6	10	7	18	*	2	8	10	3
Parent–School Communication	27	29	26	41	19	40	49	43	41	41
Organize Parents	4	5	9	5	7	*	4	5	8	1
School Board Elections	6	2	2	3	1	2	8	*	8	3
Other	4	7	8	9	11	18	3	7	10	7
Total	100%	100%	100%	100%	100%	100%	100%	100%	100%	100%
(N)	(176)	(180)	(316)	(300)	(134)	(45)	(131)	(176)	(145)	(184)

Note: Percentages based on total number of responses for each city, not the number of people responding.
*Less than 0.5 percent.

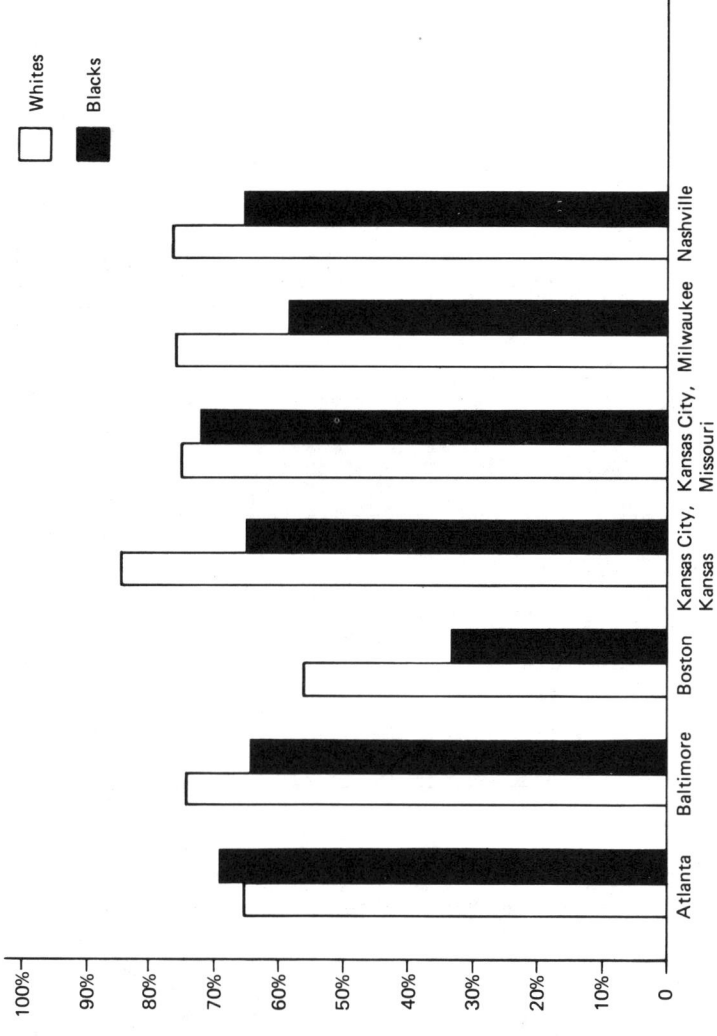

Figure 9-7. Percent Who Say Parents Have Enough Say in School Policy, by Race

Note: Data reflects only response of those who answered question, about 75% "No response" not shown.

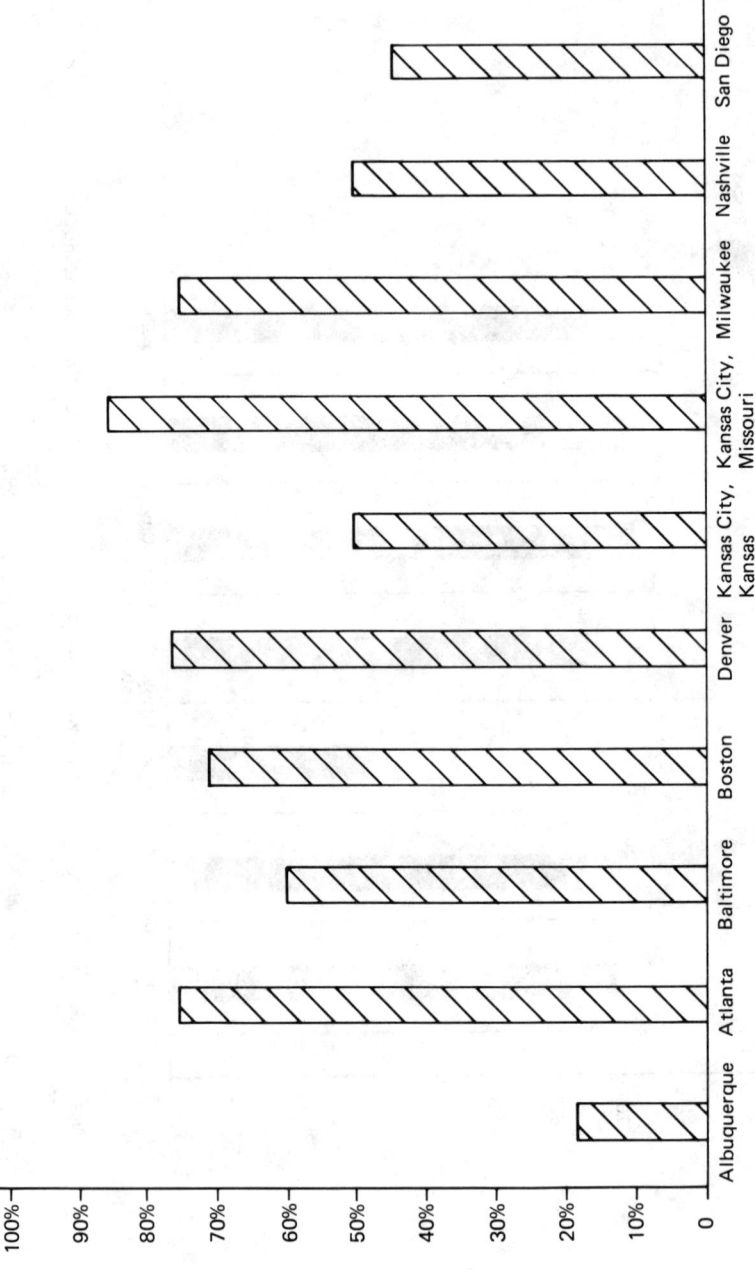

Figure 9–8. Percent Who Say Integration Has Been a "Serious" or "Some" Problem, by City

Figure 9-9. Percent Who Say Integration Has Been a "Serious" or "Some" Problem, by Race

alleviate the problem. We asked: "As you probably know, in some places they assign children to schools in other neighborhoods to get a more even spread of black and white children in schools. Do you think this is a good idea, or not?" A majority of black adults in all seven cities thought this was a "good idea," while 25 percent or less of the whites in these cities thought it was a "good idea" (Figure 9-10).

Consistent answers were obtained when we asked parents of school children whether they would be willing to send their children to "a school a little further away from home than the one they go to now in order to help integrate the schools . . . ?" The number of black parents in the sample was too small to reliably assess their response, though a majority of those responding said they were willing (Figure 9-11). It can be reliably stated, however, that less than a quarter of the white parents in the cities said they were willing to cooperate in such a program (Figure 9-12).

HOW WOULD ONE SUMMARIZE THE DATA ON THE SCHOOLS IN CENTRAL CITIES?

It appears that people living in cities were not obviously dissatisfied with schools in cities. This does not mean they were or were not getting what educators think they ought to get, but by and large, the people were getting schools that seemed to them appropriate. In a couple of cities, blacks were exceptions to this, but generally the problem in most cities was not that blacks were less satisfied with schools than whites, but that they perceived schools in their neighborhoods to be of lower quality than the city average. It was most noteworthy that there was no apparent association between income and satisfaction with schools. Overall, low-income people were as satisfied with schools as high-income people.

Curriculum changes and parental control of schools did not appear to have gained a great deal of popular support. Although sex education and black studies might get a great deal of support when they are introduced, most people did not volunteer them as needed additions to the school curriculum. Parent involvement in school policy was seen primarily on an individual basis—that is, talking with teachers and principals. Setting up neighborhood school committees was not a widespread idea in most cities.

On the topic of parochial school financing, Catholics generally favored public tax support for parochial schools, though less than a third of the Catholic families in any city relied solely on parochial schools for elementary and high school education. Because only a minority of Protestants favored such support, there were only four cities in which a majority of all citizens favored tax support for parochial schools.

While there was widespread willingness to continue to support and improve schools in cities, the quality of education that children receive in schools was not particularly a priority issue in most of the cities studied, and there was

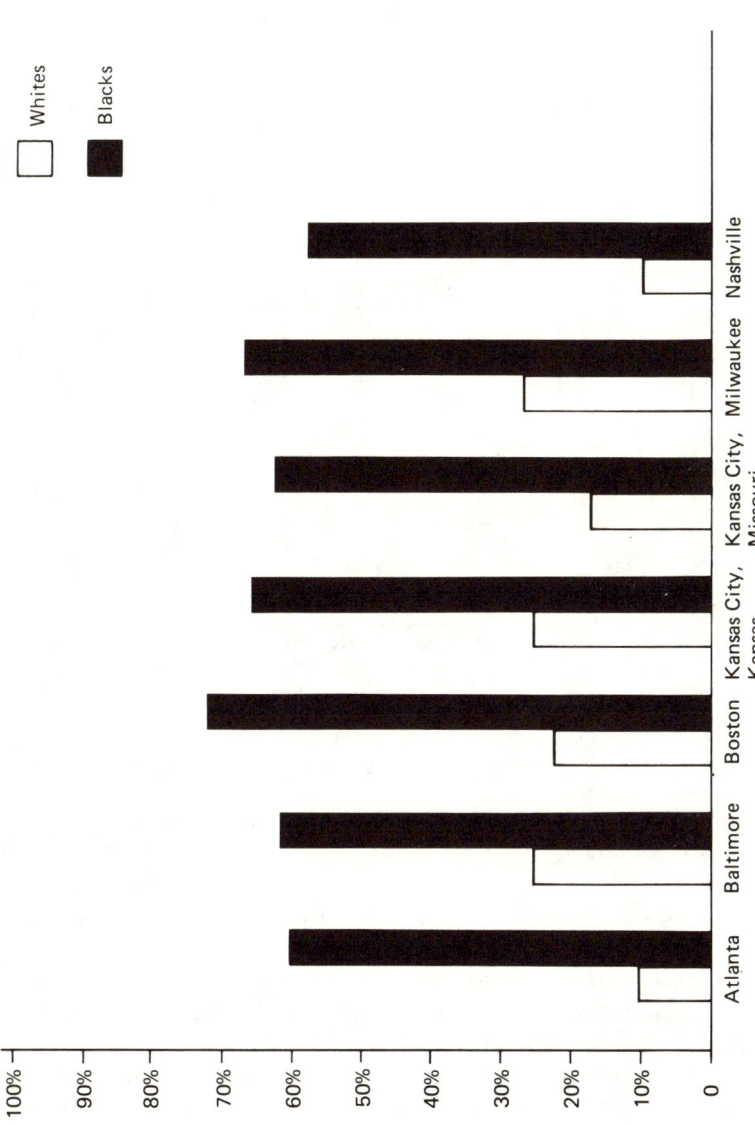

Figure 9–10. Percent Who Say Assigning Children to Schools in Other Neighborhoods Is a "Good Idea," by Race

196 Citizen Attitudes Toward Local Government, Services, and Taxes

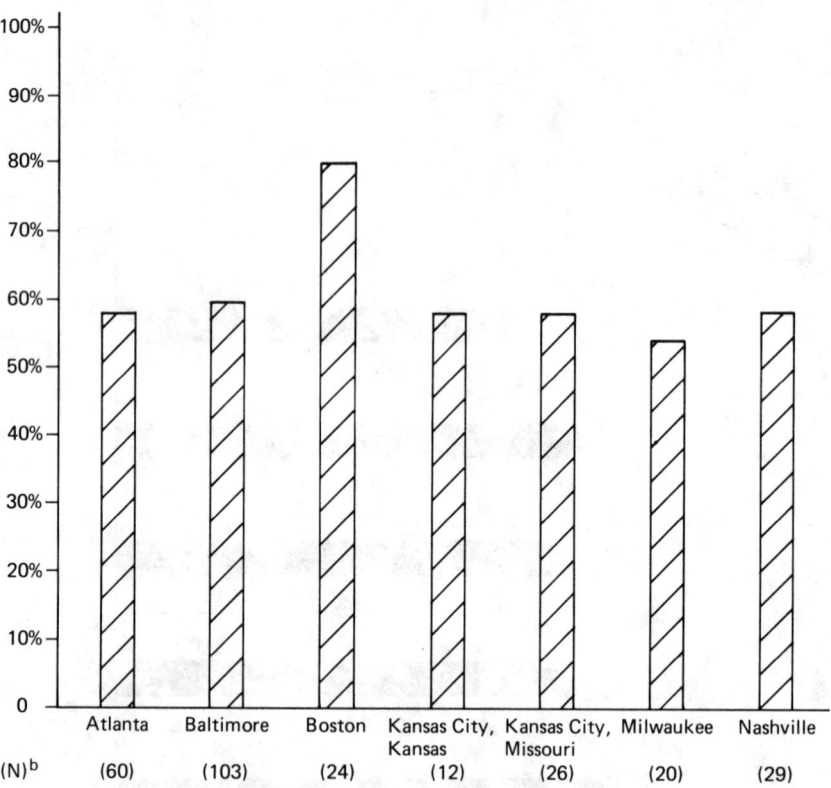

aFigures include only adults with children in public schools.
b"N's" under 50 are not very reliable estimates and should be treated accordingly.

Figure 9-11. Percent of Blacks Who Say They Are Willing to Have Their Children Bused, by City[a]

little evidence of widespread pressure for fundamental change from the citizens' point of view.

Finally, there were some cities in which racial integration was seen as a serious problem. Blacks and whites were very consistent in the extent to which they though it was or was not a serious problem in any given city. Blacks, but not whites, supported re-districting and deviation from strict proximity assignment of children to schools as strategies for dealing with the problem.

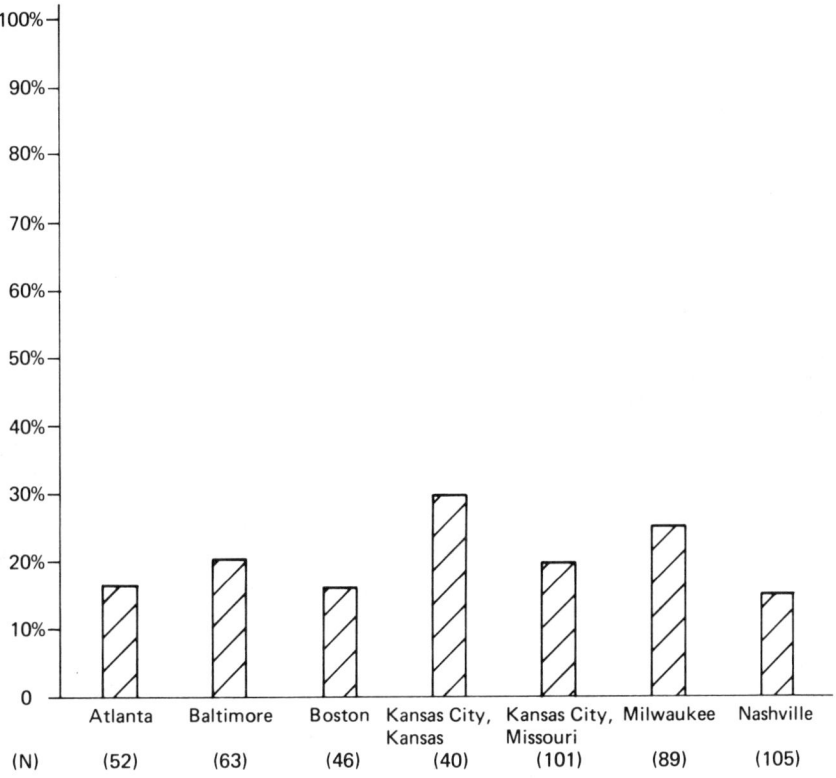

aFigures weighted for number of adults with children in public school.

Figure 9-12. Percent of Whitesa Who Say They Are Willing to Have Their Children Bused, by City

Chapter Ten

Images of City Government

Responses to questions about specific services and activities, reported in the previous chapters, are easier to understand and interpret than responses to questions seeking more generalized evaluations. But, in addition to their attitudes about taxes and services, people were asked about their perceptions of local government efficiency, honesty, and responsiveness to their problems. This permitted identification of the extent to which these concerns were more prevalent in some cities than in others, and the way these concerns were distributed among the populations of cities.

Specifically, the responses allow for interpretation of citizens' perceptions of the value obtained for their tax dollar, honesty among public officials, the ability of city officials to work on the right problems, and generally how well the city is run.

Although the data reported here on citizens' general attitudes toward their city governments indicate several notable results, it is difficult to extrapolate any significant policy implications from them. The perceptions of city government, however, tend to be negative as well as positive, and such perceptions may be tied to the way people behave in the voting booth, the pride they take in their city, and the likelihood that people with options will decide to stay in the city.[1]

WHAT WAS THE PERCEPTION OF CITY GOVERNMENT EFFICIENCY?

The main question that related to efficiency was discussed in some detail in Chapter 5: "Considering what people pay in local taxes do you think the people generally get their money's worth in services or not?" The data in Chapter 5 showed that less than half of the people in every city except San Diego said they felt they received their money's worth in services. As noted, there was also a tendency for better-educated persons and those with higher incomes to have a more positive view of the services they received for their tax dollars; this was also true more for whites than for blacks.

WHAT WAS THE PERCEPTION OF HONESTY IN CITY GOVERNMENT?

A majority of respondents in all cities said they thought their local elected officials were as honest as people in other walks of life—for example, people in business (Table 10-1). However, among the minority that did not feel this way, those who said officials were "less honest" generally outnumbered those who thought their elected officials were "more honest" than most other people.

When people were asked how much illegal activity they thought went on in their city government, more than half the people said "a great deal" or "some" in seven cities; in the other cities, the prevalence of such responses was between 40 and 50 percent (Table 10-2). In general, neither race nor education was consistently related to responses about the amount of illegal activity in the city (Figure 10-1 and Table 10-3). Although there were some fairly significant differences between cities in how citizens described their city government along this dimension, the perceptions of illegal activity seem fairly evenly spread about the population within cities.

What Kinds of Illegal Activities Were People Thinking Of?

The most common response was payment to police or other officials to ignore illegal activity (Table 10-4). The second most common concern was kickbacks on contracts let by the city. A significant portion of the population in most cities, up to 17 percent, thought there was a "great deal" or "some" illegal activity but they didn't really know what kind.

TO WHAT EXTENT WERE CITY GOVERNMENTS SEEN AS RESPONSIVE TO PEOPLE'S NEEDS?

One question on this topic asked how much the respondent thought that city officials were concerned about the same problems that he or she—the citizen—was concerned about (Table 10-5). It is rather difficult to interpret with any confidence the meaning of the distribution of responses to this question. Between 25 and 40 percent of the population in most cities characterized the amount of official concern as "very much." It is striking that the variation among cities in the answers to this question was considerably less than for most of the other measures discussed in this chapter.

There was also little variation within cities in the answers to this question. Blacks and whites differed significantly in three of the seven cities in which their responses can be compared, but not so much in the other four cities

Table 10-1. Citizens' Perception of Honesty of Local Officials Compared to Most Other People, by City*

	A	B	C	D	E	F	G	H	I	J
More Honest	5%	2%	5%	7%	7%	10%	6%	4%	4%	8%
Same	60	61	69	67	67	66	69	55	72	73
Less Honest	34	29	20	19	19	17	17	32	19	12
Not Ascertained	1	8	6	7	7	7	8	9	5	7
Total	100%	100%	100%	100%	100%	100%	100%	100%	100%	100%

Note: Figures are weighted for the number of adults.

Table 10-2. Citizens' Perception of Amount of Illegal Activity among Local Officials, by City*

	A	B	C	D	E	F	G	H	I	J
A Great Deal	8%	7%	11%	34%	16%	9%	34%	18%	22%	25%
Some	41	37	40	35	40	39	32	25	38	43
A Little	20	23	19	13	14	21	21	17	20	16
Almost None	11	17	13	4	9	15	2	10	5	5
Don't Know	11	15	13	10	20	14	10	29	13	8
Not Ascertained	9	1	4	4	1	2	1	11	2	3
Total	100%	100%	100%	100%	100%	100%	100%	100%	100%	100%

Note: Figures are weighted for number of adults.
*Citizens' attitudes vary over time and reflect perceptions rather than actual fact. To avoid unjustifiable and/or unwarranted reflection upon the current administration and employees of any of the participating cities, the data in the above table has been presented without designation and in random order.

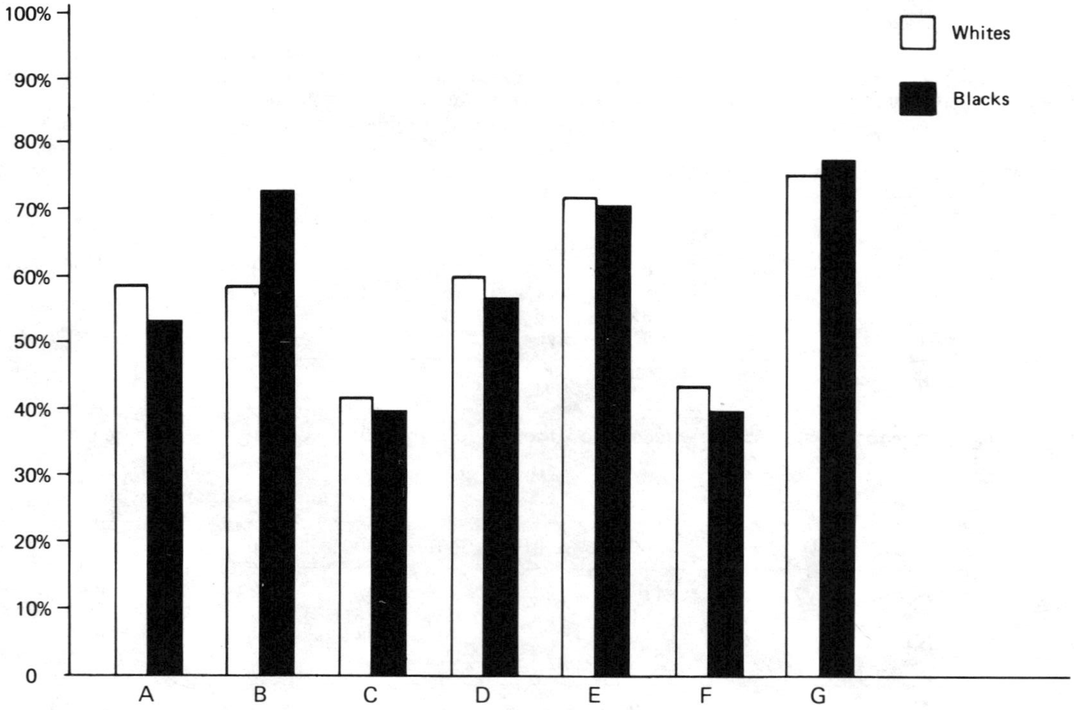

202 Citizen Attitudes Toward Local Government, Services, and Taxes

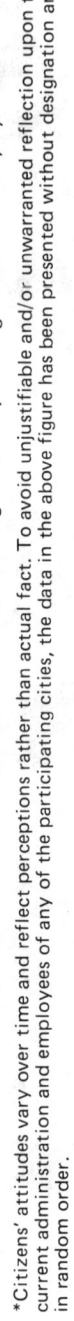

Note: Percentages exclude 10 to 30 percent for whom answer was "don't know" or not ascertained.

Figure 10–1. Percent Who Say There Is "Some" or "A Great Deal" of Illegal Activity among Local Officials, by Race*

*Citizens' attitudes vary over time and reflect perceptions rather than actual fact. To avoid unjustifiable and/or unwarranted reflection upon the current administration and employees of any of the participating cities, the data in the above figure has been presented without designation and in random order.

Table 10-3. Percent Who Say There Is "Some" or "A Great Deal" of Illegal Activity among Local Officials, by Education*

	A	B	C	D	E	F	G	H	I	J
Less than High School Graduate	64%	63%	50%	36%	50%	60%	49%	39%	64%	34%
High School Graduate	63	77	55	51	54	76	66	51	66	49
Any College	53	71	52	42	48	84	53	51	69	42

Note: Percentages exclude 10% to 30% for whom answer was "don't know," or not ascertained.
*Citizens' attitudes vary over time and reflect perceptions rather than actual fact. To avoid unjustifiable and/or unwarranted reflection upon the current administration and employees of any of the participating cities, the data in the above table has been presented without designation and in random order.

Table 10-4. Percent of Citizens Who Mention Types of Illegal Activity of Local Officials, by City*

	A	B	C	D	E	F	G	H	I	J
Bribery to Overlook Illegal Activity	30%	8%	16%	8%	15%	15%	11%	31%	16%	19%
Kickbacks	8	11	7	13	26	11	14	12	7	12
Embezzlement	1	2	1	1	3	2	1	3	3	**
Complex Activities	4	2	2	3	2	2	3	9	3	4
Jobs on City Time	**	**	1	**	1	**	**	**	**	**
Don't Know	17	11	10	17	13	17	13	4	9	14
Other General	**	**	1	2	1	1	1	2	**	2
Little Illegal Activity	32	52	56	49	31	43	52	34	57	40
No Response	8	14	6	7	8	9	5	5	5	9
Total	100%	100%	100%	100%	100%	100%	100%	100%	100%	100%

Note: Figures weighted for the number of adults.
*Citizens' attitudes vary over time and reflect perceptions rather than actual fact. To avoid unjustifiable and/or unwarranted reflection upon the current administration and employees of any of the participating cities, the data in the above table has been presented without designation and in random order.
**Less than 0.5 percent.

Table 10-5. Perception of Degree to Which Officials Are Concerned about the Same Problems as Citizens, by City

	Albuquerque	Atlanta	Baltimore	Boston	Denver	Kansas City, Kansas	Kansas City, Missouri	Milwaukee	Nashville	San Diego
Very Much	31%	37%	24%	23%	34%	28%	27%	34%	25%	29%
Some	35	35	38	38	35	40	39	38	45	39
A Little	15	12	21	15	11	13	18	11	14	12
Hardly at All	11	11	16	15	13	16	13	13	11	12
Not Ascertained	8	5	1	9	7	3	3	4	5	8
Total	100%	100%	100%	100%	100%	100%	100%	100%	100%	100%
(N)	(471)	(469)	(500)	(507)	(357)	(193)	(383)	(443)	(426)	(517)

Note: Figures are weighted for number of adults.

(Figure 10-2). In most cities there was hardly any evidence that either the better-educated or those with higher incomes found the city government more responsive or in tune with their concerns than those with lower incomes or less education (Tables 10-6 and 10-7).

How Would People Go About Getting The City Government to Do Something That They Wanted Done?

Respondents were asked what the best way was to make themselves heard by local government. Most of the answers could be classified at a general level into three categories: (1) direct contact, such as calling an elected official or the appropriate appointed official and discussing the problem with that person directly; (2) through the political process, which primarily includes either voting or working to elect candidates that a person feels will represent him well; and (3) organizing or lobbying, which primarily includes those people who were going to join together with others who had similar interests and form a pressure group outside the normal political channels. In all but one city, speaking directly to a local official was the most frequent response (Table 10-8). Those who spoke of the political process and those who spoke of organizing outside of the political process were about equal in numbers in most cities.

When we compared the answers of blacks and whites to this question, some differences appeared, though they were not the same in all cities (Table 10-9). For example, whites more than blacks said that direct contact with officials was an effective way to be heard in Milwaukee and to a lesser extent in Nashville and Atlanta. However, such a difference did not occur in the responses in the other four cities in which blacks and whites could be compared. Working through the political process to make oneself heard was seen as effective by significantly more whites than blacks in the two Kansas Cities but that was not the case in the other five cities. Organizing outside the political process was cited as an effective way to be heard significantly more often by blacks than whites in Baltimore and Kansas City, Missouri; there was a similar, though not significant, tendency in Kansas City, Kansas, and Boston. However, in the other three cities there were no such differences. Thus where differences did occur, they were consistent with the hypothesis that the normal channels of direct contact with officials and voting were seen as effective avenues more for whites than for blacks.

The data on the responses by education indicate a general tendency in some cities for better-educated people to be more likely to give more than one response (Table 10-10). There was virtually no response that less-educated people were more likely to give than people who had been to college. These data perhaps reflect more response error—i.e., error due to the method of measurement—than they do the real feelings of people about the process of city government and the way to be heard. The data do not necessarily indicate that less-educated people felt less able to be heard by city officials.

Images of City Government 207

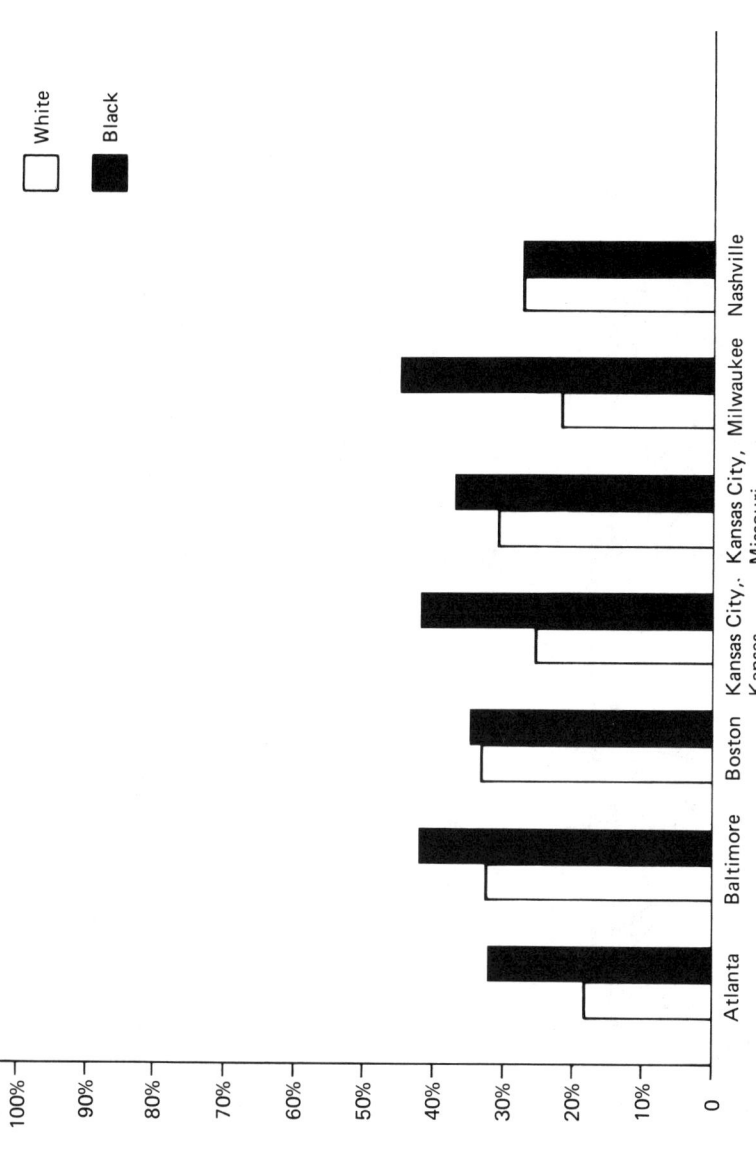

Figure 10-2. Percent Who Say Local Officials Concerned about Same Problems "A Little" or "Hardly at All," by Race

Table 10–6. Percent Who Say Local Officials Concerned about Same Problems "A Little" or "Hardly at All," by Education

	Albuquerque	Atlanta	Baltimore	Boston	Denver	Kansas City, Kansas	Kansas City, Missouri	Milwaukee	Nashville	San Diego
Less than High School Graduate	37%	28%	41%	33%	26%	36%	39%	24%	26%	25%
High School Graduate	26	25	36	32	26	23	30	23	27	27
Any College	26	20	33	32	24	29	27	31	28	24

Table 10–7. Percent Who Say Local Officials Concerned about Same Problems "A Little" or "Hardly at All," by Income

	Albuquerque	Atlanta	Baltimore	Boston	Denver	Kansas City, Kansas	Kansas City, Missouri	Milwaukee	Nashville	San Diego
Less than $5,000	33%	28%	40%	36%	35%	31%	41%	30%	29%	32%
$5,000 to $9,999	32	26	26	31	21	30	31	26	25	29
$10,000 or More	22	19	36	32	21	29	24	20	25	20

Table 10-8. Ways in Which People Can Make Themselves Heard by Local Government, by City

	Albuquerque	Atlanta	Baltimore	Boston	Denver	Kansas City, Kansas	Kansas City, Missouri	Milwaukee	Nashville	San Diego
Direct Contact	55%	46%	40%	37%	49%	57%	47%	57%	53%	64%
Political Process	20	34	31	22	29	26	32	19	24	21
Civic Organizing, Lobbying	25	22	38	30	24	22	26	22	14	24
Other	4	2	4	2	2	2	1	2	2	3
Not Possible	6	5	11	11	7	8	8	7	9	5
(N)	(471)	(469)	(500)	(507)	(357)	(193)	(383)	(443)	(426)	(517)

Note: Figures are weighted for the number of adults. The figures are the percentage of people giving each response. The percentages do not total 100% because some people mentioned two ways while others mentioned only one way.

Table 10-9. Ways in Which People Can Make Themselves Heard by Local Government, by Race

	Atlanta	Baltimore	Boston	Kansas City, Kansas	Kansas City, Missouri	Milwaukee	Nashville
Direct Contact							
White	53%	39%	37%	55%	47%	58%	52%
Black	42	35	31	52	49	34	41
Political Process							
White	34	30	22	32	34	20	25
Black	27	32	18	13	19	18	26
Civic Organizing, Lobbying							
White	20	27	29	20	22	20	13
Black	24	48	37	31	43	21	17
Other							
White	3	3	1	1	1	3	2
Black	1	3	5	4	*	*	1
Not Possible							
White	6	14	12	9	9	7	11
Black	5	7	7	6	5	12	5

Note: Percentages do not total 100 percent because some people mentioned 2 ways while others mentioned one.
*Less than 0.5 percent.

WHAT ACCOUNTED FOR THE WAY PEOPLE RATED THEIR CITY GOVERNMENT OVERALL?

The basic measure available for this analysis was the question: "How would you rate the way *[city name]* is run—excellent, very good, good enough, not so good, or not good at all." The percentage of citizens who rated their city government "excellent" or "very good" varied quite a bit from city-to-city (Table 10–11).

There are two ways to address the question of what factors relate to the way citizens feel about their city government. One approach is to look at the characteristics of those cities in which people were particularly likely to give a favorable rating to city government. However, with only ten cities it is impossible to reach firm conclusions about the bases or reasons that a citizenry as a whole felt about the way the city is run. There are literally dozens of ways in which the more positively rated cities tend to differ from the others; they are further west, they tend to have city managers, they have smaller black populations, they are even less likely to have a major league baseball team. The last item perhaps would be unlikely to explain differences in city ratings, but it illustrates the problem. The number of potential hypotheses is very large, and ten cities is not enough to successfully select those that are most accurate.

A second approach is to look at characteristics of citizens and what perceptions and responses to the survey questions go along with the way an individual rated his city government. Such an analysis does not address the question of why one city government was rated more favorably than another. It does address the question of why a given city government was rated more favorably by some people in that city than by others.

Who Was Most Positive About The Way Cities Were Run?

It was striking that there was little or no relationship between demographic variables and the way people said their city was run. The better educated rated the city government only slightly better than the less educated; significantly so in only one city (Table 10–12). Those with low incomes did not differ consistently from those with incomes over $10,000 (Table 10–13). Even though blacks were consistently more critical of services than whites, there was only one city in which there was a significant difference between blacks and whites in how they said the city government was run (Figure 10–3).

What Perceptions Went Along With The Way People Rated The Way Their City Was Run?

Six ratings were identified that often or always were correlated with the rating of city government (Table 10–14). Those who said that their city was

212 Citizen Attitudes Toward Local Government, Services, and Taxes

Table 10–10. Ways in Which People Can Make Themselves Heard by Local Government, by Education

	Albu-querque	Atlanta	Baltimore	Boston	Denver	Kansas City, Kansas	Kansas City, Missouri	Milwaukee	Nashville	San Diego
Direct Contact										
Less than High School Graduate	41%	38%	38%	28%	42%	47%	38%	46%	40%	54%
High School Graduate	52	36	35	40	44	49	47	61	50	62
Any College	65	57	37	42	53	24	57	67	62	69
Political Process										
Less than High School Graduate	7	18	25	12	22	20	25	12	28	13
High School Graduate	19	30	28	24	26	31	36	23	19	24
Any College	27	45	47	28	35	30	31	27	27	21
Civic Organizing, Lobbying										
Less than High School Graduate	23	18	30	19	15	22	23	19	10	17
High School Graduate	25	25	47	35	29	17	27	24	17	20
Any College	26	23	41	38	27	35	27	18	17	30
Other										
Less than High School Graduate	1	3	1	2	2	2	1	2	3	4
High School Graduate	3	1	4	1	1	3	1	2	3	3
Any College	5	2	6	2	4	*	2	3	1	1

Not Possible

	Albuquerque	Atlanta	Baltimore	Boston	Denver	Kansas City, Kansas	Kansas City, Missouri	Milwaukee	Nashville	San Diego
Less than High School Graduate	8	6	14	14	13	9	13	10	11	10
High School Graduate	5	6	8	10	5	3	7	4	11	4
Any College	4	3	9	10	8	14	5	7	8	3

Note: Percentages do not total 100% because some people mentioned 2 ways while others mentioned only 1.
*Too few cases.

Images of City Government 213

Table 10–11. Rating of the Way in Which the City Is Run, by City

	Albuquerque	Atlanta	Baltimore	Boston	Denver	Kansas City, Kansas	Kansas City, Missouri	Milwaukee	Nashville	San Diego
Excellent or Very Good	25%	30%	11%	7%	22%	17%	9%	31%	20%	34%
Good Enough	47	38	40	29	49	42	32	38	41	49
Not So Good or Not Good at All	24	29	48	58	25	39	55	26	36	15
Not Ascertained	4	3	1	6	4	2	4	3	3	2
Total	100%	100%	100%	100%	100%	100%	100%	100%	100%	100%
(N)	(471)	(469)	(500)	(507)	(357)	(193)	(383)	(443)	(426)	(517)

Note: Figures are weighted for the number of adults.

Table 10–12. Percent Who Rate the Way in Which the City Is Run "Excellent" or "Very Good," by Education

	Albuquerque	Atlanta	Baltimore	Boston	Denver	Kansas City, Kansas	Kansas City, Missouri	Milwaukee	Nashville	San Diego
Less than High School Graduate	27%	33%	10%	12%	21%	19%	17%	31%	17%	38%
High School Graduate	24	24	15	5	25	11	7	30	23	32
Any College	28	33	9	4	20	22	9	44	20	37

Table 10–13. Percent Who Rate the Way in which the City Is Run "Excellent" or "Very Good," by Income

	Albuquerque	Atlanta	Baltimore	Boston	Denver	Kansas City, Kansas	Kansas City, Missouri	Milwaukee	Nashville	San Diego
Less than $5,000	32%	31%	11%	10%	22%	23%	16%	31%	22%	35%
$5,000 to $9,999	22	27	10	5	23	15	6	33	18	37
$10,000 or More	29	32	14	5	22	10	10	36	21	36

Images of City Government 215

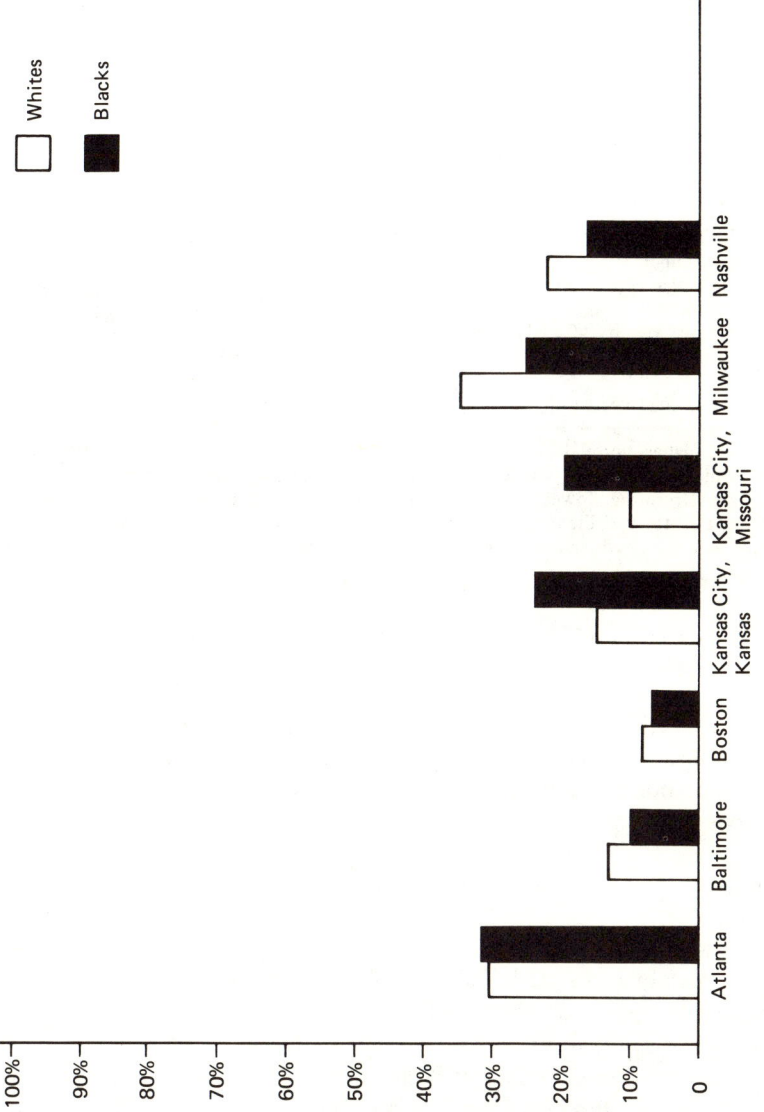

Figure 10—3. Percent Who Rate the Way in Which the City Is Run "Excellent" or "Very Good," by Race

Table 10-14. Correlations of Selected Measures with Rating of How City Government Is Run

	Correlations[a]		Number of Cities In Which Association Was Significant
	Lowest	Highest	
Demographic Characteristics			
Education	−.13	.21	1
Income	−.13	.12	0
Race	*	*	1
Other Ratings			
"Get money's worth for taxes."	.31	.57	10
"Are taxes too high."	−.08	−.32	7
"Amount of illegal activity in city government."	−.19	−.38	9
"How concerned are city officials."	.18	.44	10
"Quality of neighborhood schools."	.29	.43	10
"Rating of police."	.21	.42	9
"How safe feel on streets at night."	.02	.20	0

[a]Lowest and highest correlations refer to lowest and highest of the ten cities. Figures are gammas, which approximate correlation coefficients for ordinal data. The range of obtained correlations is from the "lowest" to the "highest." Negative numbers mean that a person who is lower on the variable in the left column (e.g., his education) is more likely than others to say the way the city is run is "very good" or "excellent."
*Not appropriate to compute gammas.

run in an "excellent" or "very good" way were also significantly more likely in every city to say:

1. They got their money's worth of service for their tax dollar.
2. City officials were concerned about the same problems as they.
3. The education children got in their neighborhood schools was "good" or "very good."

In most cities, they were also more likely to say:

4. Taxes were not too high.
5. There was not a great deal of illegal activity in city government.
6. Police did a "good" or "very good" job.

Were These The Criteria People Used to Decide How Well Their City Was Run?

These were perceptions that went along with the way a city was rated. When a person said his tax money was well spent, he also was likely to say his city was well run; and vice versa. These two perceptions in particular were very closely related in people's minds. There is no reason why every reader should understand correlation coefficients.[2] However, for those who do, it is interesting to note that the gamma values exceeded .47 in all but one city, which is a relatively high level of association for measures of this type.

It is likely that changes in people's feelings about how their city is run would be associated with changes in how they felt about the issues listed. However, what is not known is the extent to which the list encompasses all the salient issues and the extent to which the answers resulted from a generalized feeling about the city government rather than the other way around.

HOW WOULD THE DATA BE SUMMARIZED?

In every city, there were many people who said they were getting good services for their taxes, who saw little dishonest activity in government, who said city officials were working on the right problems, and who thought their city was well run. At the same time, in every city there were people who said that they were not getting full value for their tax dollar, that there was illegal activity in city government, and that there was a lack of identity between the concerns of city officials and of citizens. How people perceived and rated their city government was not consistently related to race and was even less related to income and education. It was found, however, that a number of perceptions tended to go together with how a city government is rated: honesty, fiscal efficiency, responsiveness, and the quality of schools and police. Not resolved at all is whether these were the issues on which the rating of city government was based; or whether a generally negative or positive view of a city as a whole affected a person's feelings about this diverse set of issues.

NOTES TO CHAPTER TEN

1. These data cannot be interpreted as directly reflecting on the quality of any given administration. First, we lack comparable data over a period of time. Without similar measures in 1960 or 1965, it is impossible to say how the administration in 1970 compares with previous administrations. Second, we do not know very much about the extent to which people's perceptions reflect what is going on in city government at any point in time. Third, in many cities the mayor and other elected city officials are not responsible for all the services in a city. Schools, for example, are often run by elected school committees that are independent of the mayor. Other systems, such as transportation and recreation facilities, which may be relevant to the way people feel about their city government, often are run by metropolitan or county organizations.
2. Correlation coefficients range from −1.00 to 1.00. A figure of .00 means two variables are not related at all. Negative figures mean that when a person is "high" on one variable, he is likely to be "low" on the other. Positive numbers mean that people who are "high" on one are also likely to be "high" on the other variable.

Chapter Eleven

Conclusion

POLICY IMPLICATIONS

The preceding chapters have dealt very little with the policy implications of the data. Some of the policy implications of the data depend on the answer to the question of how attitudes relate to reality. It has been said that what people think is a reality in itself. Regardless of how well informed people are, if they are unhappy about the quality of their trash collection or the way they think their tax money is spent, the city government may have to cope with this feeling in some way. However, in some cases one must then ask whether the way to change attitudes is in fact to change a service. When people say that the police do not come quickly when they are called, would this feeling change if in fact the response time were reduced? A first step in answering questions such as these would be to obtain some objective measures of police response time and see how well citizen perceptions reflect reality. It has been seen that, for example, concern about city taxes appeared to be fairly well related to how high taxes really are in a city. Also, citizens' reported concern about crime corresponded generally, but not perfectly, with the rates of crimes against people. It is clear that reality plays a part in the way people feel, but we have not adequately documented how much of a part it plays and what other factors enter into the way city government and services are evaluated in survey interviews. Until there is better research on the origins and meanings of attitudinal responses, many of the policy implications of attitudinal data will remain in question.

A second reason this report has dealt little with policy is that, at best, the opinions people express will only be one basis on which specific policy recommendations are made. Within each city, there will be a number of local conditions to take into account in order to understand fully the meaning of citizens' responses and to assess the costs and benefits of various alternative programs. A basic part of the Urban Observatory Program is acknowledgement of the importance of local solutions to problems. The ten-city perspective of this research can provide some important general guidelines, but specific steps are probably best worked out by the local research teams and officials who have intimate knowledge of the variety of issues to be considered in formulating an effective approach to problems.

While the complexity of problems may be acknowledged, and the emphasis on local action may be appropriate, people may still ask whether or not the data will be used in local decision-making and policy. One of the local research directors wrote, at the time when the questionnaire was being designed, that it was essential to address directly the question of why city officials might be interested in survey data. Included among his hypotheses were: (1) an interest in finding out how to be re-elected; (2) an interest in finding out what was politically feasible, which new programs would get a reasonable amount of popular support, and which would receive a considerable amount of opposition; and (3) an interest in how the government and its services could be changed to better meet the needs and goals of the citizens. Although one must interpret the data with care, it is possible to see how the data could be used to meet the first two interests without worrying too much about how attitudes are formed. The third interest, however, is the most important in the long run. When administrations have changed and opinions have changed, the people and their needs and interests will still be there.

FINDINGS

Despite all the caveats cited above, there are a number of findings common to almost all the cities that at the very least highlight areas for official attention:

1. The interest people expressed in having the local government take a more active role in enforcing standards for housing maintenance and repair.
2. The evidence of greater concern among minority groups with the quality of police services than with police–community relations.
3. The widespread dissatisfaction with the property tax as a source of local revenue and the general preference for taxes based on consumption.
4. The almost universal concern about the drug problem.
5. The comparative lack of concern about crimes which do not directly threaten people such as gambling, prostitution, and even car theft.
6. The absence of evidence for widespread interest in or concern about changing the school system in basic or fundamental ways.
7. The evidence that the way people rate their city government is closely tied to their perception of whether or not they are getting their money's worth in services for their tax dollar.

The Urban Observatory has established a mechanism whereby these and other data can be developed and discussed. The real question and test of the Urban Observatory concept is whether any changes will result. Can the researchers adequately develop and present data so that their relevance for city officials is clear? Can the city officials recognize the significance of the research products and will they act upon them to improve the governance of cities and the well-being of residents? The real conclusion for an effort such as this should not be a summary of findings but a set of decisions in ten cities reflecting the broader perspective and enhanced understanding that this endeavor should have wrought.

Appendix A

Tables A-1 Thru A-13

The tables that follow present the number of interviews in various sub-groups by city. Throughout the report, there are some tables presenting percentages for sub-groups within cities for which N's are not presented. The numbers presented, when used in conjunction with Tables 2-3 and 2-4, can be used to estimate the reliability of any given percentage figure or difference between groups for the tables

Table A-1. Sex of Respondents by City

	Albuquerque	Atlanta	Baltimore	Boston	Denver	Kansas City, Kansas	Kansas City, Missouri	Milwaukee	Nashville	San Diego
Female	277	276	288	295	200	114	227	257	230	293
Male	194	193	212	212	156	79	156	186	196	224
Total	471	469	500	507	357	193	383	443	426	517

Table A-2. Age of Respondents, by City

	Albuquerque	Atlanta	Baltimore	Boston	Denver	Kansas City, Kansas	Kansas City, Missouri	Milwaukee	Nashville	San Diego
Less than 30	119	141	119	158	115	56	91	119	96	126
30 to 44	144	129	164	111	98	45	106	120	115	140
45 to 64	155	134	157	155	87	55	120	121	142	140
65 or More	45	54	55	73	50	37	62	81	50	62
Not Ascertained	8	11	5	10	7	0	4	2	23	49
Total	471	469	500	507	357	193	383	443	426	517

Table A-3. Education of Respondents, by City

	Albuquerque	Atlanta	Baltimore	Boston	Denver	Kansas City, Kansas	Kansas City, Missouri	Milwaukee	Nashville	San Diego
Less than High School	119	173	229	185	93	85	112	190	155	101
High School Graduate	155	116	161	171	133	71	148	157	123	184
Some College or More	195	178	108	147	129	37	122	96	143	232
Not Ascertained	2	2	2	4	2	0	1	0	5	0
Total	471	469	500	507	357	193	383	443	426	517

Table A-4. Family Income, by City

	Albuquerque	Atlanta	Baltimore	Boston	Denver	Kansas City, Kansas	Kansas City, Missouri	Milwaukee	Nashville	San Diego
Less than $5,000	102	141	103	165	87	57	88	115	87	101
$5,000 to $9,999	159	151	206	176	145	81	128	143	140	160
$10,000 or More	169	153	168	134	100	49	152	152	148	231
Not Ascertained	41	24	23	32	25	6	15	33	51	25
Total	471	469	500	507	357	193	383	443	426	517

Note: Income figures in all tables include income of the respondent, plus that of any related persons living in the same household.

226 Citizen Attitudes Toward Local Government, Services, and Taxes

Table A-5. Ethnicity, by City

	Albuquerque	Atlanta	Baltimore	Boston	Denver	Kansas City, Kansas	Kansas City, Missouri	Milwaukee	Nashville	San Diego
White, not Spanish	316	256	235	385	274	135	288	374	337	429
White Spanish	127	4	3	12	47	4	11	5	3	30
Black	13	209	261	100	26	48	75	61	76	28
Oriental	3	0	0	8	1	0	1	0	0	13
Other	9	0	0	2	2	4	8	3	3	13
Not Ascertained	3	0	1	0	7	2	0	0	7	4
Total	471	469	500	507	357	193	383	443	426	517

Table A-6. White Protestant and White Catholic Respondents, by City

	Albuquerque	Atlanta	Baltimore	Boston	Denver	Kansas City, Kansas	Kansas City, Missouri	Milwaukee	Nashville	San Diego
White Protestant (Non-Spanish)	235	219	130	70	178	99	205	151	293	298
White Catholic (Non-Spanish)	63	17	79	252	52	32	64	198	31	95
All Other	160	213	283	163	90	55	105	77	91	97
Not Ascertained	13	20	8	22	22	7	9	17	11	27
Total	471	469	500	507	357	193	383	443	426	517

Table A–7. Presence of Minor Children in the Household, by City

	Albuquerque	Atlanta	Baltimore	Boston	Denver	Kansas City, Kansas	Kansas City, Missouri	Milwaukee	Nashville	San Diego
With Children	243	209	262	184	169	94	187	202	210	234
Without Children	228	256	238	323	181	99	196	241	213	283
Not Ascertained	0	4	0	0	7	0	0	0	3	0
Total	471	469	500	507	357	193	383	443	426	517

Table A–8. Whether Households Will Send or Are Sending Their Children to Public Schools, by City

	Albuquerque	Atlanta	Baltimore	Boston	Denver	Kansas City, Kansas	Kansas City, Missouri	Milwaukee	Nashville	San Diego
Yes*	197	156	193	100	134	68	153	140	163	187
No	26	26	28	53	24	10	15	40	28	24
Households Without Children	242	284	270	348	191	111	212	259	232	299
Not Ascertained	6	3	9	6	7	4	3	4	3	7
Total	471	469	500	507	356	193	383	443	426	517

*These figures include some households with children attending both public and private or parochial schools.

Table A-9. Condition of Housing by City

	Albuquerque	Atlanta	Baltimore	Boston	Denver	Kansas City, Kansas	Kansas City, Missouri	Milwaukee	Nashville	San Diego
Dilapidated	7	9	20	19	7	4	4	7	5	4
Deteriorating	35	50	104	64	40	13	22	46	39	26
Generally Sound	423	409	374	416	300	170	353	387	373	480
Not Ascertained	6	1	2	8	10	6	4	3	9	7
Total	471	469	500	507	357	193	383	443	426	517

Table A-10. Tenure, by City

	Albuquerque	Atlanta	Baltimore	Boston	Denver	Kansas City, Kansas	Kansas City, Missouri	Milwaukee	Nashville	San Diego
Owners	310	211	232	132	188	128	261	209	274	289
Renters	144	256	265	371	164	65	116	231	144	213
Other	17	2	3	4	5	0	6	3	8	15
Total	471	469	500	507	357	193	383	443	626	517

Table A-11. Renters by Race, by City

	Albuquerque	Atlanta	Baltimore	Boston	Denver	Kansas City, Kansas	Kansas City, Missouri	Milwaukee	Nashville	San Diego
White, Non-Spanish	86	125	82	272	118	37	78	185	105	164
White Spanish	42	2	0	10	23	1	4	3	1	16
Black	9	126	177	73	13	25	28	37	35	12
Other	4	0	0	9	2	1	3	3	0	16
Not Ascertained	3	3	6	7	7	1	3	3	3	4
Total	144	256	265	371	163	65	116	231	144	212

Table A-12. Renters by Income, by City

	Albuquerque	Atlanta	Baltimore	Boston	Denver	Kansas City, Kansas	Kansas City, Missouri	Milwaukee	Nashville	San Diego
Less than $5,000	58	110	74	138	57	23	39	86	51	59
$5,000 to $9,999	53	70	127	137	68	28	39	78	60	85
$10,000 or More	23	62	53	75	22	11	30	49	25	57
Not Ascertained	10	14	11	21	16	3	8	18	8	11
Total	144	256	265	371	163	65	116	231	144	212

Table A-13. Number of Cars Owned by Respondents' Families, by City

	Albuquerque	Atlanta	Baltimore	Boston	Denver	Kansas City, Kansas	Kansas City, Missouri	Milwaukee	Nashville	San Diego
None	48	103	186	234	58	34	72	103	52	52
One	187	211	218	216	159	85	168	242	193	216
Two	179	123	86	51	112	62	114	80	152	193
Three or More	56	30	9	5	28	12	29	17	29	55
Not Ascertained	1	2	1	1	0	0	0	1	0	1
Total	471	469	500	507	357	193	283	443	426	517

Appendix B

The Questionnaire

THE QUESTIONNAIRE

The questionnaire consisted of two parts. The cover sheet, on which sample addresses were written, was basically the interviewer's worksheet, to record her calls, to obtain household composition, including the ages of each household member and the way each was related to the household head. Using this information, the interviewer identified the adult who was to be the respondent and arranged to interview that person.

The following is a list of the questions which constituted the common interview schedule administered in all ten cities. Although the format was, of course, different for interviewer use, the wording of the questions interviewers read is reproduced verbatim.

First, we are going to ask you about the government here in (CITY)–(the mayor), (the city manager), the city (councilmen/aldermen) and others who govern the city and provide services here. First ......

A1. Over the past five or ten years, do you think that local government here in (CITY) has gotten *better,* has stayed about the *same,* or do you think it is *not as good* as it used to be?

A2. In what ways, if any, could the local government do a better job here in (CITY)? (Anything else?)

A3. And overall, how would you rate the way (CITY) is run–*excellent, very good, good enough, not so good,* or *not good at all?*

A4. Which officials or other people do you think really run the local government here in (CITY)–which people make the most difference in how well the city is run? (Anyone else?)

A5. Think about the things in this city that you think need to be changed, fixed up, or given special attention. What things do you think of as most important in making this city a better place to live?

A6. How much do you think the people who count in local government in (CITY) are concerned about the same problems you are concerned about— *very much, some, a little* or *hardly at all?*

A7. What do you think is the best way people like you can make themselves heard by the city government?

A8. Considering what people in (CITY) pay in local taxes, do you think the people generally get their money's worth in services, or not?

A9. (IF NO) What is the main reason for this—why don't people get their money's worth?

A10. Thinking of all public services—fire and police protection, schools, parks, transportation, (trash collection), street maintenance, and other things—do you think the services here in your neighborhood are generally *better* than in other parts of (CITY), are they about the *same,* or are they *not as good* as in other parts of the city?

A11. Are there any public services or facilities in this neighborhood you especially would like to see improved?

A12. (IF YES) which ones? (Anything else?)

A13. Do you, or any of your close relatives, work for the city government here in (CITY)?

A14. (IF YES) What (does he) (do they) do? (What type of job (does he/do they) have?)

A15. Do you think that people who work for the city government usually make *more,* make the *same,* or make *less* than they would make if they worked for someone else—say in a business?

A16. And do you think city (and county) wages and salaries generally should be *higher* than they are now, are they *about right,* or do you think they should be *lower?*

A17. Some people say that people who provide public services should be able to strike for more pay just like other workers. Others say that city services are too important to let these people strike.

Do you think, for example, that teachers or trash collectors should be able to go on strike, or not?

A18. How about policemen and firemen—should they be able to go on strike, or not?

A19. On the whole, do you think local government officials are *more honest,* on their jobs than most other people, say people in business, are about *the same,* or are they *less honest* than most people?

A20. In some cities, officials are said to take bribes and make money in other ways that are illegal. In other cities, such things almost never happen. How much of that sort of thing do you think goes on in (CITY)—*a great deal, some, a little,* or *almost none at all?*

A21. (IF GREAT DEAL OR SOME) What are the ways you've heard people make money like that in (CITY)?

SCHOOLS

B1. (INTERVIEWER: CHECK)

B2. (IF R HAS CHILDREN UNDER 18) (Are your children going to/Will your children go to) public schools here in (CITY), private schools or parochial schools?

B3. As you know, many children go to Catholic or other church-supported parochial schools instead of to public schools. Some people have said that local tax money should be used to help support such schools. Do you think this is a good idea or not?

B4. Now thinking of the public schools, how good would you say is the education children get in the schools in this neighborhood—*very good, good enough, not so good,* or *not good at all?*

B5. What, if anything, could be done to make the schools in this neighborhood better?

B6. Compared with schools in the rest of (CITY) do you think the schools in this neighborhood are *better, the same,* or *not as good* as those in other parts of the city?

B7. Are there any courses or subjects that are not taught in public schools now that you think ought to be taught?

B8. Do you think that parents and citizens in this neighborhood have had the right amount of say in important decisions about education in the neighborhood schools, or not?

B9. What things should be done so they would have more say in the schools?

B10. (INTERVIEWER: CHECK)

B11. How much of a problem has racial integration of schools been here in (CITY) in the past three or four years—*a serious problem, some problem, a little problem* or *no problem at all?*

B12. And how do you think school officials here have handled school integration—*very well, well enough, not too well,* or *not well at all?*

B13. As you probably know, in some places they assign children to schools in other neighborhoods to get a more even spread of black and white children in schools. Do you think this is a *good idea,* or *not?*

B14. Why do you say that?

B15. (INTERVIEWER: CHECK)

B16. (IF R HAS CHILDREN IN PUBLIC SCHOOL) Suppose people in your neighborhood were asked to send their children to a school a little farther away from home than the one they go to now to help integrate the schools in (CITY). Would you be *willing* to do this or *not?*

TRANSPORTATION

C1. Now we have some questions about transportation.
First, how many cars do you (and your family) own?

C2. What sorts of transportation do you (and your family) use most often to get around the city—car, bus (or trolley), taxi, or walking, or what?

C3. About how often do you (or someone in your family) ride the bus (or trolley)—*almost every day, a few times a week, once a week, less often,* or *never?*

C4. (IF R RIDES LESS THAN ALMOST EVERY DAY) Are there any changes that could be made in the public transportation system so that you (and your family) would use it more often?

C5. What changes?

C6. Do you think tax money should be used to help support the public transportation system, or do you think that fares should be high enough to pay for the whole cost of the system?

C7. From your point of view, would you prefer that the city work more on making it easier to drive a car in the city or work more on improving the public transportation system?

HOUSING

C8. What things should be done to make it easier to drive a car in the city?

C9. And are there any other problems concerning traffic or parking you would like to see something done about?

HOUSING

D1. Now we want to talk about housing here in (CITY). First,,how long have you lived in the (CITY) area?

D2. Where did you live before you moved to (CITY)?

D3. And how long have you lived in this (house/apartment)?

D4. Do you own this home, are you renting, or what?

D5. (R RENTS) Including your rent and everything you pay for utilities—heat and gas—about how much does this (house/apartment) cost per month? Just give me the letter next to the amount you (and those living with you) pay altogether. (SHOW CARD A)

D6. (INTERVIEWER: CHECK)

D7 (IF THERE ARE ROOMMATES) And how much is your share? Give me the letter next to the amount you (and your family) pay. (SHOW CARD A)

D8. (R OWNS) Including your payment on your mortgage, your taxes, your home insurance, and all your utilities—heat, gas and electricity—about how much are you paying per month? Just give me the letter next to the amount you are paying altogether. (SHOW CARD A)

D9. Does the cost of your housing seem *about right* to you for what you are getting or do you think you pay *too much* for housing?

D10. Are there any (other) serious ways that either this house or this neighborhood is not a good place for you (and your family) to live?

D11. (IF YES) What is that) (Anything else?)

D12. What are the main reasons you live in this (house/apartment) rather than some place else?

D13. Have you heard about urban renewal here in (CITY)?

D14. Has urban renewal in (CITY) affected you personally in any way?

D15. (IF YES) How is that?

D16. Do you think overall, urban renewal has made (CITY) a *better* place to live, or a *worse* place to live, or *hasn't it made much difference?*

D17. As you probably know, in most cities there is not enough low-cost and moderate-cost housing. Do you think the local government should be responsible for having more housing like that built, or not?

D18. How would you feel about low-cost housing being built in this part of (CITY)—would you think it was a *good idea,* would you just *accept* it, or would you be *against* it?

CODE ENFORCEMENT

E1. Has a fireman or building inspector been out to inspect this (house/building) in the last year or two?

E2. (IF YES) Did he find anything that needed to be changed or fixed?

E3. (IF YES) What was that?

E4. Has that been taken care of now, or not?

E5. (INTERVIEWER: CHECK)

E6. (RENTERS ONLY) In some neighborhoods people tell us about problems with the way houses are kept—things like dangerous floors, poor heating, bad wiring, toilets that don't work, rats and other things. Do you have any problems like that here now in this (house/building)?

E7. (IF YES) What?

E8. Do you think (this is a serious problem/these are serious problems), or not?

E9. And how well do you think local agencies do in inspecting houses and getting owners and landlords to make needed repairs—*very well, well enough, not too well,* or *not well at all?*

LAW AND ORDER

F1. There has been a lot of discussion about law and order. Who—that is, which people or groups—do you think is the biggest problem here in this city?

F2. Here is a list of some things that many cities are concerned about. Please tell me which you think is worst—the one you would like the local government and the police to work most to try to stop.

    a. prostitution
    b. gambling, making book, numbers

c. breaking into houses, burglary
d. robbing people on the street
e. stealing cars
f. demonstrations in the streets
g. selling drugs, dope
h. speeding, reckless driving

F3. And which is the next most important problem?

F4. How safe do you feel walking around your neighborhood alone at night— *very safe, pretty safe, pretty unsafe,* or *very unsafe?*

F5. Do you think there is *more* crime here in this neighborhood than in the rest of the city, is there *less* crime, or is it *about the same* here as in the rest of the city?

F6. In general, how would you rate the job the police do of protecting people in this neighborhood—*very good, good enough, not so good,* or *not good at all?*

F7. Compared with the rest of the city, how would you rate the job the police do in fighting crime here in this neighborhood—do they do a *better* job, the *same,* or *not as good* a job in this neighborhood as in other parts of (CITY)?

F8. When someone in this neighborhood calls the police for help, do they usually come right away, or do they take quite a while to come?

F9. And how would you rate the way police usually treat people in this neighborhood—*very good, good enough, not so good,* or *not good at all?*

F10. Here is a list of some crimes that happen to people. In the past year, has anything like this happened to you or anyone living with you?

a. house broken into or robbed
b. pocket picked or purse snatched
c. mailbox robbed
d. property damaged or destroyed
e. people attacked or beaten up
f. car stolen
g. anything else

F11. Could you tell me about (EACH)? (Was that in this neighborhood or somewhere else?) (What was taken or damaged?)

F12. Was (EACH) reported to the police?

F13. There has been a lot of concern about drug use among teen-agers and other young people. How much of a problem do you personally think this is here in (CITY)—*a serious problem, some problem, a little problem,* or *no problem at all?*

F14. Is there anything city agencies should be doing, more than they are doing now, to deal with this problem?

F15. (IF YES) What is that?

F16. When people are arrested or go to trial in (CITY), do you think the courts are *always fair, usually fair, sometimes unfair,* or *often unfair?*

F17. (IF UNFAIR) In what ways are they unfair?

BACKGROUND

H1. Now I need some background information. First, where were you born?

H2. (INTERVIEWER: CHECK)

H3. (INTERVIEWER: CHECK)

H4. (IF U. S. OR CANADA) What country did most of your family come from originally on your father's side—that is, before they came to the United States (or Canada)?

H5. Who first came to this country (or Canada), your father, your grandfather, or was it earlier than that?

H6. And what country did most of your family come from on your mother's side?

H7. Who first came to this country (or Canada), your mother, your grandfather, or was it earlier than that?

H8. And in what religion were you raised—Protestant, Catholic, Jewish or something else?

H9. Do you belong to any clubs, neighborhood groups or other organizations that are working on city problems in any way?

H10. Which are those?

H11. How interested would you say you are in city problems and city politics—*very interested, fairly interested,* or *not too interested?*

H12. And where do you get most of your news about the city—from radio, television, newspapers, or somewhere else?

SERVICES

J1. Here is a list of services and problems. Some we have talked about already, others we have not. For each, I want you to tell me whether you think the local agencies should spent *more money, less money,* or *about as much money* as is now spent on these services, or problems. Remember, that to spend more on something, the local government either has to spend less on something else or it has to raise taxes.

   a. public schools
   b. police patrolling the streets at night
   c. giving tickets and towing cars parked in illegal places
   d. street lighting
   e. cleaning and repairing streets
   f. providing medical care to people who cannot afford to pay for it themselves
   g. cleaning up parks and playgrounds for small children
   h. places for teen-age boys to go when they want to play a game, have some recreation or a good time
   i. trash and garbage collection
   j. inspecting and making owners clean up houses that are run down, or have rats or other safety hazards
   k. helping kids and others who are on drugs
   l. building low-cost housing
   m. controlling air pollution
   n. improve public transportation
   o. building freeways
   p. welfare and aid for dependent children (AFDC)

J2. I know there are a lot of things on this list. But could you pick out the three where you think increased efforts are most needed?

J3. And if some things had to be cut back on, which three would you choose?

J4. As you know, costs keep going up. If a choice has to be made, do you think taxes should be raised or services like those on the list should be cut down?

J5. Here are five ways that local governments can raise money. If more tax money is needed, which do you think is the best way to raise it?

   a. Tax on property
   b. Tax on income or earnings
   c. Tax on utilities—like electricity, gas or water
   d. Sales tax
   e. Tax on automobile owners

J6. What is the next best way?

J7. From what you know, do you think taxes are *too high* here in (CITY), *about right,* or are they *too low* to pay for needed services?

J8. Do you think that trash and garbage collection should be paid for by taxes, or should people hire and pay for their own trash collection service?

J9. How about libraries and museums—should tax money be used to help support these, or should people who use them have to pay enough to support them?

J10. As you probably know, land that is owned by private schools and universities in the city by law cannot be taxed. Do you think this law should be changed or not?

J11. Also, as you probably know, land that is owned by churches in the city by law cannot be taxed. Do you think this law should be changed or not?

J12. Why do you feel that way?

SOCIO-ECONOMIC

K1. Now I just have a few final questions so we can compare your answers with other people's answers.

First, how much education have you had? (IF HIGH SCHOOL OR COLLEGE, ASK: Did you graduate?)

K2. (INTERVIEWER: CHECK)

K3. And how much education has (HEAD) had?

K4. Is (HEAD) working now (in school/retired/keeping house), unemployed or what?

K5. What kind of work (does/did) (HEAD) do on his (last) job?

K6. What kind of business or organization (is/was) that in? (What do they do?)

K7. (Does/did) (HEAD) work for himself or someone else?

K8. (INTERVIEWER: CHECK)

K9. Is there anyone else in your family who is employed at all now?

K10. And is (EACH EMPLOYED PERSON) employed full time or part time?

K11. And besides pay for work, did you (and your family) receive any other kind of income during 1969—like Social Security, rents, welfare, or anything else? (What was that?) (Anything else?)

K12. There is a lot of talk about the cost of living these days. How hard is it for you to make ends meet—would you say it is *very hard, pretty hard, not too hard,* or *not hard at all?*

K13. And considering all sources of income and all salaries for everyone who worked—before deduction for taxes or anything—what was your total family income in 1969?

K14. (INTERVIEWER: CHECK)

K15. And how much of your family income came from (HEAD'S) salary or wages?

INTERVIEWER RATINGS (AFTER INTERVIEW)

1. Literacy rating
2. R's cooperativeness towards the interview
3. Type of structure in which respondent lives
4. Is this public housing?
5. Quality of housing:
    a. Dilapidated, very substandard—has defects that are either so critical or so widespread that the structure should be extensively repaired, rebuilt or torn down
    b. Deteriorating—needs more repair than would be provided in the course of regular maintenance; defects are signs of neglect or which lead to serious structural deterioration or damage if not corrected
    c. Generally sound—has no defects or only slight defects which normally are corrected during the course of regular maintenance.
6. Language in which interview was taken.
7. Ethnicity of respondent:
    a. White (not of Spanish descent)
    b. White (of Spanish descent)
    c. Negro
    d. Oriental
    e. American Indian
    f. Other (Specify):

About the Author

Dr. Fowler specialized in interview methodology at the University of Michigan, where he worked at the Survey Research Center while obtaining his doctorate in social psychology. While serving as Assistant Director of the Community Research Project in Boston, he worked with several social welfare agencies in the collection, interpretation and utilization of survey data in planning for community needs. In particular, he studied and wrote about the needs of the Jewish population and the aged.

As Assistant Director of the Survey Research Program at the Joint Center for Urban Studies of M.I.T. and Harvard University, Dr. Fowler worked on a number of projects that involved the application of survey research data to local policy. The Boston Area Survey project, in particular, attempted to obtain key baseline measures relating to housing, satisfaction with city services, crime— the range of problems cities deal with.

Since 1971, Dr. Fowler has been Director of the Survey Research Program, now also affiliated with UMass/Boston and continued his primary research interest in local service policy, as well as survey methodology.